P9-BIN-645

The Complete Sentence
Workout Book

Introduction

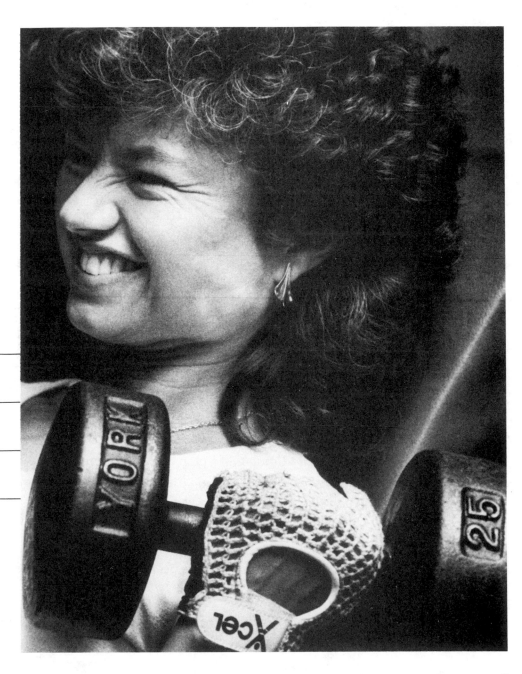

OBJECTIVES: 1. To review the parts of speech.

2. To introduce identification of subjects and verbs.

3. To introduce four basic sentence formats.

KEY CONCEPT: A sentence must fulfill two requirements:

1. It must have a subject and a verb.

2. It must express a complete thought.

Parts of Speech

There are eight parts of speech. Because most of these terms will be used throughout the book, it is helpful if you can recognize these terms.

1. **Nouns** name people, places, or things. There are two kinds of nouns: common and proper. A common noun provides a general name for a person, place, or thing; a proper noun identifies a specific person, place, or thing and is capitalized.

   Examples: The *doctor* operates daily.   (*Doctor* is a common noun naming a person.)
   Captain Lewis whistled softly.
   (*Captain Lewis* is a proper noun naming a person.)

   We crossed the *valley*.   (*Valley* is a common noun naming a place.)
   We saw the *Grand Canyon*.
   (The *Grand Canyon* is a proper noun naming a place.)

   The *boat* raced away.   (*Boat* is a common noun naming a thing.)
   We visited the *Queen Elizabeth II*.
   (The *Queen Elizabeth II* is a proper noun naming a thing.)

   A noun can also be abstract or concrete. Abstract nouns name intangible ideas, ideals, or qualities. Concrete nouns name tangible people, places, or things. Concrete nouns can be perceived through at least one of the five senses: touch, taste, smell, sight, or sound.

   Examples: The terms *love, honor,* and *patriotism* are difficult to define precisely.
   (*Love, honor,* and *patriotism* are abstract nouns.)

The *animals* at the *zoo* pleased the *tourists.*
(*Animals, zoo,* and *tourists* are concrete nouns.)

2. **Verbs** are words that describe action or existence.

 Examples: Each afternoon, the children *run, skip,* and *jump* during recess.
     (*Run, skip,* and *jump* are verbs that show action.)

     Ellen *seems* very happy. She *is* a certified public accountant.
     (*Seems,* the present tense of the verb *seem,* and *is,* the present tense of the verb
     be, are verbs that show existence.)

In addition to describing action or existence, some forms of specific verbs can be used as *helping verbs;* these helping verbs aid the reader in determining the correct time and conditions of an action. (These helping verbs are always used with another *main verb* that shows action or describes existence.) The chart below lists a number of helping verbs that can be used to determine the time and condition of the verb *to go.*

 Examples:

is going, are going	will go
was going, were going	has gone, have gone
will be going	had gone
has been going, have been going	will have gone
had been going	shall go
will have been going	did go
should have gone	may go
can go	could go
could have gone	might go
might have gone	would have gone

Although the basic action in each of the above examples is the same (*to go*), the time (present, past, and future) and the conditions (obligation, possibility, ability, emphasis, and permission) of the action change in each example.
 Below is a list of the most common helping verbs:

can	is/are/am	may	shall
could	was/were	might	should
do	has/have	must	used to
does	had	ought to	will
did			would

3. **Pronouns** are words that take the place of nouns.

 Examples: The pronoun *he* can take the place of the nouns *Bill, Jack,* or *man* (or any other
     noun that is masculine and singular).

     The pronoun *they* can take the place of a number of people.

The many types of pronouns are listed below.

• Personal Pronouns
 Subjective or Nominative case: I, you, he, she, it, we, they
 Objective case: me, you, him, her, it, us, them
 Possessive case: my, mine, your, yours, his, her, hers, its, our, ours, their, theirs

- Indefinite Pronouns

    all, anyone, anything, anybody, each, everybody, everyone, everything, no one, nobody, nothing, several, some, someone, somebody

- Relative Pronouns

    who, whom, whose, which, that, whoever, whomever, whichever

- Demonstrative Pronouns

    this, that, those, these

- Intensive/Reflexive Pronouns

    myself, yourself, himself, herself, itself, ourselves, yourselves, themselves

- Interrogative Pronouns

    who, which, whom, whose, what

4. **Adjectives** describe nouns. They tell what color, shape, size, amount, mood, or temperature a noun is.

Examples: Our trip to the beach was marred by the *cold, gray* day.
(The words *cold* and *gray* describe the day in terms of temperature and color.)

The *large, octagonal,* brightly *colored* rug was a gift.
(The words *large, octagonal,* and *colored* describe the rug in terms of its size, shape, and color.)

NOTE: The words *a, an,* and *the* are adjectives; these three words are called articles.

5. **Adverbs** modify verbs, adjectives, or other adverbs. They tell when, where, how, and to what degree.

Examples: The cat jumped *gracefully*.   (*Gracefully* tells how the cat jumped.)

We have been *here before*.   (*Here* tells where, and *before* tells when.)

She thanked him *very graciously* for the flowers.
(*Very* tells to what degree she thanked him; *graciously* describes how she thanked him.)

6. **Conjunctions** join words or groups of words. There are three major types of conjunctions. *Coordinate conjunctions* join words, word phrases, or sentences of equal value.

Examples: Ann *and* Hilda   (*And* joins the names of two people.)

The girls tried to open the window, *but* it was painted shut.
(*But* joins two sentences.)

There are seven coordinate conjunctions: *for, and, nor, but, or, yet,* and *so*.
Subordinate conjunctions join a dependent clause (a group of words with a subject and a verb which does not make a complete thought) and an independent clause (a group of words with a subject and a verb which does form a complete thought).

Examples: *After* the flood waters had receded, the townspeople began to remove the debris left behind.
(*After,* a subordinate conjunction, joins the dependent clause to the independent clause, "the townspeople began to remove the debris left behind.")

19. The kindergarten students laughed *gleefully as* they *quickly* raced *through* the tunnel.

20. "I *have been rejected* for a promotion once *too* often!" he shouted.

Check the answer key.

Subjects and Verbs

Subjects and verbs provide the core portion of a sentence, because they tell who performed an action and what the action was. **Subjects** must be nouns or pronouns. **Verbs** show action or existence. The easiest test for locating the subject and verb in a sentence is to ask these questions:

1. What is the action? or What word shows existence? The answer is the *verb*.
2. Who or what is performing the action? The answer is the *subject*.

Locate the subject and verb in the following sentence.

Example: Barry sang.

1. What is the action? *sang* (the verb)
2. Who is performing the action? *Barry* (the subject)

Sentence Formats

There are four basic sentence formats in American English. You should be able to recognize each of these, because they are used frequently. These formats give information about the construction of sentences.

1. Format 1 is **Subject/Verb.**

   Example: Teresa laughed.

   > The subject is *Teresa*.
   > The verb is *laughed*.

2. Format 2 is **Subject/Verb/Direct Object.**

   Example: The lawyer won the case.

   > The subject is *lawyer*.
   > The verb is *won*.
   > The direct object, which receives the action of the verb, is *case*.

3. Format 3 is **Subject/Verb/Indirect Object/Direct Object.**

   Example: She handed him a plate.

   > The subject is *she*.
   > The verb is *handed*.
   > The direct object is *plate*.
   > The indirect object, which tells to whom the plate was handed, is *him*.

The dog acted *as if* he had never seen a cat before.
(*As if,* a subordinate conjunction, joins the dependent clause to the independent clause, "The dog acted.")

Below is a list of frequently used subordinate conjunctions:

after	since	whenever
although	so that	when
as (as if)	unless	where
because	until	whether
even though	wherever	while
if		

Conjunctive adverbs (or *adverbial conjunctions*) are used with a semicolon to join two or more independent clauses to form one compound sentence.

Examples: The house was overpriced; *moreover,* the couple did not need so many rooms.
(*Moreover* joins two independent clauses.)

The couple planned a small wedding; *however,* their parents invited over two hundred friends.
(*However* joins two independent clauses.)

Below is a partial list of conjunctive adverbs:

consequently	however	otherwise
furthermore	moreover	therefore
hence	nevertheless	thus

7. **Prepositions** are used to show the relationship between a noun or a pronoun and another word in a sentence.

Examples: The island *across* the bay is owned *by* the city.
(*Across* is a preposition. It helps describe which island, and it connects *bay* and *island* to describe the location. *By* is also a preposition; it describes who owns the island.)

The thief ran *behind* the house *on* the corner.
(*Behind* is a preposition; it describes the location of the hiding place of the thief. *On* is a preposition; it identifies the location of the house.)

Here is a sample list of prepositions:

about	inside
after	outside
around	since
behind	through
below	to
during	under
due to	with

8. **Interjections** are words that are used to express strong emotions, such as anger, joy, sorrow, or surprise. Often an exclamation point comes after the interjection.

Examples: *Wow!* She won five million dollars in the weekly state lottery.
(*Wow* expresses happiness and surprise.)

Whew! It sure is hot today.
(*Whew* expresses discomfort.)

PRACTICE

Write the part of speech of each italicized word in the following sentences above the word.

1. *In* the past four years, college *tuition has risen* three times faster than the rate of inflation.

2. *Boy!* That's a *gorgeous* Maserati.

3. Alice *and* Arlene *must serve* detention for a week.

4. The air conditioner *seems* to be malfunctioning.

5. Each *society* photographer seeks to catch his subject in a *revealing* and *memorable* pose.

6. The dancers swayed *slowly* and *gracefully; however,* they did not win a prize.

7. *Although she* had walked on the moon *and* flown to Jupiter, she decided to retire from the space program.

8. *Oh my gosh!* The *kerosene* heater *has* exploded.

9. *Everyone should* complete one year of service *to* the community.

10. *Warden James* just paroled "The Shark," a *vicious mass* murderer.

11. The children *danced* and *sang before* the program ended.

12. A car *with* a blue hood and *purple* wheels has been found abandoned *by* the railroad tracks.

13. *Shyness* and introspection are the *characteristics of* an introvert.

14. *We* can go to the movies, *or* we can go *to* the beach.

15. *You* lost *my* book; *that* wasn't *very* nice.

16. *Jerome failed his* comprehensive examination, *for* he had not completed the required course work.

17. *On* our vacation this *summer,* we saw Naples *by* the sea, *Andorra near* the Pyrenees, and Oslo *at* the tip *of* a fjord.

18. Even though a thesaurus is helpful, I find a dictionary more *useful* and *informative.*

4. Format 4 has two forms:

A. **Subject/Linking Verb/Predicate Adjective**

Example: Grammar seems difficult.

> The subject is *grammar*.
> The linking verb, which shows existence, is *seems*.
> The predicate adjective, which modifies the subject, is *difficult*.

B. **Subject/Linking Verb/Predicate Nominative**

Example: Writing is an exercise in thought.

> The subject is *writing*.
> The linking verb is *is*.
> The predicate nominative, which renames the subject, is *exercise*.

NOTE: See Chapters 4 and 5 for further explanation of subjects, verbs, and sentence formats.

PART I

The Sentence Core: Verbs and Subjects

OBJECTIVES:
1. To recognize and use the basic verb tenses—past, present, and future.
2. To form correctly regular and irregular verbs in past, present, and future tenses.
3. To use a consistent and appropriate verb tense when writing.

KEY CONCEPT: To communicate accurately and effectively, a writer must know and use the correct present, past, and future tenses of the appropriate verb.

Action Verbs and Linking Verbs

Verbs are divided into two categories:

1. **Action verbs** are words that show movement. For example, *to run, to dance,* and *to see* are action verbs.
2. **Linking verbs** are verbs that do not show action. Instead, they convey existence, being, becoming, and, sometimes, one of the five senses (touch, taste, smell, hearing, or sight). For example, the verbs *to be, to seem,* and *to become* are linking verbs. Linking verbs connect, or make equal, the subject and the word after the linking verb.

NOTE: The basic verb form is the word *to* plus the basic verb—*to be, to run.* This form is called the **infinitive.** All verb forms are made from the infinitive.

PRACTICE 1

Identify the following verbs as action verbs or linking verbs.

1. to jump _____
2. to be _____
3. to drive _____
4. to dance _____
5. to seem _____

6. to become _____
7. to sing _____
8. to work _____
9. to draw _____
10. to read _____

Check the answer key.

Conjugating Verbs

In order to use the various forms of a verb correctly, you must learn to **conjugate** the verb—that is, produce its different forms from the basic form, the infinitive. You can determine the verb forms by using the following pronouns as subjects (a pronoun takes the place of a noun—a person, place, or thing):

First Person: *I* is singular (you are talking about your own actions)
       we is plural (you are talking about your actions and the actions of one or more people; for example, if you wanted to substitute a pronoun for "Joe and I," you would use the pronoun *we*)

Second Person: *you* is singular (you are talking directly to another person)
       you is plural (you are talking directly to two or more people)

Third Person: *he, she, it* are singular (you are talking about one other person or thing)
       they is plural (you are talking about two or more people or things)

Pronouns must agree in number (the number of people, places, or things) and in gender (masculine, feminine, or neuter) with the nouns they replace.

PRACTICE 2

Substitute pronouns for the nouns listed below.

Example: Joe and I *we*

1. Tom _____
2. Mrs. Jones _____
3. a horse _____
4. the test _____
5. a rose _____

6. the house _____
7. Sam, Tim, and Helen _____
8. the buildings _____
9. the firefighters _____
10. Mr. Duff and I _____

Check the answer key.

When you conjugate a verb, use the following chart:

	Singular	*Plural*
	I _____	we _____
	you _____	you _____
	he, she, it _____	they _____

PRACTICE 4

Fill in the blanks with the appropriate present-tense form of the verb. Use the verbs provided for the sentences.

Example: I _____*go*_____ to school each weekday.
(to go)

1. He _____ to his girlfriend every day.
   (to talk)

2. Doris _____ four miles each day.
   (to run)

3. You _____ one library book, but he _____ the one you need.
   (to have)   (to have)

4. It _____ a very hot August day.
   (to be)

5. The Allegheny Mountains _____ a lovely sight in the fall.
   (to be)

6. Ted and I _____ a joint checking account.
   (to have)

7. Many thousands of people _____ the state of Kentucky.
   (to visit)

8. She _____ very well; her sketches _____ now on display at the
   (to draw)   (to be)
   local museum.

9. On family trips, my father _____ .
   (to drive)

10. Many luxuries _____ now necessities. The telephone _____
    (to be)   (to be)
    one example.

Check the answer key.

The Past Tense

The *past tense* of verbs describes an action that took place in the past and that was completed before the present time. Look at the following sentence:

Example: Bill Rodgers *won* the New York City Marathon in 1980.

The verb *won* is in the past tense. The action took place in 1980, so it was in the past. Also, the action was completed before the current year.

Look at the following conjugations of the verbs *to walk* and *to revolve* in the past tense:

to walk

I walked	we walked
you walked	you walked
he, she, it walked	they walked

to revolve

I revolved	we revolved
you revolved	you revolved
he, she, it revolved	they revolved

Because these are regular verbs, what conclusion can you draw about how regular verbs are formed in the past tense? Both verbs add what endings? *d* or *ed*

You have now developed a rule for forming the past tense of regular verbs: add *d* or *ed* to the basic form of the verb.

NOTE: See Chapter 22, *Spelling,* for rules on doubling the final consonants of words.

PRACTICE 5

Form the past tense of the following regular verbs:

1. to dance: I _____ we _____

   you _____ you _____

   he, she, it _____ they _____

2. to pour: I _____ we _____

   you _____ you _____

   he, she, it _____ they _____

3. to mark: I _____ we _____

   you _____ you _____

   he, she, it _____ they _____

4. to paint: I _____ we _____

   you _____ you _____

   he, she, it _____ they _____

5. to call: I _____ we _____

   you _____ you _____

   he, she, it _____ they _____

Check the answer key.

Irregular verbs in the past tense are formed in a number of ways:

1. by changing the vowels in the basic verb form. For example, *to know* becomes *knew* in the past tense.
2. by changing the vowels and adding a *t*. For example, *to teach* becomes *taught* in the past tense.
3. by changing a *d* to a *t*. *To build* becomes *built* in the past tense.
4. by changing the entire form. For example, the verbs *to be, to have,* and *to do* follow no set pattern.

NOTE: If you are uncertain about the formation of a verb in the past tense, check a dictionary. Look at the following entry for the verb *to draw* from *Webster's Collegiate Dictionary*. (9th ed.).*

¹**draw** \'drȯ\ *vb* **drew** \'drü\; . . .

The second form of the verb is the past tense. Therefore, to conjugate the verb *to draw* in the past tense, one would write the following:

I drew	we drew
you drew	you drew
he, she, it drew	they drew

The following chart identifies many frequently used irregular verbs in their infinitives, past tenses, and present and past participles. (Present participles are used to form the progressive tenses. Past participles are used to form the perfect tenses. In the progressive and perfect tenses, present and past participles require helping verbs, such as *is, am, are, has, have,* or *had,* to identify the time periods. See Chapter 2 for information on the progressive and perfect tenses.)

Infinitive	Past	Present Participle	Past Participle
1. to be	was or were	being	been
2. to become	became	becoming	become
3. to begin	began	beginning	begun
4. to bite	bit	biting	bitten
5. to blow	blew	blowing	blown
6. to break	broke	breaking	broken
7. to bring	brought	bringing	brought
8. to build	built	building	built
9. to burst	burst	bursting	burst
10. to buy	bought	buying	bought
11. to catch	caught	catching	caught
12. to choose	chose	choosing	chosen
13. to come	came	coming	come
14. to deal	dealt	dealing	dealt
15. to dive	dove (dived)	diving	dived
16. to do	did	doing	done
17. to draw	drew	drawing	drawn
18. to drink	drank	drinking	drunk
19. to drive	drove	driving	driven
20. to fall	fell	falling	fallen
21. to feel	felt	feeling	felt
22. to fly	flew	flying	flown
23. to forget	forgot	forgetting	forgotten
24. to freeze	froze	freezing	frozen
25. to go	went	going	gone

*By permission. From *Webster's Ninth Collegiate Dictionary*, © 1984 by Merriam-Webster, Inc., publisher of the Merriam-Webster ® Dictionaries.

Infinitive	Past	Present Participle	Past Participle
26. to grow	grew	growing	grown
27. to have	had	having	had
28. to hit	hit	hitting	hit
29. to hold	held	holding	held
30. to know	knew	knowing	known
31. to lay (place)	laid	laying	laid
32. to lead	led	leading	led
33. to lie (recline)	lay	lying	lain
34. to make	made	making	made
35. to read	read	reading	read
36. to ride	rode	riding	ridden
37. to ring	rang	ringing	rung
38. to rise	rose	rising	risen
39. to run	ran	running	run
40. to see	saw	seeing	seen
41. to shake	shook	shaking	shaken
42. to shrink	shrank (shrunk)	shrinking	shrunk (shrunken)
43. to sing	sang	singing	sung
44. to sink	sank	sinking	sunk
45. to sit	sat	sitting	sat
46. to speak	spoke	speaking	spoken
47. to spring	sprang	springing	sprung
48. to sting	stung	stinging	stung
49. to stride	strode	striding	strode
50. to strike	struck	striking	struck
51. to swim	swam	swimming	swum
52. to take	took	taking	taken
53. to teach	taught	teaching	taught
54. to tear	tore	tearing	torn
55. to tell	told	telling	told
56. to throw	threw	throwing	thrown
57. to wake	woke	waking	waken
58. to wear	wore	wearing	worn
59. to weave	wove	weaving	woven
60. to write	wrote	writing	written

PRACTICE 6

Fill in the blanks with the correct form of the past-tense verb. Use the verbs provided.

Example: The dog _____*ran*_____ down the street.
(to run)

1. Julie _____ the same song over and over for an hour.
(to sing)

2. Faulkner _____ many of his stories about a mythical county in Mississippi.
(to write)

3. Sherri _____ home early because she _____ ill.
   (to go)   (to feel)

4. The spring of 1987 _____ many unusual weather patterns; many states
   (to bring)

   _____ excessive rainfall and floods.
   (to experience)

5. We _____ the book *Animal Farm* by George Orwell.
   (to read)

6. Pope John Paul II _____ many countries in 1983; he _____
   (to visit)   (to go)

   to Poland and countries in Central America.

7. India _____ part of the British Empire until 1947.
   (to be)

8. The American Revolution _____ a new country into existence.
   (to bring)

9. During World War I and World War II, many Americans _____ in the
   (to enlist)

   armed services.

10. Unemployment _____ 10 percent in 1982; it subsequently
    (to reach)

    _____ to 6 percent in 1987.
    (to drop)

Check the answer key.

The Future Tense

The *future tense* indicates actions that will take place in the future. The time could be within the next few minutes: I *will begin* dinner in five minutes. Or it could be in thousands of years: In the year 3000, the world *will be* very different from what we know today.

Look at the following conjugations of the verbs *to write* (a regular verb) and *to be* (an irregular verb):

to write

I shall/will write	we shall/will write
you will write	you will write
he, she, it will write	they will write

to be

I shall/will be	we shall/will be
you will be	you will be
he, she, it will be	they will be

What pattern is followed? The word *will* is combined with the infinitive base of the verb. Thus, the rule for forming the future tense for both regular and irregular verbs is to add the word *will* to the infinitive base of the verb.

When the future tense is used to form a question, the helping verb *will* precedes the subject of the sentence and the infinitive base of the verb follows.

Example: *Will* you *meet* us for dinner tonight at the new French restaurant?

NOTE: In first-person singular and plural forms of the future tense, the word *shall* is used (for example, I *shall go* home). However, in current American English, many people prefer to use *will* in place of *shall*. When you use *will* and the *infinitive base* in first-person singular and plural forms in the future tense, you indicate a great conviction (for example, I *will go* home). This form of the future shows that you are determined to go and that you have made a definite choice.

PRACTICE 7

Supply the future-tense forms of the verbs in the following sentences. Use the verbs provided.

Example: Harry ____*will come*____ to dinner on Thursday.
(to come)

1. I _____ my homework tonight.
(to complete)

2. Jason _____ Mary to the Senior Dance.
(to ask)

3. _____ you _____ home tonight?
(to be)

4. A serious runner _____ over fifty miles a week.
(to run)

5. Before we move to Seattle, we _____ our house in Los Angeles.
(to sell)

6. _____ they _____ their father at the airport?
(to meet)

7. Each presidential candidate _____ across the country to gain the
(to travel)

voters' support.

8. The new industry _____ the town in a number of ways.
(to benefit)

9. College _____ a testing ground for many students.
(to be)

10. With determination and effort, students _____ academically in college.
(to succeed)

Check the answer key.

Consistency of Verb Tenses

Since verbs indicate the time an action occurred, you should make certain that all verbs in a sentence use the appropriate tense. For example, if you are describing an event from your childhood, then you should use only the past tense. You would confuse your reader if you included future or present actions in the paragraph. Examine the following sentences with inconsistent verbs tenses and their revisions.

Example: When she *was* fifteen years old, Barbara *trains* horses.
Revision: When she *was* fifteen years old, Barbara *trained* horses.

Example: As soon as the train *arrived*, we *board* it quickly.
Revision: As soon as the train *arrived*, we *boarded* it quickly.

APPLICATION I

In the following sentences, change the italicized present-tense verbs to the correct past-tense forms.

Example: I ~~walk~~ *walked* home.

1. The library *is* open during the winter break.

2. The space shuttle *flies* a mission each month.

3. It *is* difficult to find good craftspeople.

4. This year's crop of summer movies *offers* adventure and romance.

5. The fitness craze of the 1970s *continues* to increase; more people *express* concern about their physical condition.

6. The exhibit of Ansel Adams's photographs *pleases* the museum patrons.

7. The essay *is* to be five pages long.

8. The children *know* their multiplication tables.

9. Because we *want* to see everything, we *sit* in the first row at the theater.

10. The museum *contains* a great number of paintings by the Impressionists.

Check the answer key.

APPLICATION II

In the following sentences, change the italicized past-tense verbs to the correct future tense forms.

Example: He ~~brought~~ *will bring* roses to Faye.

1. We *danced* all night long at the prom.

2. The students *enjoyed* the trip to the Bronx Zoo.

3. The scuba diver *explored* the sunken ship.

4. Harold *participated* in the triathalon, an event that includes three sports: swimming, bicycling, and running.

5. I *watched* the children at the playground.

6. Sara *made* tea for dinner.

7. Thieves *stole* the famous painting by Monet.

time to study for exams, to enjoy his family and friends, to relax, or just to have a social life. (10) Although a part-time job *gives* a student an income and work experience, it *requires* him to sacrifice his time.

Check the answer key.

APPLICATION VI

Read the following paragraph carefully. Check all italicized verbs for consistent tense. Change any verb that is not consistent.

(1) My first cooking experience *was* a memorable one. (2) I *decide* to bake some chicken; not knowing what to do, I *will fumble* my way through all the steps of a recipe. (3) The end result *is* a cooked piece of rawhide; the chicken *was* so tough that it *begun* to solidify while it *cooks*. (4) Not knowing where I *went* astray, I *will scrape* the contents of my plate into the garbage can and *proceeded* to go out to dinner. (5) When I *return* home, the dirty pots, pans, and dishes *wait* to be cleaned; I *will toss* them into the sink where they *sat* for nearly a week. (6) In addition, this cooking experience *created* an aversion to doing the dishes. (7) In my house, I *will do* the dishes when I *ran* out of plates, or I can no longer find the sink. (8) In either case, I eventually *did* the dishes. (9) However, I *am* too lazy to scrub them, and into the dishwasher they *went* untouched. (10) After the dishwasher *completes* its cycle, I *will put* the clean dishes away; the dirty ones *remained* in the dishwasher for another wash. (11) Fortunately, I *will learn* to correct my cooking errors and cleaning habits.

Check the answer key.

APPLICATION VII

Proofread a rough draft of a paper of your own. Check the verbs in the present, past, and future tenses. Did you form each one correctly? Do *regular* past-tense verbs have *d* or *ed* as endings? Correct any problems with tense. Show your revisions to your instructor or tutor.

2

Verbs II: The Perfect Tenses and the Progressive Forms

2. that an action took place in the past and is continuing in the present.

    Example: He *has attended* this school for two years.
              He obviously started in the past, and he is presently a student.

The **present perfect tense** is formed by using *has* or *have* (the present tense of the verb *to have*) and the past participle of the verb. Your use of *has* or *have* is determined by the noun. If it is third-person singular, use *has*. If it is plural or first- or second-person singular, then use *have*. Consider the following conjugation of the verb *to walk* in the present perfect tense:

I have walked	we have walked
you have walked	you have walked
he, she, it has walked	they have walked

EXERCISE   Write the rule for forming the present perfect tense:

_____

_____

Have your instructor or tutor check your work.

PRACTICE 2

Fill in the blanks with the correct form of the present perfect tense of the verb. Use only the verbs given.

Example: He ___*has strolled*___ down this street many times.
                    (to stroll)

1. I _____ a good school year.
       (to have)

2. Terry _____ to Europe several times.
        (to be)

3. In presidential campaigns, foreign policy _____ a major issue between
                                                    (to be)

   the two candidates.

4. They _____ us many times.
        (to visit)

5. He _____ a fine young man.
      (to become)

6. Women _____ many of the rights they fought for during the 1960s and
          (to receive)

   1970s.

7. Stella _____ the dress she wanted.
         (to buy)

8. He _____ in several marathons.
   (to race)

9. Mary and I _____ the movie *Psycho* four times.
   (to see)

10. Students _____ for the fall semester at the college.
    (to enroll)

Check the answer key.

The Past Perfect Tense

The past perfect tense describes a time in the past that occurred before another past action.

Example: Bob *had passed* his examination before he received his license.
By the time he received his license (an action that took place in the past), he had already passed the exam (an action that took place *before* he got the license).

Examine this sentence and explain the time sequence:

Example: After he *had run* ten miles, he *fainted*.
Which past action occurred first? *had run*
Which past action occurred last? *fainted*

The rule for forming the past perfect tense is a simple one: use *had* and the *past participle*. Here is the conjugation of the verb *to drive* in the past perfect tense:

I had driven	we had driven
you had driven	you had driven
he, she, it had driven	they had driven

PRACTICE 3

Fill in the blanks with the correct form of the past perfect tense of the verb. Use the verbs given.

1. If he _____ home, we would have visited him.
   (to be)

2. When the teacher _____ the lesson, the class applauded.
   (to finish)

3. After the bank teller _____ the transaction, the robbers left.
   (to complete)

4. The lawyer _____ his star witness before the defendant confessed.
   (to call)

5. Before the bomb could have exploded, the police officers _____ it.
   (to defuse)

6. Before the referee blew his whistle, he _____ the foul.
   (to determine)

7. After the star basketball player _____ his foul shot, the crowd in the gym exploded.
   (to make)

8. After the college students _____ their tour of London, they boarded a train to Scotland.
   (to complete)

9. The student _____ his topic before he began to write his essay.

(to choose)

10. After we _____ the heavy chest upstairs, we decided that it was too

(to move)

large for the small room.

Check the answer key.

Future Perfect Tense

The future perfect tense tells about a future event that will have been completed before another event. Look at the following sentence:

Example: I *will have worked* for three months by the time I start school this fall.

     Both actions will take place in the future. Which action will be completed first? *will have worked*. This action must be in the future perfect tense.

The rule for forming the future perfect tense is simple: add *will have* or *shall have* to the *past participle of the verb*. Here is the verb *to go* in the future perfect tense:

I will have gone	we will have gone
you will have gone	you will have gone
he, she, it will have gone	they will have gone

NOTE: See "The Future Tense" in Chapter 1 for a discussion of *shall* and *will*.

PRACTICE 4

Fill in the blanks with the correct form of the future perfect tense of the verb. Use only the verbs given.

1. The satellite _____ in orbit for five years before its power source is

(to be)

depleted.

2. The archaeologists _____ for seven years at the dig before they un-

(to work)

cover the first layer of the forgotten city.

3. By the end of the week, Kerri _____ her project.

(to finish)

4. When he completes graduate school, he _____ in school continuously

(to be)

for twenty years.

5. By the year 2000, Disney World _____ over three billion visitors.

(to welcome)

6. Professor Abbot _____ for thirty years by the end of this semester.

(to teach)

7. Sheila _____ the novel *Crime and Punishment* by Friday.

(to read)

8. By July, the North Carolina Outer Banks _____ their four hundredth
   (to celebrate)

   anniversary.

9. By March, the architects _____ their proposals for the new city hall.
   (to submit)

10. When he wins his 300th game, the pitcher _____ about 10,000
    (to throw)

    baseballs.

Check the answer key.

The Progressive Forms

The progressive forms of verbs indicate an action that is, was, or will be in progress. The progressive form requires a present participle as the base of the form. The present participle is formed by adding *ing* to the infinitive base. For example, *jumping* is the present participle of *to jump*.

EXERCISE Form the present participle of the following verbs.

1. to hop _____

2. to sleep _____

3. to become _____

4. to honk _____

5. to work _____

Have your instructor or tutor check your work.

The progressive forms exist in the present, past, and future. The forms are constructed by adding the appropriate form of the verb *to be* to the present participle.

Look at the following conjugations of the verb *to show*:

- **Present Progressive** (The action is taking place now.)

I am showing	we are showing
you are showing	you are showing
he, she, it is showing	they are showing

NOTE: Use the *present* tense of the verb *to be* to form the present progressive.

- **Past Progressive** (The action was taking place in the past.)

I was showing	we were showing
you were showing	you were showing
he, she, it was showing	they were showing

NOTE: Use the *past* tense of the verb *to be* to form the past progressive.

- **Future Progressive** (The action will be taking place in the future.)

I will be showing	we will be showing
you will be showing	you will be showing
he, she, it will be showing	they will be showing

NOTE: Use the *future* tense of the verb *to be* to form the future progressive.

The three perfect tenses—the past perfect, the present perfect, and the future perfect—also have progressive forms. These perfect progressive forms follow the rules of the perfect tense (in telling when an action occurred) and the progressive (an action in progress).

Here are the conjugations of the verb *to practice* in the perfect progressive forms. These are also constructed by adding the appropriate form of the verb *to be* (to indicate the time) to the present participle:

- **Present Perfect Progressive** (The action began in the past and continues to the present; this form stresses the continuing action.)

I have been practicing	we have been practicing
you have been practicing	you have been practicing
he, she, it has been practicing	they have been practicing

Example: The band *has been practicing* for five weeks for the state contest.

- **Past Perfect Progressive** (The action in progress was completed in the past before another event.)

I had been practicing	we had been practicing
you had been practicing	you had been practicing
he, she, it had been practicing	they had been practicing

Example: I *had been practicing* my violin when Mother told me to stop.

- **Future Perfect Progressive** (The action will continue into the future and be completed before another future action.)

I will have been practicing	we will have been practicing
you will have been practicing	you will have been practicing
he, she, it will have been practicing	they will have been practicing

Example: We *will have been* practicing our songs for three weeks before the contest begins.

PRACTICE 5

Complete the progressive forms of the verbs indicated below.

1. The present progressive of *to ask*   I _____

2. The past perfect progressive of *to do*   They _____

3. The future progressive of *to sing*   We _____

4. The present perfect progressive of *to hit*   He _____

5. The future perfect progressive of *to deal*   You _____

6. The past progressive of *to swim*   They _____

Check the answer key.

PRACTICE 6

Fill in the blanks with the correct progressive forms of the verbs indicated. Pay particular attention to the time sequence; the time will tell you which tense to use.

1. We _____ for four hours when the fireworks begin.
   (to dance)

2. He _____ his work now.
   (to complete)

3. She _____ the dog when the phone rang.
   (to bathe)

4. The lawyer _____ on this case for two years.
   (to work)

5. Jean _____ to her grandmother's house since she was five.
   (to go)

6. The guests _____ soon.
   (to leave)

7. Last year, she _____ on her law degree; this year, she
   (to work)

   _____ law.
   (to practice)

8. The toaster _____ not _____ properly; I _____ my toast
                      (to work)   (to burn)

   every morning for the past week.

9. Last year, Harold _____ for a city council post; this year, he
   (to run)

   _____ a concession stand at the stadium.
   (to operate)

10. The college football team _____ its rivals next week.
    (to play)

Check the answer key.

Helping Verbs

As you have seen in the perfect tenses and progressive forms, some verbs have a dual function. When acting alone, they describe action or existence; when acting as part of a verb phrase, they help the reader correctly determine the time frame, conditions, and tone (in some tenses) of an action. When they act as **helping verbs,** these verbs will precede the main verb.

Helping Verbs (Condition)

meaning	*verb*	*tense*	*example*
able to	can could	present past	I can pay I could pay, I could have paid
permitted to	may might	present past	I may pay I might pay, I might have paid
expected to	shall should	present past	I shall pay I should pay, I should have paid
willing to	will would	present past	I will pay I would pay, I would have paid

Helping Verbs (Time and Tone)

helping verb	*tense*	*example*
has, have	present perfect	I have swum He has swum
had	past perfect	He had swum
shall, will	future perfect	I shall have swum He will have swum
am, is, are	present progressive	I am swimming He is swimming They are swimming
was, were	past progressive	I was swimming They were swimming
will be	future progressive	He will be swimming
has been, have been	present perfect progressive	He has been swimming They have been swimming
had been	past perfect progressive	He had been swimming
will have been	future perfect progressive	He will have been swimming

Helping Verbs (Time and Tone)

helping verb	tense	example
do, does	present emphatic	I do swim He does swim
did	past emphatic	He did swim

PRACTICE 7

Fill in the blank with the verb and tense that are requested in the parentheses.

1. My mother told me that I _____ with my cousin at least once tonight. (conditional past tense of *to dance*)

2. This professor _____ at the college for over thirty years. (present perfect progressive of *to teach*)

3. The candidate _____ to correct the misstatements in his résumé. (present emphatic of *to plan*)

4. The infant _____ across the floor to retrieve his favorite toy. (past perfect of *to crawl*)

5. Her counselor indicated that she _____ able to take physics if she wanted to, but she opted for a calculus course instead. (past tense of *to be*)

6. The patient _____ well after surgery, but then his condition deteriorated. (past perfect progressive of *to do*)

7. Even though the patient died, let us remember that he _____ for over one hundred days with an artificial liver. (past emphatic of *to live*)

8. By the time he qualifies for the Olympic team, Charles _____ for more than ten years. (future perfect progressive of *to compete*)

9. If the party _____ me, I would have been proud to serve in the office. (past perfect of *to nominate*)

10. She _____ the committee's draft report. (present perfect of *to accept*)

Check the answer key.

Consistency of Verb Tenses

Verb tenses should be consistent in most cases. Because verb tenses show time, it is important that they express exactly what time you wish to describe. For example, if you are writing about an event that occurred in the past, use the past tense. Imagine how confused your reader would be if he read a sentence like this:

Example: Tomorrow, the pilot *flew* the plane.

When is the action taking place? The verb *flew* is the past tense form of *to fly*, yet the time is *tomorrow*.

With this confusion corrected, the sentence would read:

Example: Tomorrow, the pilot *will fly* the plane.

When you write a paragraph or an essay, make sure that the verb forms you use are in the same tense, or time period.

PRACTICE 8

Make the verb tenses of the underlined verbs consistent. Use the first verb in the sentence as your guide. If it is present tense, make the second verb present tense, also. If it is past tense, make the second verb past tense, also.

Example: When I ran home, I ~~find~~ *found* the front door open.

1. Before he <u>called</u> Alice to ask her for a date, he <u>takes</u> a deep breath.

2. As the band <u>marched</u> onto the football field, the football players <u>are</u> still on the gridiron.

3. College <u>offers</u> many activities to students, yet many students <u>failed</u> to take advantage of the extracurricular activities.

4. The mechanic <u>tested</u> the car's engine, only to find that it <u>is</u> not <u>working</u>.

5. Dreiser's novel *An American Tragedy* <u>was written</u> in 1925; the same year, Fitzgerald's novel *The Great Gatsby* <u>is published</u>.

6. The typewriter <u>will become</u> obsolete one day because the word processor <u>replaced</u> it.

7. When the football player <u>caught</u> the ball, he <u>turns</u> to look at his coach.

8. After the photographer <u>took</u> the picture, he <u>will develop</u> the film.

9. Before the Olympic Games <u>begin</u>, many thousands of athletes <u>arrived</u> in Seoul.

10. The train trip across Canada <u>took</u> so many days that we <u>will miss</u> our appointment in Seattle, Washington.

Check the answer key.

PRACTICE 9

Read the following paragraph carefully. Check the italicized verbs for consistent tense. Change any verb that is not consistent.

(1) "If I had been able to study, I *will have passed* the test," exclaims a distraught teenager. (2) "But I *do* not *have* a sufficient amount of time." (3) All parents *have heard* this excuse at one time or another. (4) Helping teenagers become mature, responsible adults *was* a difficult job. (5) Unfortunately, some parents do not succeed, but that it is not because they *had* not *tried*. (6) They diligently read books and articles on the topic; they faithfully *attended* parenting classes, and they regularly set aside "quality time" for family discussions. (7) But all their efforts *have been* in vain. (8) Some people *managed* to cross the threshold into so-called adulthood even though they are still self-indulgent, egocentric, and petty.

Check the answer key.

APPLICATION I

Change the verbs listed below from past, present, or future tense to the corresponding perfect tense and progressive form.

Examples: *saw* (past tense)
had seen (past perfect)
was/were seeing (past progressive)

run (present)
has/have run (present perfect)
am/are/is running (present progressive)

will sing (future)
will have sung (future perfect)
will be singing (future progressive)

Verb	Perfect Tense	Progressive Form
1. ride (present)	_____	_____
2. will consider (future)	_____	_____
3. evolved (past)	_____	_____
4. draws (present)	_____	_____
5. will answer (future)	_____	_____
6. will build (future)	_____	_____
7. solved (past)	_____	_____
8. remembers (present)	_____	_____
9. made (past)	_____	_____
10. will discover (future)	_____	_____

Check the answer key.

APPLICATION II

Read the following paragraph carefully. Check the italicized verbs for consistent tense. Change any verb that is not consistent.

(1) When I *was* ten, visiting my grandparents' farm in Georgia *is* a great deal of fun. (2) There *are* many activities I *enjoy*. (3) For example, each day my grandfather and I *went* fishing. (4) It *is* so easy to catch the fish we *need* for dinner. (5) In fact, one time I *had caught* twelve small fish before we *leave*. (6) Another example of the delights of the farm *is* the pony. (7) My

cousins and I *will take* turns riding him. (8) That poor pinto *has trotted* many a mile in a day just to please us. (9) Finally, my grandmother's meals *will please* everyone. (10) Each supper *brought* a new dessert made from fresh fruit or pudding. (11) It *is* a marvelous place for a child's summer vacation.

Check the answer key.

APPLICATION III

Read the following paragraph carefully. Check the italicized verbs for consistent tense. Change any verb that is not consistent.

(1) Fortunately, the homes of many famous American writers *have been preserved.* (2) Two of these homes *will be* quite remarkable, for they *give* us literary and social history. (3) In the late nineteenth century, Samuel Clemens, better known as Mark Twain, *had paid* $131,000 for a large house in Hartford, Connecticut. (4) The house itself *was* a wonder. (5) A greenhouse *will be occupying* the end of the house, and a fireplace *has had* a glass insert so that Clemens *could watch* snow fall into the chimney as a fire *was burning* below. (6) In addition, the Thomas Wolfe residence in Asheville, North Carolina, *will have* a profound effect upon Wolfe. (7) He and other members of the family *were forced* to share the house with a constant stream of boarders and roomers. (8) Wolfe later *immortalized* the house and its occupants in his first novel, *Look Homeward, Angel*, which *had been published* in 1929. (9) Built in 1883, the house now *is containing* most of the family's original furniture dating from the decade 1910–1920. (10) With its sleeping porches, chamber pots, Victrolas, and wood stoves, the house *will be* a study in an America of long ago. (11) From these two houses, Americans *will be* able to understand the environments that *shelter* the two authors and to glimpse a way of life that *has been replaced* by computers and fast-food restaurants.

Check the answer key.

APPLICATION IV

Proofread a rough draft of a paper of your own for verb consistency. Correct any problems you find, and show your revisions to your instructor or tutor.

3

Verbs III: The Finer Points—Voice, Mood, Verbals, and Style

OBJECTIVES: 1. To recognize transitive and intransitive verbs in context.

2. To recognize and use active and passive voice.

3. To recognize the three moods of verbs.

4. To recognize and use verbals—infinitives, gerunds, and participles.

5. To use verbs in developing writing style.

KEY CONCEPT: To communicate effectively, the writer must choose the proper voice and mood for the verb used, learn to use verbal forms when needed, and use verbs to develop an effective style.

Transitive and Intransitive Verbs

Consider a typical English sentence:

Example:
subject verb object
Helen wrote a paper.

The sentence moves from *Helen* (the subject, who performed the action) to the verb *wrote* (the action) to *paper* (the object that received the action, or what was written).

In the first chapter on verbs, you learned that there are two types of verbs: action verbs and linking verbs. Action verbs can be further divided into transitive and intransitive verbs. Linking verbs are always intransitive.

Transitive Verbs

A **transitive verb,** such as *build,* has an object. The transitive verb's action is transferred from the subject to the object, as we saw in the sentence *Helen wrote a paper.* To test for transitive verbs, simply ask, "What receives the action of the verb?" or "What was acted upon (in this case, what was written)?" For your use, substitute the verb in your sentence. Test the following sentence:

Example: Jerry threw the ball.

The subject (the actor) is *Jerry.*
The verb (the action) is *threw.*
What was thrown? *ball.* So, *ball* is the object of the verb *threw,* a transitive verb.

Intransitive Verbs

An **intransitive verb** does not have an object.

Example: She laughed.

The subject (the actor) is *She.*
The verb (the action) is *laughed.*
But there is no word to receive the action, so there is no object; therefore, the verb *laughed* is intransitive.

PRACTICE 1

Determine whether the following italicized verbs are transitive or intransitive.

Example: Captain Williams *caught* a shark.   ___*transitive*___

1. He *caught* a fish.

2. Susie *swam.*

3. The choir *sang* an opera.

4. He *drove* the car.

5. The children *cleared* the table.

6. It *rained.*

7. Sara *baked* a cake.

8. The gorilla *frightened* the child.

9. Steve *jumped.*

10. The goat *climbed.*

Check the answer key.

The same verb can be transitive or intransitive, depending upon how it is used in the sentence.

Example: The four-year-old child *acts* like an adult. (*Acts* is intransitive; there is no word that receives the action.)

He *acted* the role of Othello. (*Acted,* in this case, is transitive; *role* is the object—it receives the action of the verb.)

NOTE: Check a dictionary if you are unsure whether a verb is transitive or intransitive. A good dictionary will list the word and categorize it. Here is an entry from *Webster's Dictionary*:

> ²**act** *vt* [verb transitive] . . . **1** *obs:* ACTUATE, ANIMATE **2a:** to represent or perform by action esp. on the stage . . . *vi* [verb intransitive] **1a:** to perform on the stage. . . .*

Voice

Transitive verbs have voice. A transitive verb can have either active or passive voice. A transitive verb with **active voice** will carry the action to an object. The subject actually performs the action of the verb. Look at this sentence:

Example:
subject verb   object
Ted played tennis.

Ted is the subject, and he is also the actor.

Examine this sentence:

Example:
subject   verb   object
Jane is playing basketball.

Does *Jane* (the subject) actually perform the action? If the subject performs the action, then the verb is in active voice. In this case, the verb, *is playing,* is active.

A transitive verb with **passive voice** will not carry the action forward to an object. Instead, the subject will be acted upon:

Example: The ball *was caught* by Bill.

The subject of the sentence is *ball.* But did the ball perform the action of the verb? No, it was simply caught. Bill, the person who caught the ball, is not the subject. Instead, the actor, Bill, has been placed in a prepositional phrase. Actually, the normal order of the sentence (subject-verb-object) has been reversed. The action of the verb moves backwards to *ball,* not forward as in active voice. In fact, the sentence could easily be rewritten in normal order:

Example: Bill caught the ball.

In most cases, the active voice is more powerful and more realistic than the passive voice. The reason for this is simple: in a sentence with active voice, the subject *performs* the action of the verb. In a sentence with passive voice, the subject *receives* the action of the verb, a job usually performed by the object of the sentence.

---

*By permission. From *Webster's Ninth New Collegiate Dictionary,* © 1984 by Merriam-Webster, Inc., publisher of the Merriam-Webster Dictionaries.

However, there are two cases in which the passive voice is the better choice:

1. when you don't know who performed an action.

    Example: The door was slammed.

    This sentence indicates that you do not know who slammed the door.

2. when, for whatever reason, you do not wish to disclose the name of the actor.

    Example: The report was submitted late.

    In this case, the author of the report does not want to admit that he submitted the paper after the deadline.

PRACTICE 2

Change the following passive verbs to active ones.

Example: The report *was delivered* by David.

Correction: David ___*delivered*___ the report.

1. The announcement *was made* by John.

    John _____ the announcement.

2. The horse *was saddled* by the jockey.

    The jockey _____ the horse.

3. Birthday presents *were received* by the child.

    The child _____ birthday presents.

4. The radio station *was changed* by me.

    I _____ the radio station.

5. The dinner *was cooked* by the gourmet chef.

    The gourmet chef _____ the dinner.

6. The fire *was lit* by Sam.

    Sam _____ the fire.

7. The proclamation *was announced* by the president.

    The president _____ the proclamation.

8. A new law *was passed* by Congress.

    Congress _____ a new law.

9. The ruling *was made* by the Supreme Court.

   The Supreme Court _____ the ruling.

10. The gift *was given* by my aunt.

   My aunt _____ the gift.

Check the answer key.

Transitive verbs can be conjugated in passive voice through all the tenses. Compare the following conjugations of the verb *to give* in active and passive voice.

	Active Voice	*Passive Voice*
Present	gives/give	am/is/are given
Past	gave	was/were given
Future	will give	will be given
Present Perfect	has/have given	has/have been given
Past Perfect	had given	had been given
Future Perfect	will have given	will have been given
Present Progressive	am/is/are giving	am/is/are being given
Past Progressive	was/were giving	was/were being given
Future Progressive	will be giving	will be being given
Present Perfect Progressive	has/have been giving	has/have been being given
Past Perfect Progressive	had been giving	had been being given
Future Perfect Progressive	will have been giving	will have been being given

PRACTICE 3

Change the following active verbs to passive voice; use the same verb tense given in the sentences.

Example: I *gave* the present.

Correction: The present ___*was given*___ by me.

1. He *will give* the speech.

   The speech _____ by him.

2. The Joneses *sent* the roses.

   The roses _____ by the Joneses.

3. James *had driven* the car.

   The car _____ by James.

4. The major *will have commanded* the troops.

   The troops _____ by the major.

5. I *wrote* the report.

   The report _____ by me.

Check the answer key.

Mood

Verbs are classified also by mood. There are three moods: indicative, imperative, and subjunctive.
The **indicative mood** makes a statement.

Example: I *ran* home.

The indicative mood is most frequently used. In fact, almost all the verbs in the book have been in the indicative mood.

The **imperative mood** expresses a command or a request.

Example: Please *close* the door.

The **subjunctive mood** has been replaced in everyday spoken English, for the most part, by the indicative mood. However, the present and past tenses of the subjunctive mood are still valuable in expressing certain concepts, and the subjunctive mood is required in formal writing.
The present tense of verbs in the subjunctive mood is conjugated the same throughout the form. The present subjunctive is the same as the infinitive. The present subjunctive is used rarely and only in conjunction with verbs of insistence (verbs like *demand, insist, require,* and *request*). In the sentence construction, the speaker demands that someone complete an action.
Here is the present-tense conjugation of the verb *to be* in the subjunctive mood:

I be	we be
you be	you be
he, she, it be	they be

Examples: John requires that we *be* on time.
The president demands that all citizens *be* registered voters.
It is necessary that Mary *be* ready at five o'clock exactly.

The past subjunctive is formed from the past tense of a verb. The verb used most frequently in the past subjunctive is the verb *to be*. Look at the past subjunctive of the verb *to be*:

I were	we were
you were	you were
he, she, it were	they were

The past subjunctive is used in one of two cases:

1. *To express a situation contrary to fact.* Use an *If . . . then* sentence construction.

   Example: If I *were* a millionaire, then I would buy a huge estate.

   The implication is obvious: I am not a millionaire. This use of the past subjunctive shows that the premise (the phrase following *If*) is not true.

2. *To express a wish.* Use a sentence construction that includes a verb that **expresses a wish,** hope, or desire.

   Example: I wish that it *were* Saturday.

   The statement was made on a day other than Saturday. The speaker wants the weekend to come.

PRACTICE 4

Insert the correct form of the subjunctive of the verb *to be* into the following **sentences.**

1. I wish that Mary _____ here.

2. If Tom _____ a scientist, then he would qualify as an **astronaut.**

3. My job demands that I _____ at work at 5:00 a.m.

4. The senator requests that aides _____ at the briefing.

5. If you _____ the instructor, then I know you would correct the **problems.**

Check the answer key.

Verbals

Infinitives, gerunds, and participles are derived from verbs and are used frequently. These verbals and verbs share some characteristics. For example, verbals can describe actions and have objects. Verbals also can describe states of existence and have subject complements. However, these verbals are *not* the verbs in sentences. Instead, verbals act as different parts of speech.

Infinitives

You should recognize these as the basic form of verbs. The infinitive consists of the word *to* plus the verb. An infinitive can function as a noun (a person, place, or thing), an adverb (modifies a verb, adverb, or adjective), or an adjective (modifies a noun or pronoun).

Consider the following sentences:

Examples: 1. *To run* is my favorite sport.

   To run is a noun used as the subject of the sentence.

2. His desire *to eat too much* made him gain weight.
   The infinitive phrase *to eat too much* is used as an adjective; it describes his desire.

3. She ran *to see who was at the door*.
   The infinitive phrase *to see who was at the door* is used as an adverb; it tells why she ran.

EXERCISE Underline the infinitives and the infinitive phrases in each of the following sentences. Identify each infinitive by its part of speech: noun, adjective, or adverb.

1. To become a good pianist, you must practice an hour each day.

2. His ability to run quickly made him an excellent sprinter.

3. Terrance hopes to travel to Europe next summer.

4. To enjoy a visit to another country, you should be willing to explore the country's cities and to visit historical sites.

5. Our trip to the library allowed us to complete our research.

Have your instructor or tutor check your work.

Gerunds

A gerund is used frequently. It is made by adding *ing* to the verb. A gerund has only one function: it serves as a noun. The words *rowing, sailing,* and *hiking* in the following sentences are all gerunds and used as nouns.

Examples:
1. *Sailing* is a favorite sport on the Gulf of Mexico.
   Sailing is a gerund and is used as the subject of the sentence.

2. The campers enjoyed *rowing, hiking, sailing,* and *backpacking*.
   The words *rowing, hiking, sailing,* and *backpacking* are all gerunds used as objects of the verb.

EXERCISE Underline the gerunds and gerund phrases in each of the following sentences. Identify each gerund by its part of speech.

1. Many adventurous tourists enjoy rafting down the Colorado River.

2. Hiking the length of the Appalachian Trail requires at least six months.

3. Wind surfing has become a popular sport.

4. Many actors and actresses like preparing for the annual *Circus of the Stars*.

5. Many people appreciate picnicking on warm spring days.

Have your instructor or tutor check your work.

Participles

A participle is a verbal used only as an adjective to modify a noun or pronoun.

A **present participle** is made from the verb and *ing*. You constructed these when you studied the progressive forms of verbs. Although a present participle and a gerund are constructed in the same manner, you can tell them apart. Remember that a gerund is used solely as a noun, and a participle is used only as an adjective.

Examples: 1. People of all ages enjoy *dancing*.
             Dancing is a gerund, a noun.

             2. *Dancing* gracefully, they won the audience's heart.
                In this sentence, *dancing* is the present participle of the verb *to dance*; it describes the subject *they*.

You have already seen past participles when you constructed the perfect tenses of verbs. The past participle is the form of the verb that follows *has* or *have* and *had*. A past participle is usually made from the verb and *d* or *ed*. However, past participles derived from irregular verbs do not follow this rule. To review the formation of irregular past participles, check the list of the various formations in "The Perfect Tenses," Chapter 2.

The participle, present or past, is used as an adjective to describe a noun or pronoun. Look at the following sentences:

Examples: 1. He is a well-*known* author.
             Known is the past participle of the verb *to know*; it modifies *author*.

             2. After *hitting* the ball, she ran to first base.
                The participial phrase *After hitting the ball* modifies the subject *she*; it tells what she did.

             3. The baseball, *hit* by Mickey Mantle, sailed over the outfield wall.
                The participial phrase *hit by Mickey Mantle* describes the baseball by telling who hit it.

NOTE: By themselves, present and past participles cannot be the verbs in sentences; instead, these participles will modify nouns or pronouns. However, present and past participles are used to construct the perfect tenses and the progressive forms of verbs. In this usage, the participles are preceded by helping verbs, such as *am, is, are, have, has,* or *had*. Review the conjugations of the perfect tenses and the progressive forms in Chapter 2.

EXERCISE   Underline the participles and participial phrases in each of the following sentences. Identify each participle by its part of speech.

1. Sharon is an accomplished pianist; she recently won the coveted Prix de France.

2. Jumping for joy, the children raced to the entrance of the amusement park.

3. The recently injured man applied for government benefits.

4. Listening intently to the radio, Jules failed to hear the ringing telephone.

5. The steaming soup quickly boiled over the sides of the pot.

   Have your instructor or tutor check your work.

PRACTICE 5

Identify all verbal phrases in the sentences by circling them, and label each type of verbal. The verbs in the sentence have been identified for you; they are in italic type.

Example: Roller (skating) *is* great fun.   _____ *a gerund* _____

1. To earn an *A* on the test *is* my goal.   _____

2. Their mother, a noted scientist, *received* the Nobel Prize.   _____

3. Driving to the store, I *saw* an old friend.   _____

4. He *wants* to earn extra money this summer.   _____

5. Water skiing *is* a marvelous way to spend a summer afternoon.   _____

6. The child playing in the yard *is* Hank's brother.   _____

7. We *took* a well-deserved vacation.   _____

8. Shakespeare's famous line "To be, or not to be" *is* often *quoted*.   _____

9. The middle-aged man *enjoyed* photographing birds.   _____

10. He *enjoys* his job of ringing the church bells.   _____

11. Dashing to the finish line, Jenny *placed* first in the 800-meter race.

    _____

12. After receiving her bachelor's degree, Carrie *plans* to attend law school.

    _____

13. Typing the final word, the novelist *finished* her first work.   _____

14. To dance the limbo, you *must* be very flexible.   _____

15. The couple *planned* to see a movie, dine at a good restaurant, and dance until midnight.   _____

16. The quarterback, fading back for a pass, *was hit* by the rushing tackles.

    _____

17. Pivoting quickly, the band members *marched* past the parade judge.

    _____

18. The feuding families *decided* to settle their differences in court.   _____

19. Building a fire *requires* effort, skill, and a little luck.   _____

20. Frank *enjoys* camping and biking as his hobbies.   _____

Check the answer key.

Style

Verbs are the core portion of a sentence. Therefore, they are vitally important when you write a sentence, a paragraph, or an essay. The following guidelines will help you when you write:

1. *Use action verbs.* These convey more movement than the linking verbs. They also convey a visual image, much more so than the verb *to be*. Compare these sentences:

    Examples: The horse *was* in the pasture.
    The horse *grazed* in the pasture.

    Which verb gives a better image of the scene? *grazed,* the action verb.

2. *Use active voice in preference to the passive voice.* The active voice conveys action from the subject (the actor) to the object (the receiver of the action). In other words, the subject fulfills its function—to act. Compare these two sentences:

    Examples: a. The article was written by Ms. Abrams.
    b. Ms. Abrams wrote the article.

    Which is the stronger sentence? *b*

3. *Keep verb tense consistent.* Do not confuse your reader by changing tenses unnecessarily.

4. *To give a clear, visual image, use more verbs and verbals than adjectives.*

APPLICATION I

Rewrite the following sentences to eliminate the weak verbs. Supply action verbs in place of the linking verbs.

1. Five people *are* on the committee.

   _____

2. The book *is* on the library shelf.

   _____

3. This pen *is* Jacob's.

   _____

4. The blue car *is* Harriet's.

   _____

5. There *are* many things students enjoy.

   _____

6. The horse *is* slow.

   _____

7. San Francisco *is* a great place to visit.

   _____

8. There *were* five people who applauded the speech.

   _____

9. Exercise *is* good for us.

   _____

10. Swimming *is* her favorite sport.

    _____

Have your instructor or tutor check your work.

APPLICATION II

Read the following paragraph carefully. Change the passive verbs to active voice by rewriting the entire sentence. All verbs have been italicized.

(1) Baseball *is loved* by the American people. (2) It *is viewed* as the true American sport.

(3) Baseball *was invented* by an American, Abner Doubleday, in 1839. (4) Since that time, the game *has been dominated* by many great players. (5) For example, Babe Ruth, Ted Williams, Jackie Robinson, and Ty Cobb *are* just a few of the many men who *made* the game a national passion. (6) Today, the ball parks and stadiums *are filled* with millions of people each year. (7) From sandlots and school playgrounds to superdomes, baseball *is played* by everyone. (8) After all, *is* there a better way to spend a lazy summer day? (9) The green field, the colorful uniforms, the gentle contest between two teams, and the refreshments *bring* millions to the stadiums.

_____

_____

_____

_____

_____

_____

_____

_____

_____

Check the answer key.

APPLICATION III

Read the following paragraph carefully. Check all italicized verbs for consistent tense. Change any verb that is not consistent.

(1) The Battle of Antietam, which *had claimed* over 22,000 casualties on September 17, 1862, *marks* a turning point in America's history. (2) Robert E. Lee, commander of Confederacy's Army of Northern Virginia, *had wanted* to divert the Union's attention away from Richmond. (3) Moreover, his men badly *needed* food, which he *was thinking* would be available in the lush Maryland countryside, and he *had* his eye on the federal armaments in Harper's Ferry to the west. (4) Lee *hoped* that Maryland, a border state, *will be won* over to the Confederate cause. (5) Ultimately, Lee *plans* to invade Pennsylvania and cut the federal railroad lines. (6) Lee's

opponent in this ambitious scheme *was* Major General George B. McClellan, noted for his extreme caution. (7) After discovering Lee's battle plan, McClellan *will be failing* to press his advantage sufficiently and *was allowing* the badly hurt Confederate army to withdraw across the Potomac back into Virginia. (8) Had he pursued, McClellan *might* then *have ended* the Civil War in the East. (9) At any rate, the Confederacy never again *will have* such an opportunity for victory. (10) The Union *was remaining* intact, and American history *will take* its present course with an America that *was* not *divided*.

Check the answer key.

APPLICATION IV

Proofread a rough draft of a paper of your own for the following three items: verbs in active voice, action verbs, and verb consistency. Correct any problems and show your revisions to your instructor or tutor.

Subjects, Verbs, and Prepositional Phrases

OBJECTIVES: 1. To identify subjects, verbs, and prepositional phrases.

2. To recognize parts of speech and their use in sentences.

KEY CONCEPT: A complete sentence requires a subject and a verb; it also must express a complete thought.

Subjects

A sentence must have a subject. A **subject** is a *noun* (a person, place, or thing) or a *pronoun* (a word that takes the place of a noun).

Types of Nouns

Nouns can be classified in a number of ways. A **proper noun** names a specific person, place, or thing. It is always capitalized.

> Examples: *Mr. Smith, Professor Thomas, New York City, Ford*

A **common noun** names an object, place, or person. It does *not* name a *specific* object, place, or person.

> Examples: *dog, animal, tree*

A **concrete noun** names anything you can perceive through one of the five senses: touch, taste, smell, hearing, or sight.

> Examples: *chair, room, ball, wind, music, paint*

An **abstract noun** names an emotion, quality, or idea. You cannot perceive this noun through one of the five senses.

> Examples: *love, hate, anger, philosophy*

A **collective noun** names a group of individuals.

Examples: *army, jury, team, committee*

Types of Pronouns

A **pronoun** takes the place of a noun.

Example: Meredith went to the movies; she saw the Bogart movie *The African Queen*.
In this sentence, *she* is a pronoun that takes the place of the proper noun *Meredith*.

Each of the following pronouns could be used as the subject of a sentence:

Personal Pronouns: *I, you, she, he, it, we, you, they*

Indefinite Pronouns: *everyone, everybody, somebody, someone, each, nobody, no one, none, anybody, anyone, some, all, several*

PRACTICE 1

A. List five proper nouns:

1. _____

2. _____

3. _____

4. _____

5. _____

B. List five common nouns:

1. _____

2. _____

3. _____

4. _____

5. _____

C. List five concrete nouns:

1. _____

2. _____

3. _____

4. _____

5. _____

D. List five abstract nouns:

1. _____

2. _____

3. _____

4. _____

5. _____

E. List five collective nouns:

1. _____

2. _____

F. List five pronouns:

1. _____

2. _____

3. _____   3. _____

4. _____   4. _____

5. _____   5. _____

Have your instructor or tutor check your work.

Verbs

A sentence also must contain a **verb.** There are two types of verbs:

1. **Action** verbs show movement. For example, *to sing, to joke, to run,* and *to walk* are action verbs.

2. **Linking** verbs do not show action. Instead, they convey existence, being, becoming, and, sometimes, one of the five senses. For example, the verbs *to be, to seem,* and *to become* are linking verbs. Linking verbs connect, or make equal, the subject and the word after the linking verb.

PRACTICE 2

A. List five action verbs: B. List three linking verbs:

1. _____   1. _____

2. _____   2. _____

3. _____   3. _____

4. _____

5. _____

Have your instructor or tutor check your work.

Identifying Subjects and Verbs

To identify the subject and verb in a sentence, ask these questions:

- What is the action? or What word links two or more other words? the *verb.*
- Who or what is performing the action? the *subject.*

Examples: 1. Barbara sang.
                   What is the action? *sang* (verb—action)
                   Who sang? *Barbara* (subject)

              2. Robert leaped.
                   What is the action? *leaped* (verb—action)
                   Who leaped? *Robert* (subject)

3. The bird is ill.
   What word joins the other words? *is* (verb—linking)
   Who is ill? *bird* (subject)

4. The children were happy.
   What word joins the other words? *were* (verb—linking)
   Who were happy? *children* (subject)

PRACTICE 3

Identify the subjects and verbs in the following sentences.

1. Terry laughs.

   verb _____

   subject _____

2. I swam.

   verb _____

   subject _____

3. Elvis Presley is world-famous.

   verb _____

   subject _____

4. Children play.

   verb _____

   subject _____

5. The defendant read his statement.

   verb _____

   subject _____

6. The homework seemed complete.

   verb _____

   subject _____

7. Prom night will be a disaster.

   verb _____

   subject _____

8. The doctor fainted.

   verb _____

   subject _____

9. The bullet hit the target.

   verb _____

   subject _____

10. This Porsche is a popular gift.

    verb _____

    subject _____

Check the answer key.

Simple and Compound Subjects and Verbs

The sentences you have worked with up to this point have contained only one subject and one verb. A single subject is referred to as a **simple subject;** a single verb is referred to as a **simple verb.**

Example: The police officer quickly drew his pistol.

    Subject—police officer (one actor—simple subject)
    Verb—drew (one action—simple verb)

However, a sentence may also contain a **compound subject:** two or more stated nouns or pronouns perform the same action.

Examples: Charles and the boys have gone to the movies.
What is the action? *have gone* (one action—simple verb)
Who has gone? *Charles and the boys* (two stated actors—compound subject)

He and I decided to backpack through South America.
What is the action? *decided* (one action—simple verb)
Who decided? *He and I* (two stated actors—compound subject)

A sentence may also contain a **compound verb:** the subject performs two or more actions.

Example: Trendy people frequently drink, dance, and party through the night.

What is (are) the action(s)? *Drink, dance, and party* (three actions—compound verb)
Who drinks, dances, and parties? *Trendy people* (one stated group—simple subject)

NOTE: In the last sentence, the fact that the subject *people* is a plural noun is not significant. Only *one* performer of the action—people—is given; therefore, there is only one subject and it is a simple subject.

In addition to sentences with simple subjects and verbs, there are three other possible combinations of simple and compound subjects and verbs.

Compound Subject/Simple Verb. In this case, two or more subjects perform one action.

Example: George and Frank went to Mexico.

What is the action? *went*
Who went? *George and Frank*

In this sentence, both *George* and *Frank* are performing the same action. The compound subject is *George and Frank*.

Simple Subject/Compound Verb. The simple subject of the sentence performs two or more actions. Answer the questions in this example:

Example: The audience booed and hissed the performer.

What are the two actions performed? _____

What is the subject? _____

In this sentence, the audience performed two actions—booed and hissed. The compound verb is *booed* and *hissed*.

Compound Subject/Compound Verb. This means that two or more subjects perform two or more actions. Answer the questions in this example.

Example: Curly, Larry, and Moe danced and ate all night.

What is the compound verb? _____

What is the compound subject? _____

Curly, Larry, and *Moe* are all performing the same actions—*danced* and *ate*.

PRACTICE 4

Find the verbs and subjects in the following sentences. Indicate whether they are simple or compound by writing *S* (for simple) or *C* (for compound) beside the verbs and subjects.

1. Fords and Chevrolets are two makes of American cars.

   verb(s) _____ subject(s) _____

2. The cat hissed and scratched.

   verb(s) _____ subject(s) _____

3. Caleb and I read and study.

   verb(s) _____ subject(s) _____

4. Angela became a doctor.

   verb(s) _____ subject(s) _____

5. He and Martha took a vacation last spring.

   verb(s) _____ subject(s) _____

6. Tina seemed sad.

   verb(s) _____ subject(s) _____

7. Ice cream and cake are his favorite foods.

   verb(s) _____ subject(s) _____

8. Puerto Rico and St. Thomas are beautiful vacation spots.

   verb(s) _____ subject(s) _____

9. Nita appears happy.

   verb(s) _____ subject(s) _____

10. The dolphin leaped and swam.

   verb(s) _____ subject(s) _____

Check the answer key.

Exceptions

The words *there*, *here*, and *where* can never be the subject of a sentence, so you must look for another word—a noun or a pronoun—as the subject of the sentence.

Example: There is my car.

What is the verb? *is*
What is the subject? *car*

PRACTICE 5

Find the verbs and subjects in the following sentences. Indicate whether they are simple or compound by writing *S* (for simple) or *C* (for compound) beside the verbs and subjects.

1. There are my best friends.

   verb(s) _____   subject(s) _____

2. Here is the manuscript for the new television series.

   verb(s) _____   subject(s) _____

3. Where are Harry's ball and bat?

   verb(s) _____   subject(s) _____

4. Here is the answer to your question.

   verb(s) _____   subject(s) _____

5. Here come Linda's boyfriend and another girl.

   verb(s) _____   subject(s) _____

Check the answer key.

Helping Verbs

In the previous examples and practice exercises, you might have noticed that most of the verbs have consisted of only one word. Because most of the sentences used the present tense (present time), only one word was needed for the verb. However, because verbs tell us about time, it is sometimes necessary for a verb to have more than one word in order to convey a particular time. The **main verb** (major action) may be accompanied by **helping verbs** that help describe the time of the action.

Example: Look at the following sentences. All of them contain a form of the verb *to ask*. Notice the helping verbs.

I ask.	I am asking.
I asked.	I was asking.
I will ask.	I will be asking.
I have asked.	I have been asking.
I had asked.	I had been asking.
I will have asked.	I will have been asking.

NOTE: See Chapters 2 and 3 for more information on helping verbs and tenses.

PRACTICE 6

Find the verbs and subjects in the following sentences. Be sure to include any helping verbs.

NOTE: Do not include negatives (such as the word *no*) in the verb.

Example: Helen is not going to the dance.

The subject is *Helen*.
The verb is *is going*.

1. Tom will not have left school by four o'clock.

   verb _____   subject _____

2. The senator will have been in office four years this spring.

   verb _____   subject _____

3. The car had been demolished in the wreck.

   verb _____   subject _____

4. The animals at the zoo will be released into a natural-habitat park.

   verb _____   subject _____

5. The disc jockey was playing records by Willie Nelson and Hank Williams, Jr.

   verb _____   subject _____

Check the answer key.

Prepositional Phrases

A sentence may have many phrases and additional words. One type of phrase that can seem confusing and make a sentence seem more complex is a prepositional phrase. A prepositional phrase consists of a **preposition** (for example: *of, for, to, in, out, around, through*) and a noun or pronoun (called the **object of the preposition**); it may also contain adjectives and/or adverbs.

Prepositions are easily recognized. Prepositional phrases provide additional information to the reader of the sentence. Usually, prepositions express the time of the action or other relationships. The following prepositions introduce information in the categories of time, place, and other:

Time	*Place*		*Other*	
after	under	behind	about	for
before	in/into	through	against	at
during	out	up	off	onto
until	around	inside	past	of
	outside	to	with	from
	between	among	except	in order of
	over	by	due to	because of
	above	across	by	like
	below	beneath	such as	
	beside	beyond		
	near	without		
	within			

The following are examples of prepositional phrases:

under the forbidding mountain	behind the door
into the green room	since May
after the game	with her

NOTE: To help determine if a word is a preposition, use this test: a preposition expresses any relationship that makes sense with regard to a house.

Example: *into* the house
around the house
to the house
outside the house
into, around, to, and *outside* are prepositions
This test will help you locate most prepositions that describe place; it will not help locate those that express time.

A number of prepositional phrases in a sentence may make it difficult to find the subject and the verb. Remember that the *noun* or *pronoun* in a prepositional phrase is *the object of the preposition;* this word can never be the subject of the sentence!

To find the subject and verb in a sentence, simply eliminate the prepositional phrases in the sentence.

Example: The Board of Trustees of the college is meeting now in the conference room of the Administration Building.

Cross out the prepositional phrases (as well as any other adjectives and adverbs) in the above sentence, and find the subject and the verb. Your sentence should now look like this:

The Board ~~of Trustees of the college~~ is meeting ~~now in the conference room of the Administration Building.~~

What is the verb? *is meeting*
What is the subject? *Board*

PRACTICE 7

Cross out any prepositional phrases in the following sentences. Then, underline the subjects and the verbs and label them.

Example: ~~In the center of the room~~ stood Jim.   *verb subject*

1. The cat ran under the porch.

2. Bronco Davis was a famous football player for twenty years.

3. The greyhound with the matted coat and an evil look in his eyes frightened the school-children.

4. The drive to Orlando is a pleasant one.

5. Bing Crosby and Bob Hope were a successful team for more than fifteen years.

Check the answer key.

APPLICATION I

Find the subjects and verbs in the following sentences and underline the subject once and the verb twice. Cross out any prepositional phrases. Then, in the appropriate column, indicate whether the subjects and verbs are simple or compound by writing S (for simple) or C (for compound).

	Subject	*Verb*
1. At night, it usually becomes colder.	_____	_____
2. President and Mrs. Reagan greeted the guests.	_____	_____
3. Will Julio help me?	_____	_____
4. Where did Bob and Ted go after football practice?	_____	_____
5. The members of the Board of Trustees chose a new chairperson.	_____	_____
6. Jerry is planning to take a trip to the Far East.	_____	_____
7. Do you ever watch soap operas?	_____	_____
8. Dr. Harper, the famous anthropologist, climbed Mt. McKinley and then reported her findings to the American Academy of Scientists.	_____	_____
9. Professors James and Harvey played in the student-faculty basketball game and scored 15 points each.	_____	_____
10. There are many fine, old homes in Concord, Massachusetts.	_____	_____
11. Many of the U.S. presidents encouraged the country to remain isolated from the rest of the world.	_____	_____

12. Children and adults both like to visit Disneyland.

   _____ _____

13. Call the doctor and make an appointment for Friday afternoon.

   _____ _____

14. Mr. Avery, my tax accountant, has saved me money each year by itemizing my deductions.

   _____ _____

15. In the distance were two Air Force planes.

   _____ _____

16. In the morning, the Department of History will announce its decision about the new history course.

   _____ _____

17. Why did Chad go to Alaska this winter?

   _____ _____

18. My friend Juanita is going to school this fall and is going to work at the same time.

   _____ _____

19. It is important for students to write down all their assignments.

   _____ _____

20. Firefighters and police officers have dangerous jobs and often are injured.

   _____ _____

21. Math and science are Helen's favorite subjects.

   _____ _____

22. The Broncos tried hard to win the Super Bowl but couldn't do it.

   _____ _____

23. All of the students requested a change of schedule.

   _____ _____

24. The basketball team and the baseball team practiced in the gym during the winter. _____ _____

25. Have Delores and Ann decided where to go on their vacation? _____ _____

26. Jim sold his Ford and bought a Chevrolet. _____ _____

27. Many of the new businesses require college graduates. _____ _____

28. Talk to Sara and ask her to help us. _____ _____

29. All of the members of the Women's Club sold flowers in order to earn extra money for their annual dance. _____ _____

30. People need to be recognized and praised for their good deeds. _____ _____

Check the answer key.

APPLICATION II

A. Write two sentences that each contain a simple subject and a simple verb.

1. _____

2. _____

B. Write two sentences that each contain a simple subject and a compound verb.

1. _____

2. _____

C. Write two sentences that each contain a compound subject and a simple verb.

1. _____

2. _____

D. Write two sentences that each contain a compound subject and a compound verb.

1. _____

2. _____

E. Write two sentences that each contain a helping verb and a main verb.

1. _____

2. _____

Have your instructor or tutor check your work.

APPLICATION III

In a paragraph you wrote, identify the subjects and verbs. Show your list of subjects and verbs to your instructor or tutor.

5

Sentence Formats and Sentence Classes

OBJECTIVES: 1. To recognize and write sentence formats.

2. To identify and write the major classes of sentences.

KEY CONCEPT: The position of words in a sentence helps to convey the sentence's meaning.

The words in a sentence are not randomly thrown into the sentence; they are arranged according to specific patterns. These patterns make it easier for the reader to understand the writer's idea and to organize the relationship between concepts. Without these generally recognized patterns, or formats, communication would be difficult. Without them, writing and reading would be very individualized activities. Each reader would have to become familiar with each writer's specific style before communication could begin. That would be a time-consuming process.

Example: Towards the launch delta the sleek and gray safety sped mouth motor of the.

Obviously, this sentence is not easy to read or understand. It does contain a complete thought, but because the words are not in their accustomed position, that thought is not communicated.

Revised: The sleek gray motor launch sped towards the mouth of the delta and safety.

Now the sentence can be understood, and its thought can be communicated, solely because the words have been unscrambled.

Sentence Formats

Sentence Format 1: Subject and Verb

Here is an example of a Format 1 sentence: Birds sing.

The abbreviation for Sentence Format 1 is S-V. Consider the abbreviation and explain it by using terms you have already encountered.
(S stands for _____ . V stands for _____ .)

The Subject. What words other than *birds* can be substituted into the sentence? Remember, construct a sentence that will have meaning.

_____ sing.   _____ sing.

_____ sing.   _____ sing.

_____ sing.   _____ sing.

What types of words are *birds* and the ones you substituted? Words that can be substituted for each other belong to the same format. The words you supplied have the same relationship with *sing* as the word *birds* has with *sing*. They are all the same type of words—nouns or pronouns.

If you used *I, we, you,* or *they* for the subject, then you used pronouns, not nouns. Pronouns take the place of nouns, so they can be used as the subject of a sentence.

EXERCISE   Fill in the blanks with words that follow Sentence Format 1.

1. _____ squawk.   5. _____ jump.

2. _____ yell.   6. _____ sink.

3. _____ meow.   7. _____ swim.

4. _____ dance.   8. _____ leap.

Have your instructor or tutor check your work.

The Verb. The noun or pronoun—the subject—is only part of Sentence Format 1; the second portion of the format is the **verb.** In the example sentence, *Birds sing,* what words can be substituted for *sing*? These are **action verbs,** because they name an action.

Birds _____   Birds _____   Birds _____ .

A word that can be substituted for *sing* is a verb.

EXERCISE   Fill in the blanks with verbs to complete the sentences.

1. Dogs _____ .   5. Windows _____ .

2. Monkeys _____ .   6. Joggers _____ .

3. Cars _____ .   7. Airplanes _____ .

4. Houses _____ .   8. Radios _____ .

Have your instructor or tutor check your work.

Next, using Sentence Format 1 (S-V), write your own sentences.

1. _____ .

2. _____ .

3. _____ .

4. _____ .

5. _____ .

Have your instructor or tutor check your work.

EXERCISE   Using Format 1, write five sentences with pronouns as the subjects.

1. _____

2. _____

3. _____

4. _____

5. _____

Have your instructor or tutor check your work.

Not all Format 1 sentences consist of only two words. Modifiers, such as adjectives, adverbs, and prepositional phrases can be added without changing the fundamental pattern of the sentence.

Example: The world-famous soprano sang mournfully at the funeral.
What is the subject?   *Soprano.*   What is the verb?   *Sang.*

The above sentence conforms to Format 1 because it has two essential elements: the subject and verb. The other words (*world-famous* and *mournfully*) describe the subject and verb, but they do not carry the meaning of the sentence. Likewise, the prepositional phrase says where the singing occurred, but it does not convey the basic message.

PRACTICE 1

In each sentence, underline the subject once, the verb twice, and write its format in the blank to the right.

Example: Each proud <u>graduate</u> <u>walked</u> swiftly to the podium.   *1*

1. The cheerful child hopped merrily across the pavement.   _____

2. The lamb cried loudly.   _____

3. At night, hundreds of bats fly out of that cave.   _____

4. The price of milk has just been increased by 20 percent. _____

5. Jumpin' Jack sings nightly at the Go-ahead Lounge.   _____

Check the answer key.

Sentence Format 2: The Direct Object

Sentence Format 2 builds upon Sentence Format 1 (S-V). It simply adds another word and relationship to the format.

Example: Harry hit the baseball.

Consider carefully the relationships among the words. You should recognize that *Harry* is the subject and *hit* is the verb. However, what relationship does *baseball* have to *hit*? *Baseball* is the **direct object** of the verb. Nouns and pronouns can act as direct objects. The direct object receives the action of the verb. When you ask, "What was hit?" and locate an answer, then you have found the direct object.

The abbreviation for Sentence Format 2 is S-V-DO.

EXERCISE   Fill in the blanks with one word that will complete the sentence. Identify the word you used. Is it a subject, a verb, or direct object?

1. _____ threw a ball.

2. Rob _____ his lunch.

3. I dropped my _____ .

4. Grandmother _____ her knitting.

5. _____ read the book.

6. Dad drove the _____ .

7. My little brother _____ the dog.

8. The bus hit the _____ .

9. He bought the _____ .

10. The cat _____ its kittens.

Have your instructor or tutor check your work.

You should be familiar with this format; it is Sentence Format 2. Now, label the next sentence:

Hector threw me the ball.

In the sentence above, *Hector* is the subject; *threw* is the verb, and *ball* is the direct object. But the sentence has an additional word—*me*. *Me* is a pronoun; it tells to whom the ball was thrown. A pronoun or a noun with this relationship to the verb is called an *indirect object*. You could construct the sentence in this manner: Hector threw the ball to me. Notice that *me* is now the object of the preposition *to*. You can place *to* or *for* in front of the indirect object.

To test for indirect objects in a sentence, follow these two steps:

1. Rewrite the sentence to follow Format 2 (S-V-DO).
2. Add *to* or *for* plus the word in question to the end of the sentence.

> Example: May gave me the book.
>
> In order to decide if *me* is the indirect object, follow the two steps of the test:
>
> Step 1. Rewrite the sentence to follow Format 2:
> May gave the book. (S-V-DO)
>
> Step 2. Add *to* or *for* plus the word in question to the end of the sentence:
> May gave the book to me.

Because *me* can be placed into a prepositional phrase, *me* is the indirect object.

> Examples: Harold gave Tracy the roses.
>
>   Apply the two-step test:
>
> _____
>
> Dad gave Vicki her allowance.
>
> Apply the two-step test:
>
> _____

Do the sentences make sense? If they do, you have found the indirect objects.

The abbreviation for Sentence Format 3 is S-V-IO-DO.

PRACTICE 4

Label all subjects, verbs, indirect objects, and direct objects.

        S   V   IO   DO
Example: I gave Anwar the award for academic excellence.

1. Pablo awarded Henry the prize.

2. The boy bought the girl a flower.

3. The nervous young man handed his girlfriend a diamond ring.

4. My English teacher gave me a high mark on my test.

5. Hector fed the dog his dinner.

6. The bird built his mate a nest.

7. I gave my friend an umbrella.

8. She brought Darryl a soda.

9. The kidnappers gave the child a candy bar.

10. Sharon bought her father a wool sweater.

Check the answer key.

EXERCISE   Write ten sentences of your own that follow Format 3.

1. _____

2. _____

3. _____

4. _____

5. _____

6. _____

7. _____

8. _____

9. _____

10. _____

Have your instructor or tutor check your work.

EXERCISE   The following questions will test your understanding of the first three sentence formats.

1. What is the relationship of a direct object to the verb?

_____

2. What is the relationship of a direct object to the subject?

_____

3. What is the relationship of an indirect object to the verb?

_____

4. What is the relationship between the subject and the verb?

_____

5. Give the codes for the first three sentence formats.

_____

Have your instructor or tutor check your work. If you had trouble answering any of these questions, review the sections on Formats 1, 2, and 3 before you continue.

Sentence Format 4: The Predicate Adjective and the Predicate Nominative

The fourth sentence format introduces two new elements. Look at these examples.

Examples: Harry is tall.
            Harry is a freshman.

Notice that a new type of verb is included: a **linking verb.** Any form of the verb *to be* is a linking verb, as are the verbs *seem, feel, appear,* and *become.* Linking verbs (LV) connect the word that follows them to the subject in a special relationship. It almost seems as if the linking verb equates both sides.

The Predicate Adjective. Consider these Format 4 sentences:

Examples: Cathy is cute.
            The sky appears cloudy.
            Horses are strong.
            The runners seem tired.

In these sentences, the words connected to the subjects by the linking verbs are **adjectives;** they describe or characterize the nouns that are the subjects. You could write *cute Cathy, cloudy sky, strong horses,* or *tired runners.* These adjectives in Sentence Format 4 are called **predicate adjectives,** because they describe the subject.

NOTE: If you took only the subjects and verbs of the sentences, then you would not have complete sentences: *Cathy is, The sky appears, Horses are,* and *The runners seem.* The predicate adjective is needed to describe the subject and to complete the sentence.

The format for the sentence *Harry is tall* is: S-LV-PA.

PRACTICE 5

In the following sentences, underline the linking verbs. Write the predicate adjective and the subject together and identify the format.

	PA-S	LV	Format
Example: The weather is bad.	*bad weather*	*is*	S-LV-PA

	PA-S	LV	Format
1. The weightlifter is powerful.	_____	_____	_____
2. Tom appears sad.	_____	_____	_____
3. May looks happy.	_____	_____	_____
4. The dinner tasted good.	_____	_____	_____
5. Earl Bruce was cooperative.	_____	_____	_____
6. The cat sounds angry.	_____	_____	_____
7. He seems tired.	_____	_____	_____
8. The onion smells sour.	_____	_____	_____
9. The road becomes rough.	_____	_____	_____
10. The apple was red and delicious.	_____	_____	_____

Check the answer key.

EXERCISE Complete the following sentences by adding predicate adjectives.

1. He becomes _____ .

2. The mouse was _____ .

3. The movie seemed _____ .

4. The sky turned _____ .

5. Sam is _____ .

6. Baseball seems _____ .

7. The book appeared _____ .

8. The oranges are _____ .

9. The cake tasted _____ .

10. The dessert was _____ .

Have your instructor or tutor check your work.

PRACTICE 6

Both Format 2 and Format 4 sentences will be found in the following exercise. Identify each format. Underline the linking verb twice, write the predicate adjective in the blanks, and label them. Underline action verbs once and write the direct objects in the blanks and label them DO.

NOTE: Linking verbs never take direct objects.

		Format
Examples:	1. He suddenly <u>became</u> weak.	*weak* PA
	2. Tom <u>bounced</u> a ball.	*ball*, DO

Format

1. The cowboy branded the calf.   _____

2. His car looks expensive.   _____

3. I enjoy comic books.   _____

4. The arrow struck a rock.   _____

5. His shoes are dirty.   _____

6. The girls were pretty.   _____

7. Gerry's Restaurant serves good food.   _____

8. The Gulf of Mexico has quite blue water.   _____

9. The teacher looks interested.   _____

10. The audience seemed uneasy.   _____

Check the answer key.

EXERCISE   Write five sentences of your own that follow the format S-LV-PA.

1. _____

2. _____

3. _____

4. _____

5. _____

Have your instructor or tutor check your work.

The Predicate Nominative. The second example sentence for Format 4 is below:

Harry is a freshman.

The format is basically the same as S-LV-PA. *Harry* is the subject, and *is* is the linking verb. However, *freshman* is a noun, not a predicate adjective. A noun following a linking verb is called a **predicate nominative.** The predicate nominative might define the subject, identify it, or rename it. In other words, the predicate nominative, a noun, is equal to the subject, a noun. For instance, in the example sentence, *Harry* and *freshman* are equivalent. The abbreviation for this second type of Format 4 sentence is: S-LV-PN.

S   LV   PN
Harry is a freshman.

PRACTICE 7

Identify the predicate nominatives in the following sentences. Write the predicate nominative and the subject on the lines to the right of the sentence. Use an equal-sign to indicate their equality. Also, label the subjects and linking verbs.

Example: S LV   PN   *captain = Tom*   PN = S
  Tom is the team captain.

1. The senator is the head of a major committee. _____

2. Annapolis is the state capital of Maryland. _____

3. The mahogany desk is an antique. _____

4. Shawn became an astronaut. _____

5. Because of his ability as a blocker, John is a complete foot-

   ball player. _____

6. With her ability as a writer of feature stories, Jane is a con-

   siderable force in Houston journalism. _____

7. Television is one of the primary news media today. _____

8. She is a good actress. _____

9. The girl with the red hair is my cousin. _____

10. An alligator on a shirt is a symbol of preppies. _____

Check the answer key.

EXERCISE   Complete the following sentences by adding predicate nominatives.

1. Novels are _____ .

2. My car is _____ .

3. The captain was _____ .

4. Besides being test pilots, astronauts must also be _____ .

5. The pretty little girl became _____ .

6. Besides being students, many college students are also _____ .

7. The cowboy is also a _____ .

8. Ricardo is a _____ .

9. To Michelangelo, sculpture was _____ .

10. Multinational corporations are _____ .

Have your instructor or tutor check your work.

EXERCISE   Write five sentences of your own that conform to the format S-LV-PN.

1. _____

2. _____

3. _____

4. _____

5. _____

Have your instructor or tutor check your work.

PRACTICE 8

Label each sentence as one of two formats: S-LV-PA or S-LV-PN. Label each part of the sentence.

Example: S LV   PN

Example: Harry is a good debater.   S - LV - PN

1. She is an attractive girl in my opinion.   _____

2. His ideas about politics are ambiguous.   _____

3. Students always seem busy with their work.   _____

4. Doctors and lawyers are our most highly paid professionals.   _____

5. Most teachers are enthusiastic. _____

6. Discos, once places of popular entertainment, are now

   bowling alleys. _____

7. Records and tapes are expensive. _____

8. The latest dress craze is the mini-skirt. _____

9. William Faulkner was one of the greatest American novelists. _____

10. Silence and patience are virtues. _____

Check the answer key.

PRACTICE 9

Identify each sentence as either Format 1, 2, 3, or 4. Label each part of the sentence.

	Abbreviation	Format
Example: S LV He is my basketball coach. PN	S - LV - PN	4
	Abbreviation	Format

1. She is the star of our class play. _____ _____

2. The coach gave Paul his football equipment. _____ _____

3. The bread tastes stale. _____ _____

4. The dog caught the stick. _____ _____

5. The wealthy man gave the poor child a dollar. _____ _____

6. I walked into the room. _____ _____

7. The marathon runner became an Olympic hero. _____ _____

8. Women have joined many traditional men's clubs. _____ _____

9. Kim sang an aria from *Aida*. _____ _____

10. The horse tripped on the last jump. _____ _____

11. Jimmy Connors is a marvelous tennis player. _____ _____

12. The lawyer gave his client some advice. _____ _____

13. The student was sick yesterday. _____ _____

14. Maria invited Brad to the dance. _____ _____

15. The dog growled at the letter carrier.   _____ _____

16. Freshly cut roses are an expensive gift.   _____ _____

17. Alice caught a fish for dinner.   _____ _____

18. Doctors seem quite intelligent.   _____ _____

19. He gave me a present for my birthday.   _____ _____

20. The television picture appears faded.   _____ _____

Check the answer key.

Verbals

As you learned in Chapter 3, both the infinitive and the gerund can function as nouns. Because they can fulfill a noun's function, infinitives and gerunds can be found acting as subjects and direct objects in the sentence formats.

Remember: An *infinitive* is made by adding the word *to* to the verb; for example, *to run, to swim, to bowl.*

A *gerund* is made by adding *ing* to the verb; for example, *running, swimming, bowling.* (For a more complete discussion of verbals, see Chapter 3, *Verbs III*).

Examples: 1. *To hike* is my favorite pastime.
The infinitive *to hike* is functioning as a noun in this sentence, and it is the subject of the sentence.
2. She decided *to party* on her birthday.
The infinitive *to party* is functioning as a noun in this sentence, and it is the direct object in the sentence.
3. *Parasailing* is Acapulco's favorite sport.
The gerund *parasailing* is functioning as a noun in this sentence, and it is the subject of the sentence.
4. Many jet-setters enjoy *dancing* from dusk to dawn.
The gerund *dancing* is functioning as a noun in this sentence, and it is the direct object in the sentence.

PRACTICE 10

Identify the infinitives and gerunds in the sentences by circling them and label your answers. Also, indicate whether the verbal is being used as the subject or the direct object. Finally, write the code and format for each sentence.

	Verbal	Function	Code	Format
Example: (Motorcycling) is a dangerous sport.	*gerund*	*subject*	S-LV-PN	_____

1. To give is good; to receive is best.   _____ _____ _____ _____

2. Bailing out the boat took an incredible amount of time.   _____ _____ _____ _____

3. On her college application, Mary Jones's hobbies are partying, dancing, and swinging.   _____ _____ _____ _____

4. He tried to climb the mountain, but he failed.   _____ _____ _____ _____

5. His primary goal was to see the exploding supernova.   _____ _____ _____ _____

6. Writing is a thankless task to most people.   _____ _____ _____ _____

7. More people enjoy reading.   _____ _____ _____ _____

8. Before daylight, each group sought to hide its provisions from the others.   _____ _____ _____ _____

9. A major tourist activity in the Caribbean is snorkeling.   _____ _____ _____ _____

10. The toddler liked mixing his milk and his chicken soup.   _____ _____ _____ _____

Check the answer key.

Parts of Speech and Their Functions

You can use the following chart to check on parts of speech and their functions in a sentence.

> **NOTE:** Since gerunds and infinitives are used as different parts of speech, they are included in this chart.

Part of Speech	Uses in a Sentence		Example
noun	subject		The *children* were playing on the corner.
	direct object		He baked a *cake* for the party.
	indirect object		I passed *Sue* a note.
	object of the preposition		The flag flew proudly over the *house*.
	predicate nominative		He is the *teacher* who inspired me.
pronoun	subject		*They* played soccer all day.
	direct object		The teacher lost *it*.
	indirect object		Her aunts sent *them* an anniversary gift.
	object of the preposition		The class arranged a surprise party for *her*.
	predicate nominative		"I am *he*," replied the dictator.
gerund	subject		*Renovating* is a major task.
	direct object		Kindergartners like *painting*.
	predicate nominative		Their favorite pastime is *eating*.
infinitive	noun	subject	*To participate* in a triathalon is my goal.
		direct object	I love *to run*.
		predicate nominative	Her last wish was *to die* at home.
	adverb	modifies the verb	The class turned *to see* the new arrival.
	adjective	modifies a noun or pronoun	His tendency *to overeat* made him fat.

NOTE: See Chapter 3, *Verbs III,* for more information on verbals.

Part of Speech	Uses in a Sentence	Example
preposition	provides relationship between two ideas	Seven cars raced *around* the track.
verb	action	The squirrel *scurried* across the field.
	linking	The manager *was* incredulous at the sales slump.
	helping	Profit margins *had been* squeezed by increasing costs for raw materials.

EXERCISE Using the preceding chart as a guide, for each italicized word write its part of speech and function in the sentence on the line under the sentence.

1. The troop *had been* planning a camping *trip*.

   _____

2. *It* was canceled *for* a variety *of* reasons.

   _____

3. Each *boy seemed* very disappointed.

   _____

4. By spring, I expect *to be* in *Colorado*.

   _____

5. *To be* an Eagle scout was his lifelong *ambition*.

   _____

   Have your instructor or tutor check your work.

Classes of Sentences

There are four types of sentences, classified according to their purpose: declarative, interrogative, imperative, and exclamatory.

A **declarative** sentence makes a statement. You have been working primarily with declarative sentences. Notice that the sentence ends with a period.

Example: The car will not start.
           It is raining today.

An **interrogative** sentence asks a question. It ends with a question mark.

Example: Will you go to the movies with me?
           Subject: *you*
           verb: *Will go*

NOTE: In a question, usually the helping verb comes before the subject and the main verb comes after it.

An **imperative** sentence expresses a command or a rhetorical question (you expect that the listener will comply with your request). It usually ends with a period, but an imperative sentence can also end with an exclamation mark (for added emphasis).

Examples: Help.
            Help!

NOTE: This particular imperative sentence contains only one word. What is the verb in the sentence? *Help.* But where is the subject? Consider this for a moment. Aren't you commanding or requesting that someone help you? Then, you are actually addressing someone else; it is as if you are saying, "*You* help." The subject of the sentence is called an **understood you.** It is written like this: (you)

Example: Please pass the cake.
            verb: *pass*
            subject: (*you*)

An **exclamatory** sentence expresses surprise or shock. It ends with an exclamation mark.

Example: The house is on fire!

PRACTICE 11

Classify each of the following sentences as one of the four classes: declarative, imperative, interrogative, or exclamatory.

1. Watch out for that man. _____

2. Have you done your homework? _____

3. Time can be measured. _____

4. The car caught fire! _____

5. Tell me your name. _____

6. Exercise is good for you. _____

7. Do you like summer sports? _____

8. Help. _____

9. I got an *A*! _____

10. Horses are patient animals. _____

Check the answer key.

EXERCISE   Now, write a sentence of your own as an example of each class.

1. Declarative: _____

2. Interrogative: _____

3. Imperative: _____

4. Exclamatory: _____

Have your instructor or tutor check your work.

APPLICATION I

Write the following sentences.

A. Write two sentences using Sentence Format 1.

1. _____

2. _____

B. Write two sentences using Sentence Format 2.

1. _____

2. _____

C. Write two sentences using Sentence Format 3.

1. _____

2. _____

D. Write two sentences using Sentence Format 4.

1. _____

2. _____

E. Define a declarative sentence and write an example.

Definition: _____

Example: _____

F. Define an interrogative sentence and write an example.

Definition: _____

Example: _____

G. Define an imperative sentence and write an example.

Definition: _____

Example: _____

H. Define an exclamatory sentence and write an example.

Definition: _____

Example: _____

Have your instructor or tutor check your work.

APPLICATION II

In the following sentences, label the subject (*S*), verb (*V*), direct object (*DO*), indirect object (*IO*), predicate nominative (*PN*), and predicate adjective (*PA*) above the word. Write each sentence's format on the line to the right.

(1) The teacher taught John a lesson. (2) He had been very rambunctious lately. (3) His behavior was disrupting the class. (4) That was unacceptable to her. (5) Therefore, she sent his mother a note. (6) The note asked for the mother's cooperation. (7) John's mother agreed to help. (8) Consequently, John will never forget Tuesday, March 3. (9) On that fateful day, his view of school changed radically.

1. ____________
2. ____________
3. ____________
4. ____________
5. ____________
6. ____________
7. ____________
8. ____________
9. ____________

Check the answer key.

APPLICATION III

In the following paragraph, for each italicized word identify its part of speech (such as noun, verb, gerund) and its function in the sentence (such as subject, direct object, linking verb) above the word.

Example: Howard *felt* *better* after he slept for a while. (*felt*: linking verb; *better*: predicate adjective)

(1) Many *students think* a college degree is their ticket to the land of *opportunity*. (2) In some *situations, it* is. (3) But, unfortunately, all too often a college degree merely offers its *holder* an *interview*. (4) There *is* no *guarantee* of a job. (5) Prospective employers want *to see* results. (6) They *are* not interested in *possibilities*. (7) *Talking* to them about future actions wastes *time*. (8) *They* want *to know* what has already been accomplished. (9) Students *should keep* this fact of life in mind. (10) Job *hunting* is a nasty *business*.

Check the answer key.

APPLICATION IV

In a paragraph you wrote, label each sentence's format. Show it to your instructor or tutor.

PART II

Correct Sentence Formation

6

Types of Sentences

OBJECTIVES:	1. To recognize simple sentences.
	2. To recognize compound sentences.
	3. To recognize complex sentences.
	4. To recognize compound-complex sentences.
	5. To write all four types of sentences correctly.
KEY CONCEPT:	There are four types of sentences:
	1. simple
	2. compound
	3. complex
	4. compound-complex

Because all types of sentences are built upon clauses (a group of words that has a subject and a verb), a writer must be able to recognize the two kinds of clauses:

- independent
- dependent

Simple Sentences

A **simple sentence** contains a single independent clause. A clause is a group of words that has a subject and a verb. There are two kinds of clauses:

1. independent (or main) and
2. dependent (or subordinate).

PRACTICE 1

Read each of the following groups of words and decide if the group of words is a clause. Place a C beside the groups that are clauses.

_____ 1. In the rain.

_____ 2. When he finished.

_____ 3. Because the movie is over.

_____ 4. Hilda screamed.

_____ 5. When jogging home.

Check the answer key.

An **independent clause** has a subject and a verb, and it expresses a complete thought. As its name suggests, an independent clause can stand by itself. A simple sentence is an independent clause.

Examples: The lecture was over.
              The Colorado River travels through many western states.
              In the fall, the Blue Ridge Mountains are spectacular.
              The ship is owned by Ridder Company, a firm in Miami.

PRACTICE 2

Write five simple sentences of your own.

1. _____

2. _____

3. _____

4. _____

5. _____

Have your instructor or tutor check your work.

A **dependent clause** has a subject and a verb, but it does not express a complete thought. A dependent clause does *not* make a sentence.

Example: While Dan was driving.

             This group of words does have a subject (*Dan*) and a verb (*was driving*), but it does not express a complete thought. The writer did not tell us what happened while Dan was driving.

Look at these two versions of the same idea:

Examples: The dog barked all night.
             Because the dog barked all night.

             The first sentence is complete; the second sentence is not, because it does not tell us the result of the dog's barking. Both groups of words, *While Dan was driving* and *Because the dog barked all night,* contain subjects and verbs, but do not express complete thoughts; both word groups are dependent clauses.

The following words are commonly used **subordinate conjunctions** and **relative pronouns.** If a group of words that has a subject and a verb begins with one of these subordinate conjunctions or relative pronouns, the clause is a dependent clause. Be able to recognize these words.

Subordinate Conjunctions

after	if	what
although	since	when
as	so that	whenever
as if	than	where
because	though	whereas
before	unless	wherever
even though	until	whether
how		while

Relative Pronouns

that	whoever
which	whom
whichever	whomever
who	whose

If one of these words precedes a group of words containing a subject and a verb, then you have a dependent clause.

> **NOTE:** The pronouns *who, which, that,* and *whoever* can be the subject of the dependent clause.

Since many of the words listed as subordinate conjunctions are also other parts of speech, check each group of words carefully. If one of these words precedes a group of words containing a subject and a verb, then you have a dependent clause. Consider the following example:

> While he enjoyed the play.

In this group of words, the word *while* is a subordinate conjunction since it precedes the subject *he* and the verb *enjoyed.*

However, many of the words in the list are also adverbs or prepositions. As such, they will not precede a subject and a verb; hence, the group of words will not be a dependent clause. Consider the following examples:

> While running for the train.
>
> Because of her competence.

Neither group of words above is a complete sentence nor a dependent clause. Instead, the first group, *while running for the train,* is a participial phrase. There is no subject or verb in this group of words. (See "Verbals" in Chapter 3.) The second group of words, *because of her competence,* is a prepositional phrase. The compound preposition *because of* has as its object the noun *competence.* (See "Prepositional Phrases" in Chapter 4.)

Always check the complete group of words before you determine the function of the group in the sentence.

PRACTICE 3

Read the clauses below. If the clause expresses a complete thought, place an *I* (for independent clause) next to it. If the clause does not express a complete thought, place a *D* (for dependent clause) next to it.

_____ 1. Although the day was bright and sunny.

_____ 2. Because she is so vain and conceited.

_____ 3. I believe in motherhood and apple pie.

_____ 4. When we reach our destination.

_____ 5. He completed his work.

_____ 6. If the recession ever ends.

_____ 7. Before the play starts.

_____ 8. Tonight is a night for merrymaking.

_____ 9. While Anne was driving east.

_____ 10. She received an *A* in English.

Check the answer key.

As you saw in Chapter 4, simple sentences can contain any combination of simple and compound subjects and verbs. Simple sentences may also contain prepositional and verbal phrases. In addition, simple sentences follow the formats listed in Chapter 5. For more information on word combinations that appear in simple sentences, see "Adjectives and Other Modifiers," "Appositives," "Participles," and "Beginning Sentences" in Chapter 10.

PRACTICE 4

For each of the simple sentences below, label the subject(s), verb(s), prepositional and verbal phrases, and the format.

Example: ___S – V - DO-II___ S   V   DO   PP
Tad enjoys hiking (in the mountains) each weekend.

_____ 1. Each spring, the college sponsors a career day for students.

_____ 2. During the president's vacation, the vice-president was solely responsible for the administration of the college.

_____ 3. Swimming is an excellent sport.

_____ 4. The sentry, supposedly standing guard duty, had fallen asleep at his post.

_____ 5. Harold and Maude made an improbable couple because of the contrast in their ages.

_____ 6. Our hiking club plans to visit Pike's Peak this summer.

_____ 7. Distraught, the accident victim refused to answer questions.

_____ 8. At the sound of the approaching train, the deer scrambled for safety.

_____ 9. To enjoy a stage production of one of Shakespeare's plays, you should read the play prior to the performance.

_____ 10. Sheila's chief ambition is to become an actress.

Check the answer key.

Compound Sentences

A **compound sentence** contains two or more independent clauses. Read the following sentences, and determine how they differ:

Examples: 1. Mickey and Marvin sang a song and played their guitars.
            2. Mickey sang a song, and Marvin played his guitar.

In sentence 1, both Mickey and Marvin are performing both actions—*sang* and *played*. In sentence 2, only Mickey sang, while Marvin played. Sentence 2 is a compound sentence; it is made of two independent clauses: (1) *Mickey sang a song,* and (2) *Marvin played his guitar.* A compound sentence is punctuated in one of three ways:

1. The two independent clauses are joined by a comma (,) and one of the seven coordinate conjunctions: *for, and, nor, but, or, yet,* and *so.* You can remember the coordinate conjunctions by remembering the word FANBOYS (composed of the first letter of each word).

   IMPORTANT: When you use one of these seven coordinate conjunctions, pay attention to the relationship each word stresses:

   a. *And* makes the independent clauses equal; both clauses carry the same weight and have the same value.
   b. *But* and *yet* show contrast between the two independent clauses.
   c. *Or* indicates a choice between the two statements; *nor* indicates a negative choice between the two clauses.
   d. *For* and *so* show cause and effect.

   Example: Read each of the following sentences, and determine how the coordinate conjunctions change the meaning of the sentences:

   a. Helen is going to the mall, *and* Cynthia is going to town.
   b. Helen is going to the mall, *but* Cynthia is going to town.
   c. Helen is going to the mall, *so* Cynthia is going to town.

2. The two independent clauses are joined by a semicolon (;).

   Example: Terry hurried home; the house was on fire.

   IMPORTANT: Use a semicolon only when the two independent clauses are closely related and the relationship is implied.

3. The two independent clauses are joined by a semicolon (;) and an adverbial conjunction. The adverbial conjunction indicates the type of relationship between the two independent clauses. The following list contains many of the adverbial conjunctions.

also	indeed	primarily
consequently	likewise	rather
currently	moreover	similarly
finally	nevertheless	then
hence	next	therefore
however	overall	thus

Since each adverbial conjunction stresses a particular relationship between the two independent clauses, consider your choice of an adverbial conjunction carefully. For example, the adverbial conjunctions *therefore, consequently,* and *thus* indicate that the second independent clause is a logical conclusion or result of the first clause. Check a dictionary for the relationships the other adverbial conjunctions stress.

When you use one of these adverbial conjunctions to join two independent clauses, you must place a semicolon before the adverbial conjunction and a comma after it.

Examples: Ms. McBride was the city council president for many years; currently, she is mayor.

The supply of crude oil dropped tremendously; thus, the price of gasoline climbed rapidly.

NOTE: See "Coordination" in Chapter 10 for additional information on compound sentences.

PRACTICE 5

Combine each pair of simple sentences into a compound sentence. Use six of the seven coordinate conjunctions. Remember that a comma must precede the coordinate conjunction.

1. The student was sick. She missed the test.

   _____

2. The administration has decided to raise salaries. The cost of living has risen.

   _____

3. The recession continued. Steel output increased.

   _____

4. I lost my wallet. I cannot buy the record.

   _____

5. Harold will go to law school. He will go to medical school.

   _____

6. It may snow. I am still going on my vacation.

_____

Have your instructor or tutor check your work.

PRACTICE 6

Using three of the seven coordinate conjunctions and three adverbial conjunctions from the preceding lists, write six compound sentences of your own.

1. _____

2. _____

3. _____

4. _____

5. _____

6. _____

Have your instructor or tutor check your work.

PRACTICE 7

Classify each of the following sentences as either simple or compound. Identify all subjects and verbs.

Example: _compound_ School started late today, for it had snowed.

_____ 1. Governor Toll was nominated for a second term, but he declined the opportunity.

_____ 2. The Kentucky Derby, the Preakness, and the Belmont Stakes form the Triple Crown of horse racing.

_____ 3. Before the turn of the century, firefighters used horse-drawn trucks; today, they use motorized vehicles.

_____ 4. Many musicians and composers were employed by kings in the seventeenth century.

_____ 5. Mexico has many interesting buildings; some, in fact, go back to the time of the Mayas.

Check the answer key.

Complex Sentences

A complex sentence contains one independent clause and one or more dependent clauses.

Examples:

1. They wanted to manage a restaurant.

    (s v)

    Sentence 1 is an independent clause; it has a subject and a verb, and it expresses a complete thought.

2. Although they had no cooking skills or management experience.

    This group of words is a dependent clause. It has a subject and a verb, but it does not express a complete thought, so it is not a sentence. Notice, also, that the clause begins with the subordinate conjunction *although*.

3. (Independent Clause) They wanted to manage a restaurant, (Dependent Clause) although they had no cooking skills or management experience.

    Sentence 3 is a complex sentence, because it has both an independent clause and a dependent clause.

Subordination

In a compound sentence, both independent clauses carry the same amount of weight; they are equally important. However, in a complex sentence, the independent clause is more important than the dependent clause because an independent clause can stand by itself. The dependent clause in a complex sentence should give only additional information about the independent clause.

Example:

(Independent Clause) The students finished the test (Dependent Clause) (that their teacher had given them.)

Which clause is more important? _____
The main idea of the sentence is that the students finished the test. The dependent clause, *that their teacher had given them,* is not as important; the dependent clause simply adds extra information about who gave the test to the students.

NOTE: See "Relative-Pronoun Clauses" and "Subordination" in Chapter 10 for additional information on complex sentences.

PRACTICE 8

Review the subordinate conjunctions and relative pronouns on page 100. Identify the word or groups of words by writing one of the following labels: *IC* (independent clause), *DC* (dependent clause), *PP* (prepositional phrase), *SW* (subordinate word).

_____ 1. before the storm

_____ 2. if he goes

_____ 3. since she is rich

_____ 4. because

_____ 5. millions have cable television

_____ 6. nearly every American drives a car

_____ 7. in the spring

_____ 8. beyond the blue horizon

_____ 9. when she took her seat

_____ 10. on the beach

_____ 11. when

_____ 12. after the clock struck twelve

_____ 13. he gave a dazzling performance

_____ 14. despite the blizzard

_____ 15. Henry who is a sailor

_____ 16. on the roof

_____ 17. at the party in the old house

_____ 18. Marge can be intriguing

_____ 19. after the race begins

_____ 20. while she was dancing

Check the answer key.

PRACTICE 9

Combine each pair of sentences into a complex sentence by making one of the clauses dependent. Remember to keep the most important idea as the independent clause.

1. The book was difficult. It was worth the effort.

_____

2. The brunette cried. She had won the contest.

_____

3. The riverboat capsized. It struck a log.

_____

4. The wallet was returned. The credit cards were missing.

_____

5. Jane received the school award. The teachers voted for her.

_____

Have your instructor or tutor check your work.

PRACTICE 10

Write five complex sentences of your own.

1. _____

2. _____

3. _____

4. _____

5. _____

Have your instructor or tutor check your work.

PRACTICE 11

Identify the dependent clauses and the independent clauses in each of the following sentences. Underline the independent clause and label it. Place parentheses around the dependent clause and label it.

Example: (Because it is so hot) the children want to go to the beach.
  dependent clause *independent clause*

1. Whenever the weather is beautiful, they have a picnic.

2. Although he had household chores, he decided to see a movie.

3. It began to rain before the boat reached shore.

4. We knew that he did not go home.

5. Because she has an exam tomorrow, Kate will study tonight.

6. After the movie ended, all thirty of us headed to the local pizza parlor.

7. Before Marvin could shout a warning, the firecracker exploded.

8. After they buy a house, they will purchase new furniture.

9. Harriet decided to go on the ski trip, even though she had a broken leg.

10. Because many parents believe that their children should know how to operate computers, they are purchasing home computers.

Check the answer key.

PRACTICE 12

Identify each of the following sentences by type: simple, compound, or complex. Label all clauses, as in Practice 11.

_____ 1. Betsy goes to the beach whenever she can.

_____ 2. It is a warm day; the temperature is now 95 degrees.

_____ 3. In order to earn enough money to go to college, Terry worked as a waitress all summer.

_____ 4. Jack and Mary entered the haunted house cautiously, for they believed all the stories about ghosts.

_____ 5. When the rain was over, the children ran outside.

_____ 6. Because the battery was dead, the car refused to start.

_____ 7. You must hurry, or you will miss the last bus.

_____ 8. Marcello and his brothers gritted their teeth and began the long, slow climb to the top of the mountain.

_____ 9. He told you that your plan was impossible.

_____ 10. With its varied historical background, New Orleans is a fascinating place to visit; the Mardi Gras is one example of its French heritage.

Check the answer key.

Compound-Complex Sentences

A compound-complex sentence is just what its name says: it is a compound sentence that contains one or more dependent clauses. A compound-complex sentence has two or more independent clauses and one or more dependent clauses.

Example: The doctor, (who was also a golfer,) examined his last patient; then he headed for the golf course.

Dependent Clause · *Independent Clause* · *Independent Clause*

PRACTICE 13

The following sentences are compound-complex. Underline each independent clause, and place parentheses around the dependent clause. Label the clauses.

Example: (When he listens to the radio,) he turns the volume up, and the neighbors complain.

dependent clause · independent clause · independent clause

1. When the monster appeared on the screen, one girl fainted, and the audience clapped.

2. The movie's visual effects, which cost fifteen million dollars, were fantastic; later, the graphic artists won an Academy Award for their work.

3. I wish that you had seen the film; we could discuss it.

4. Knitting, which is a relaxing pastime, can be profitable, for handmade sweaters have become a fashion item.

5. Order the pizza when you get home; I'll be there soon.

6. Because England was America's first mother country, many people believe that the English do everything better; however, these Americans are not correct.

7. If you will wait for me, I'll finish my work, and then we can go to the beach.

8. Before you purchase your textbooks, go to class; the instructor may have changed the reading list.

9. Our surprise birthday party for Jerry failed; before he entered the room, everyone was practicing "Happy Birthday."

10. My father always told me to turn the lights off when I leave a room; he claimed that such a practice would save money.

Check the answer key.

PRACTICE 14

Write five compound-complex sentences of your own.

1. _____

2. _____

3. _____

4. _____

5. _____

Have your instructor or tutor check your work.

PRACTICE 15

Identify each of the following sentences by type: simple, compound, complex, or compound-complex. Label all clauses, as in Practice 13.

_____ 1. She is a person whom we admire.

_____ 2. The dog that wins the contest will be used in the commercial.

_____ 3. Because he has left, we must stay here.

_____ 4. Because the panda's natural habitat in China is threatened, many Chinese zookeepers wish to export them to other countries, and the Chinese government has agreed.

_____ 5. Close the door when you enter.

_____ 6. Before we leave for a vacation, we always have the car checked for problems.

_____ 7. Have Dave and Hank decided when they will paint the house?

_____ 8. We decided to see *The Rocky Horror Picture Show* at midnight.

_____ 9. Curt and Stacy played the romantic leads in *Romeo and Juliet;* however, the performance reminded one of *The Taming of the Shrew.*

_____ 10. Each section of the country, from New England to the West Coast, boasts of its native foods.

Check the answer key.

A Final Hint

There is a pattern of logical steps you can follow to identify the type of sentence. Follow these guidelines, and you cannot make a mistake:

Step 1:   Circle the subordinate conjunctions or relative pronouns in the sentence. Do a subject and a verb follow a subordinate word? Does a verb follow a relative pronoun? If so in either case, label the group of words a *dependent clause.*

Step 2:   Circle any commas and the coordinate conjunctions, and circle any semicolons. If there are independent clauses on either side of the coordinate conjunction or semi-colon, label the clauses *independent clauses.*

Step 3:   Count the number of independent clauses and dependent clauses in the sentence, and decide what type of sentence you have.

   Example: Look at the following sentence:

   If you will do the dishes, I will vacuum the house, and then we can go to the movies.

dependent clause

Step 1:   (If) you will do the dishes, I will vacuum the house, and then we can go to the movies.

independent clause   independent clause

Step 2:   If you will do the dishes, I will vacuum the house, (and) then we can go to the movies.

Step 3:   one dependent clause: *If you will do the dishes*

two independent clauses: a) *I will vacuum the house*
b) *then we can go to the movies*

One dependent clause and two independent clauses make this a *compound-complex sentence.*

PRACTICE 16

Use the guidelines above to determine what type the following sentence is. Write out the steps as you apply them.

Although her father had forbidden her to see him, Maude continued to meet Harold.

Step 1: _____

_____

Step 2: _____

_____

Step 3: _____

_____

Have your instructor or tutor check your work.

Style

Ideas can be presented in any of the types of sentences; however, one way is usually more effective than others. If you understand how sentences are made, then you can begin to manipulate them to create the most effective one.

You should also strive for sentence variety and complexity in your writing. A paragraph that contains only simple sentences will probably bore your reader. On the other hand, a paragraph that contains only compound-complex sentences will cause your reader to spend more time on each sentence, and the complexity of thought may cause confusion. Try to write sentences that are effective and concise. (See Chapter 10, *Style: Sentence Combinations,* for a detailed explanation of combining sentences effectively.)

APPLICATION I

Identify each of the sentences below by type: simple, compound, complex, or compound-complex.

1. Each day during the summer, Tom drives to Malibu and stays all day.

   _____

2. Before Jean leaves for work, she reads the newspapers. _____

3. Although Custer and his men were well armed and had information about the enemy, the Indians made a surprise attack and destroyed the army. _____

4. Boxing is a demanding sport; it requires great athletic skill, determination, and self-discipline. _____

5. Call the doctor if your child has a fever. _____

6. Dogs are good friends to man, but many people prefer cats because cats are more independent than dogs. _____

7. It is imperative that you finish your work tonight. _____

8. Mr. Harris, who is a noted literary critic, just finished a book on W. H. Auden.

   _____

9. Because Jack Kennedy was a good president, it is important that we remember his death.

   _____

10. Jogging is good exercise; it helps your legs and cardiovascular system.

    _____

11. It is difficult to learn the rules of grammar, yet basic grammar skills are essential for success in college. _____

12. Georgia, Alabama, and South Carolina are southern states; Maine, New Hampshire, and Vermont are northern states. _____

13. Because television influences children so much, many parents want certain programs banned. _____

14. Quit when you are ahead. _____

15. Although summer is a pleasant season, I prefer the fall. _____

16. Writing requires a lot of work and patience and a little bit of creativity.

    _____

17. You can go to New York on the Garden State Parkway, or you can drive to New York on the

    New Jersey Turnpike. _____

18. F. Scott Fitzgerald and Ernest Hemingway were both famous American authors.

    _____

19. Did Todd tell Jane that he saw her boyfriend with Mary? _____

20. Los Angeles is a pleasant city, but I prefer New York because it has marvelous cultural

    activities. _____

Check the answer key.

APPLICATION II

Construct the sentences you are directed to write.

A. Write two simple sentences.

   1. _____

   2. _____

B. Write two compound sentences.

   1. _____

      _____

   2. _____

      _____

C. Write two complex sentences.

   1. _____

      _____

   2. _____

      _____

D. Write two compound-complex sentences.

1. _____

_____

2. _____

_____

Have your instructor or tutor check your work.

APPLICATION III

Read the following paragraph carefully. Combine the information contained in the paragraph's sentences to form different sentence types: simple, compound, complex, and compound-complex. Consider your purpose for each sentence and construct an effective sentence for the message. Identify the types of sentences you construct.

(1) One contrast to the economic realities of the Great Depression was the release of two films. (2) The contrast was sharp. (3) The films were released in 1939. (4) The two films offered Americans some measure of hope. (5) *The Wizard of Oz* was the first film. (6) The film provided a fantasy land. (7) In this land, wishes could come true. (8) In this land, good triumphs eventually over evil. (9) For example, Dorothy's desire to return to Kansas comes true. (10) She believed that there is "no place like home." (11) Her dream comes true after she recognizes that she has the ability to return. (12) Her ability comes from the magical powers of the ruby slippers. (13) During her stay in Oz, Dorothy helps to destroy the Wicked Witch of the West. (14) She also ends a reign of terror. (15) The second film uses a different approach. (16) *Gone With the Wind* shows a woman's determination to survive. (17) She survives despite overwhelming odds. (18) Scarlett O'Hara gives everything to save the family plantation. (19) The plantation was called Tara. (20) This occurred during the Civil War and Reconstruction. (21) The land also proves to be her strength. (22) Tara offers farmlands. (23) Tara offers shelter from the harsh realities of the changing world around Scarlett. (24) For Scarlett to survive, she must transport her sister-in-law through Yankee lines to the safety of Tara. (25) Scarlett must marry a man. (26) She does not love the man. (27) Scarlett must become an entrepreneur. (28) Scarlett remains strong through

all of the adverse conditions. (29) Both films presented such positive visions of life. (30) They

have been well received by later generations of American moviegoers.

Have your instructor or tutor check your work.

APPLICATION IV

Read a rough draft of a paper of your own. Identify the types of sentences you wrote. Did you write too many simple sentences? Or did you write too many compound-complex sentences? Do your sentences say exactly what you want them to say? Are the sentences effective? Make any corrections and combinations you think necessary. Then, show your revisions to your instructor or tutor.

7

Fragments

OBJECTIVES:
1. To recognize fragments, individually and in paragraphs.
2. To correct fragments.
3. To use the editing symbol for fragment (*Frag*) when proofreading.

KEY CONCEPT: A sentence is a group of words that expresses a complete thought. If a sentence is not complete, it is called a *fragment*. In other words, a fragment is an incomplete thought punctuated as if it were complete, as if it were a sentence. There are four sentence errors that can produce fragments.

Fragment Type 1: No Subject

Usually, in order to express a thought completely, a sentence must contain a subject and a verb. Sometimes, however, it may contain only a verb. This particular type of sentence, called an imperative sentence, is used to express commands: for example, "Stop!" The verb is *stop;* the subject is called an **understood you,** because the speaker is commanding someone else to stop.

A group of words written without a subject is a fragment.

Example: Were walking down the street in a great hurry.

Obviously, you don't write this type of sentence frequently, but it does happen. The mistake can be corrected by simply adding a subject.

Correction: *The children* were walking down the street in a great hurry.

EXERCISE   Follow the above example, and correct the following fragments.

1. Stopped on the side of the road.

_____

2. Hit the curb.

_____

3. Ran into the store.

_____

Have your instructor or tutor check your work.

Fragment Type 2: No Verb

A group of words written without a verb is a fragment.

Example: The woman in the yellow-striped dress.

Again, this type of fragment isn't usually mistaken for a sentence, but it can happen. When it does, the simplest way to correct the error is to add a verb.

Correction: The woman in the yellow-striped dress is my teacher.

NOTE: Often the reason for mistakenly punctuating this type of fragment as a sentence is that the group of words is used in apposition. (See Chapter 10 for additional information on appositives.)

Example: That's my teacher. The woman in the yellow-striped dress.

If this is the basis for the mistake, then correct the fragment by attaching it to the sentence to which it is related.

Correction: That's my teacher, the woman in the yellow-striped dress.

EXERCISE   Follow the example above, and correct the following fragments.

1. The child in the clown costume.

_____

2. The tiger in the cage.

_____

3. The duck pond in the center of town.

_____

Have your instructor or tutor check your work.

Fragment Type 3: -ing Verb with No Helping Verb

A sentence containing an -ing verb without a helping verb (such as *is, are, was, were, have been, will be*) is a fragment.

Example: Barry battling bravely against the encroaching ants.

This fragment can easily be corrected by adding an appropriate helping verb.

Correction: Barry *was* battling bravely against the encroaching ants.

EXERCISE   Follow the above example, and correct the following fragments.

1. The wolves circling the injured doe.

_____

2. The helicopter hovering overhead.

_____

3. The plane landing on the runway.

_____

Have your instructor or tutor check your work.

Fragment Type 4: No Complete Thought

A dependent clause (a group of words that contains a subject and a verb but does *not* express a complete thought) punctuated as a sentence is a fragment.

Example: That the children were very unhappy.

When editing very quickly, you might see a subject and verb in this dependent clause and incorrectly label it a sentence. But if you read the clause carefully, you can *hear* that it is not a complete thought. The fragment leaves the reader hanging in mid-air, asking who, when, or why.

NOTE: A dependent clause usually begins with a subordinate conjunction or a relative pronoun. (See Chapter 6, *Types of Sentences*, for a detailed explanation of dependent clauses.) The following words are some of the most common subordinate conjunctions and relative pronouns; you should be able to recognize most of them.

Subordinate Conjunctions

after	since	when
although	so that	where
as (if)	than	whereas
because	though	wherever
before	unless	whether
even though	until	while
how	what	unless
if		until

Relative Pronouns

that	which	whom
what	whichever	whomever
whatever	who	whose
	whoever	

(*Whichever, whoever,* and *whomever* are not often used.)

There are two ways to correct a dependent-clause fragment. Choose whichever method is more appropriate for your message.

1. Because it is the subordinate conjunction that transforms the independent clause (simple sentence) into a dependent clause, *get rid of the subordinate conjunction,* which will leave you with a simple sentence.

   Fragment: That the children were very unhappy.

   Correction: The children were very unhappy.

   NOTE: This method does not always work, because a relative pronoun serves as the subject of the dependent clause.

   Example: Which was difficult.

   If you omit the subordinate conjunction, you still would not have an independent clause:

   Was difficult.

   Instead, you would still have a fragment, because your group of words now does not have a subject. In such a case, use the second method to correct the fragment.

2. *Connect the dependent clause to an independent clause,* and create a complex sentence.

   Fragment: That the children were very unhappy.

   Correction: Anyone could see that the children were very unhappy.

   Fragment: Which was difficult.

   Correction: We had to take a make-up exam, which was difficult.

EXERCISE   Follow the above examples as models, and correct the following fragments.

1. Because new cars get better gas mileage.

_____

2. Because it began to snow.

_____

3. Although we raced to the scene of the accident.

_____

Have your instructor or tutor check your work.

PRACTICE 1

Decide whether each group of words below is a sentence or a fragment. If the sentence is correct, write *C* in the blank. If the group of words is a fragment, write *Frag* in the blank. Correct all fragments.

1. Man's best friend a dog.   _____

2. The summer which is a pleasant season.   _____

3. Mr. Jones is my English teacher.   _____

4. Which is a difficult subject.   _____

5. Many people vacation in Maine because the state offers outdoor activities

   and historical sites.   _____

6. Taking tests can be a grueling experience.   _____

7. The boy in the scuba outfit.   _____

8. The Roseland Ballroom a good place to dance.   _____

9. Many people buy designer jeans because they fit better.   _____

10. Harold swimming the English Channel.   _____

Check the answer key.

APPLICATION I

Decide whether each group of words below is a sentence or a fragment. If the sentence is correct, write C in the blank. If the group of words is a fragment, write *Frag* in the blank. Correct the fragments.

1. A library which can be an interesting place. _____

2. A small town in upstate New York. _____

3. Had been a shoe salesman many years ago. _____

4. The boys playing golf at the country club. _____

5. Before heading for home, their son had another cup of coffee. _____

6. Although pregnancy requires a woman to modify her diet. _____

7. After they tried to defraud the government on their federal income tax

   return. _____

8. The beautiful girl with the long blond hair and the bright red shirt. _____

9. Retired to Arizona with one cat, two dogs, and a snake. _____

10. The teacher grading the papers with a heavy heart. _____

11. Since the air conditioner broke. _____

12. He tried hard to convince the jury, but to no avail. _____

13. The car refusing to start. _____

14. Even though an attendance book is a legal document. _____

15. The canister on the right with the red flower on it. _____

16. Have been through so much, have suffered so much hardship, but have

    remained married. _____

17. The child had a lollipop which broke when she fell. _____

18. Because loneliness is a dreaded disease, too. _____

19. On a beautiful day no one wants to remain indoors. _____

20. The pack of dogs fighting on the street corner. _____

Check the answer key.

APPLICATION II

Read the following paragraph carefully. If a group of words is a sentence, write *C* above the number at the beginning of the sentence. If the group of words is a fragment, write *Frag* next to the number and correct the fragment.

(1) Summer is supposed to be an enjoyable time. (2) Going to the beach. (3) Playing tennis and other games. (4) Even just taking walks during the evening hours. (5) Unfortunately, not everyone can enjoy the season. (6) There are people for whom the summer is pure torture. (7) For instance, my aunt who has angina. (8) Suffers terribly in the heat. (9) Because her heart just can't pump fast enough to circulate her blood and to dissipate her body's heat. (10) The only solution she has found to the problem is to stay in her air-conditioned house for the whole season. (11) As you can imagine, that gets rather boring. (12) Infants and toddlers, too, playing all the time in the summer. (13) They are bothered by the heat. (14) Since their bodies haven't yet developed the ability to dissipate heat. (15) Mothers find the situation frustrating because they cannot explain the causes to their babies and they cannot force their little ones to slow down. (16) People who live in apartments can't enjoy the summer either. (17) Frequently, apartments lack cross-ventilation, so the hot air stays in the small, boxy rooms. (18) Also, apartment dwellers don't own backyards, so they have no place to go to enjoy a fine summer day. (19) Rather than just stepping out on to the lawn. (20) They must plan a major trip to a park or beach for summertime fun.

Check the answer key.

APPLICATION III

Read the following paragraph carefully. If a group of words is a sentence, write *C* above the number at the beginning of the sentence. If the group of words is a fragment, write *Frag* next to the number and correct the fragment.

(1) Once considered to be a pastime of the wealthy. (2) Reading is now accessible and interesting for all people. (3) Before the Industrial Revolution, only the wealthy could afford an education and books and had the time to read. (4) Other members of society working to survive. (5) Since mass education was introduced to the American public. (6) The number of people who read for pleasure has grown. (7) Today, the many bookstores in our shopping malls

attesting to the fact that people like to read. (8) On every subject, from astrology to zoology, books line the shelves. (9) For example, if someone is interested in science fiction and fantasy. (10) Then he has many writers to choose from: Ray Bradbury, C. S. Lewis, Ursula Le Guin, H. G. Wells, and J. R. R. Tolkien—all wrote many books. (11) The science-fiction buff can also return to nineteenth-century British and American literature. (12) Mary Shelley's *Frankenstein* was one of the first novels to introduce a man-made creature, built from spare human parts. (13) Moreover, Edgar Allan Poe's tales of horror and the supernatural providing early examples of science fiction. (14) In addition to providing escapes to imaginary worlds. (15) Books inform readers of science, technology, business, psychology, history, and a host of other subjects. (16) For the person who enjoys reading. (17) A trip to a local bookstore or library is quite rewarding. Check the answer key.

APPLICATION IV

Proofread a rough draft of a paper of your own. Check carefully for fragments. Identify each one, and correct it. Show your corrections to your instructor or tutor.

8

Comma Splices

OBJECTIVES: 1. To recognize comma splices in individual sentences and in paragraphs.

2. To correct comma splices.

3. To use the editing symbol for comma splices (CS) when proofreading.

KEY CONCEPT: A *comma splice* occurs when two independent clauses (in compound and compound-complex sentences) are spliced (joined) by a comma and punctuated as a single sentence.

Using only a comma to join two or more complete thoughts is incorrect.

Example: The teacher was not smiling, he was frowning.

In this example, there are two complete sentences: *The teacher was not smiling,* and *he was frowning.*

Identifying the Problem

Comma splices occur only in compound or compound-complex sentences; these are the sentence types that have at least two independent clauses. To identify comma splices, look at the break between the two independent clauses. If the two independent clauses are joined by only a comma at this break, then the entire sentence is a comma splice. You must then correct the comma splice.

PRACTICE 1

Read the following sentences. If a sentence is correctly punctuated, place *C* beside it. If the group of words is actually a comma splice, place *CS* beside the sentence, and draw a vertical line separating the two independent clauses.

1. The exhibit of Andrew Wyeth's paintings was excellent, we particularly appreciated the recently unveiled "Helga" series.　　　_____

2. Many films have been made of the conditions in Germany during the 1930s, *Cabaret* is one of the best of these.　　　_____

3. Jason decided to see a movie, he should have completed his work first.　　　_____

128

4. The space shuttle program has been devastated by the *Challenger* acci-

   dent, no new shuttles will be launched for eighteen months. _____

5. Before Harriet enrolled in college, she worked as a bank teller, she plans

   now to major in business. _____

Check the answer key.

Correcting the Problem

There are three acceptable ways to correct the comma splice.

1. *Make the two independent clauses into two separate, complete sentences.*

   Comma Splice: The teacher was not smiling, he was frowning.
   Correction: The teacher was not smiling. He was frowning.

EXERCISE   Correct these comma splices by making two complete sentences.

1. George is an expert skier, he won three trophies.

   _____

2. Morgan enjoys adventure movies, he saw *Raiders of the Lost Ark* ten times.

   _____

   _____

Have your instructor or tutor check your work.

2. *Join the independent clauses with a comma and an appropriate coordinate conjunction.* The coordinate conjunction tells the reader that there is a relationship between the two independent clauses; furthermore, the conjunctions provide clues to the type of relationship. There are seven coordinate conjunctions: *for, and, but, so, yet, nor,* and *or.*

   Example: The teacher was not smiling, and he seemed very grumpy.

   NOTE: Learn what types of relationships each of the coordinate conjunctions stresses (see Chapter 6, also):

   1. *For* shows cause.
   2. *And* makes two independent clauses equal.
   3. *Nor* shows negative choice.
   4. *But* shows opposition.
   5. *Or* shows choice.
   6. *So* shows result.
   7. *Yet* shows opposition.

EXERCISE   Correct this comma splice by joining the two independent clauses with a comma and a coordinate conjunction.

The blizzard forced us to change our plans for a five-mile hike, we decided to stay home and build a fire.

_____

_____

Have your instructor or tutor check your work.

3. *Join the two independent clauses with a semicolon (;).*

   Example: The dean was not smiling; he seemed very grumpy.

   NOTE: The semicolon tells the reader that a relationship exists between the two independent clauses; however, the semicolon does not identify the relationship. Although it is correct to use a semicolon to join two independent clauses, the clauses should be closely related. For example, the second independent clause can explain the first or provide an example of the first. This connection should be clear to your reader.

   Example: Many Civil War battlefields have been preserved by the Park Service; the Antietam battlefield is one of these.

In this example, the second independent clause provides a direct example of the first clause. The reader can easily understand the relationship between the two clauses.

EXERCISE   Correct these comma splices by joining the two independent clauses with semicolons.

1. We did not buy the self-cleaning oven, the high cost of electricity to operate it would be beyond our budget.

_____

_____

2. Tammi's membership in the club was important to her, the club provided her with activities and social contacts.

_____

Have your instructor or tutor check your work.

NOTE: Often when you use a semicolon, you may want to include an **adverbial conjunction** (sometimes called a **conjunctive adverb**) to indicate what kind of relationship exists between the two independent clauses. There are four major adverbial conjunctions: *however, therefore, moreover,* and *nevertheless.* When you use one of these four adverbial conjunctions, you must place a semicolon before the adverbial conjunction and a comma after it.

Example: It was raining constantly; nevertheless, we continued our climb up the mountain.

Here are the relationships that these adverbial conjunctions indicate:

1. *however* means "contradiction" or "opposition."
2. *moreover* means "in addition to" and "also."
3. *therefore* means "in conclusion."
4. *nevertheless* means "in spite of."

The following list provides additional adverbial conjunctions.

also	indeed	rather
consequently	likewise	similarly
currently	next	then
finally	overall	thus
hence	primarily	

If you are unfamiliar with these adverbial conjunctions, check a dictionary for the relationships these conjunctions stress.

If you have only a comma in front of the adverbial conjunction in a sentence with two independent clauses, you still have a comma splice, so be careful.

Comma Splice: On the Fourth of July, all the banks were closed, moreover, all of the stores were closed.

Correction: On the Fourth of July, all the banks were closed; moreover, all of the stores were closed.

Adverbial conjunctions can be used in a simple sentence, as well. If an adverbial conjunction is located in a simple sentence—one with only one independent clause—you must enclose it within commas.

Examples: A dog is, moreover, man's best friend.

Therefore, you must work harder.

EXERCISE   Correct these comma splices by joining the two independent clauses with semicolons and appropriate adverbial conjunctions.

1. Students must have free time during a school day, they must not spend all of their time in the student center.

_____

_____

2. Our opponents won the state championship three times in a row, we were confident of our abilities.

_____

_____

Have your instructor or tutor check your work.

PRACTICE 2

In the blank at the right of each sentence, write C if the sentence is correct. Write CS if the sentence is a comma splice. Correct the comma splices.

1. April is a lovely month, but I like June best. _____

2. Sally got a good promotion at her job, she also managed to take courses in the evening. _____

3. The cost of living in Paris is very high, I heard that an apartment could cost as much as a thousand dollars a month. _____

4. Last summer, Jerry spent most of his time at the beach, however, he never learned how to surf. _____

5. One of the best jobs I ever had was as a lifeguard at Wildwood State Park, I could meet many new people. _____

6. Photography is a good hobby; many people like to take pictures of people they know and places they have visited. _____

7. Teachers prefer typed papers, yet many students don't own a typewriter. _____

8. The parking facilities at this university are inadequate, each day I must drive around for at least thirty minutes before I find a space. _____

9. I prefer good restaurants, but I like fast-food places also. _____

10. Walt Whitman was a major American poet, he lived in Camden, New Jersey. _____

Check the answer key.

APPLICATION I

In the blank at the right of each sentence, write *C* if the sentence is correct. Write *CS* if the sentence is a comma splice. Correct the comma splices.

1. It is important to understand and use correct grammar, for correct usage enables your reader to comprehend your message easily. _____

2. On a clear day, you can see three states from here, on a cloudy day, you can't see across the river. _____

3. Wool retains the body's heat best, fiberfill, however, is a close second. _____

4. Taking humanities courses benefits students in many ways, students develop analytical skills, synthesize information from a number of fields, and gain insight into many contemporary problems. _____

5. Because adolescence is a difficult period, parents should try to be understanding, teenagers need to know that someone cares. _____

6. Chocolate milk is nutritious, however, unflavored milk has fewer calories. _____

7. Gold and silver have always been considered precious commodities, in recent years platinum has also been placed in that category. _____

8. Completing an income tax form requires an unconscionable amount of time, the government should streamline the form. _____

9. Typing should be a required course for students who intend to attend college, but not for those who don't have specific plans to go to college. _____

10. I've always liked studying current events, I like to know where the world is heading. _____

11. Recently the Northeast suffered a prolonged drought, this had many adverse effects on agricultural production. _____

12. My mother frequently won blue ribbons for her sour-cream coffee cake, but she never told me the recipe. _____

13. High-school graduates should work for a year before they go to college, this time could be used to save money and decide on a career goal. _____

14. Our vacation in Tahiti was great fun, it was too bad that it was over so soon.   _____

15. Video games are constantly improving, the newest games appear to be three-dimensional and allow the player to make more decisions.   _____

16. There is a chronic shortage of short-order cooks, everyone wants to be a white-collar worker.   _____

17. More people are killed each year mining coal than have ever been killed in a nuclear-power plant accident, therefore, coal mining should be banned.   _____

18. Some people think the legal driving age should be nineteen, others argue for twenty-one.   _____

19. Children can add a lot to one's life, yet they require a major investment of time and money.   _____

20. One way to prevent boredom is to have a hobby, then you always have something to do.   _____

Check the answer key.

APPLICATION II

Each sentence in the following paragraphs is numbered. If the sentence is correctly punctuated, write *C* above the number at the beginning of the sentence. If the sentence is a comma splice, write *CS*. Correct all comma splices.

(1) Birthdays are terrible days, I think they should be abolished. (2) Have you ever noticed how many people are depressed on their birthday? (3) Have you ever thought about the reason for that depression? (4) If you are one of the few people who enjoy birthdays, you probably haven't even considered the problem.

(5) There are many reasons for depression and for disliking birthdays, the classic one is that a birthday reminds us that we're getting older. (6) That may be true, but it's also better than the alternative. (7) Actually, there are two alternatives to getting older, but I'll bet that you haven't thought of either of them. (8) The first alternative is departing this world, which most people are not anxious to do, the second choice is to stay the same—not to grow older. (9) The latter choice is the one that Peter Pan and his gang of merry boys favored, we all know what

happened to them in the end. (10) Besides, would you really want to spend seventy years as a two-year-old?

(11) Another reason for birthday depression is that we're afraid no one will remember, that the day will pass as just an ordinary day. (12) Why, you ask, is that depressing? (13) It's depressing because it proves that nobody cares, it shows us that we aren't important to anybody. (14) The world is completely unaware of our existence, it doesn't even know that we're alive. (15) All of our friends and neighbors who profess to like us are simply hypocrites, they not only fail to give us the time of day, but they also neglect to wish us "Happy Birthday."

(16) Is there a cure for birthday depression? (17) I've already mentioned it. (18) Let's abolish birthdays, then each person could choose one day to celebrate being alive! (19) How does that sound?

Check the answer key.

APPLICATION III

Each sentence in the following essay is numbered. If the sentence is correctly punctuated, write *C* above the number at the beginning of the sentence. If the sentence is a comma splice, write *CS*. Correct all comma splices.

The College Application

(1) "It is to the student's benefit to begin to apply to several colleges as soon as possible." (2) This is good advice, we have heard it before. (3) In July, the deadlines are barely visible. (4) We have plenty of time, so we can wait until we are inspired to complete the forms. (5) Now it is October, we have to get to work. (6) We wonder where to begin, everything looks so confusing.

(7) The first source of information is the famous *College Handbook*. (8) Finding the right college here is like finding Tom Jones's phone number in the white pages. (9) Each college has different courses, different sports, and different requirements, they all seem the same. (10) Asking a few teachers is always a help, but each teacher recommends the college he or she attended. (11) For every ten teachers, there are ten colleges that are "just right for you." (12) Of course, for those who find the time, visiting the colleges remains the most accurate method of making the right choice, the best colleges are always located hundreds of miles from home.

(13) After receiving the many application forms, the college-bound student must now make some decisions. (14) After the stack of applications has managed to block the bedroom door, the time comes to throw away what is useless. (15) The student fills the trash can three times, enough brochures still remain to wallpaper the family room. (16) One day the process of applying finally begins.

(17) Weekdays are too hectic, and weekends disappear too quickly. (18) However, Mom demands action, so the student begins. (19) The personal-data sections and the list of activities take only a few days to complete. (20) "Now," the student mutters to himself, "I'm really rolling, I'll start the essays next Saturday morning." (21) Unfortunately, I cannot tell you how to write the essay, next Saturday morning is always a week away. (22) The completed application package must be sent to the college counselor's office, for his deadline comes months before the colleges' deadlines. (23) The application takes the student only a week to write, it takes the counselor's office over a month to mail. (24) However, this delay does not matter; the hardest part of applying is over.

(25) The next problem is finding two teachers who are willing and able to write decent recommendations. (26) Finding a slightly dishonest teacher is about as hard as finding a completely honest one. (27) The remarks on report cards are usually gratifying, a recommendation to a college takes more than a smile and a courteous remark. (28) If a student does find a teacher who will write a glowing recommendation, then his remarks often sound too good to be true.

(29) Now, it is January, the waiting game will last until March or later. (30) The spring days creep along. (31) On Saturdays, the senior occupies the recliner on the front porch and waits for the mail carrier. (32) Mothers are warned not to open other people's mail. (33) The day finally arrives, the senior tears open the letter to learn where he will go to school for the next four years. Check the answer key.

APPLICATION IV

Proofread a rough draft of a paper of your own. Check carefully for comma splices. Identify each one, and correct it. Show your corrections to your instructor or tutor.

9

Run-Ons

OBJECTIVES:

OBJECTIVES: 1. To recognize run-ons, individually and in paragraphs.

2. To correct run-ons.

3. To use the editing symbol for run-ons (RO) correctly when proofreading.

KEY CONCEPT: A run-on (sometimes called a **fused sentence** or a **run-together sentence**) contains two or more independent clauses that have been punctuated as one sentence; that is, no punctuation separates the two independent clauses.

Consider this example:

Example: The lawyer pleaded her client's case well she won the case.
In this example, there are two complete sentences:

The lawyer pleaded her client's case well, and *she won the case.*

Identifying the Problem

Run-ons are found only in compound or compound-complex sentences; these are the sentences with two or more independent clauses. To identify run-ons, look at the break between the two sentences. If there is no punctuation at this point, then the sentence is a run-on.

PRACTICE 1

Read the following sentences. If a sentence is correct, place C beside it. If the group of words is actually a run-on, place RO beside the sentence, and draw a vertical line separating the two independent clauses.

Example: __RO__ I work at a factory during the night/I go to school during the day.

__C__ Drag racing is an exciting sport.

1. Harry is my best friend he will do anything for me.   _____

2. Chemistry is a difficult subject.   _____

3. America is a nation on the move many families move four times in a ten-year

   period.   _____

4. Shelly is a good dancer she has been selected to appear with the New York

   Ballet Company.   _____

5. The United Nations was formed from an older organization, the League of

Nations.   _____

Check the answer key.

Correcting the Problem

There are three ways to correct a run-on sentence.

1. *First, break the run-on into two separate sentences with a period and a capital letter in each.*

Run-on: The dean smiled at the new freshmen they had survived their first week of classes.

Correction: The dean smiled at the new freshmen. They had survived their first week of classes.

EXERCISE   Correct these run-ons by following the above example.

1. The students went to the dean's office they wanted to complain about a teacher.

_____

2. The accountant sighed as she left her office she had worked for fifteen consecutive hours.

_____

_____

3. Smoke detectors do not cost very much they have helped save many lives.

_____

_____

Have your instructor or tutor check your work.

2. *Connect the two independent clauses with a comma and the appropriate coordinate conjunction.* There are seven coordinate conjunctions: *for, and, nor, but, or, yet,* and *so.* Each coordinate conjunction tells the reader what kind of relationship exists between the two independent clauses.

Look at the following sentences and determine the relationship between the two independent clauses. Pay particular attention to the coordinate conjunctions.

a. Sue is going shopping, and her husband is going bowling.
b. Sue is going shopping, but her husband is going bowling.
c. Sue is going shopping, so her husband is going bowling.
d. Sue is going shopping, for her husband is going bowling.

In sentence a, the *and* tells the reader that neither one of the two independent clauses is more important than the other. In other words, the fact that *Sue is going shopping* is as important as the fact that *her husband is going bowling.*

In sentence b, the *but* shows opposition; it tells the reader that Sue and her husband are doing different things.

In sentence c, the *so* tells the reader that *her husband's going bowling* is the result of *Sue's going shopping.* You might imagine that her husband didn't want to go shopping, and he decided to go bowling while Sue was shopping.

In sentence d, the *for* tells the reader that *Sue is going shopping* because *her husband is going bowling.* In other words, Sue didn't want to go bowling, and she chose to go shopping instead.

> **NOTE:** See Chapter 8, *Comma Splices,* for a list of the relationships each coordinate conjunction stresses.

EXERCISE   Following the example, correct these run-ons.

1. The snow thrilled us we wanted to go skiing.

_____

2. Doug gently unlocked the front door he did not want to awaken his parents at 4:00 A.M.

_____

_____

3. Nearly half of all car accidents involve a drunk driver many states have tightened their laws concerning driving under the influence of alcohol.

_____

_____

Have your instructor or tutor check your work.

> **NOTE:** Using only a comma is not enough. You must use *both* the comma and the coordinate conjunction.

3. *Connect the two independent clauses with a semicolon* (;). The semicolon implies to the reader that a relationship exists between the two sentences; however, it does not indicate the *type* of relationship. Use a semicolon when the two independent clauses are closely related. For instance, the second clause can provide an example of the first one or explain the first.

Run-on: The giant black and white pandas are native to China in fact they are the national animals of China.

Correction: The giant black and white pandas are native to China; in fact, they are the national animals of China.

EXERCISE   Correct these run-ons by using a semicolon to separate the two independent clauses.

1. We could not buy the house it was priced at $150,000.

_____

2. You must dress warmly in an Alaskan winter the average temperature is 0 degrees Fahrenheit.

_____

_____

3. In the 1800s, life in the American West was treacherous a pioneer might fall victim to natural disasters or wild animals.

_____

_____

Have your instructor or tutor check your work.

NOTE: Often when you use a semicolon, you may want to include an **adverbial conjunction** (sometimes called a **conjunctive adverb**) to indicate what kind of relationship exists between the two independent clauses. There are four major **adverbial conjunctions:** *however, moreover, therefore,* and *nevertheless.* When you use one of these four adverbial conjunctions, a semicolon must come before the adverbial conjunction and a comma after it.

Example: We were supposed to be at school at 9:00 A.M.; however, our car wouldn't start.

Below is a list of other adverbial conjunctions. Each of these identifies a particular relationship between the two independent clauses. Check a dictionary to learn these relationships.

also	indeed	primarily
consequently	likewise	rather
currently	next	similarly
finally	overall	then
hence		thus

PRACTICE 2

In the blank at the right of each sentence, write *C* if the sentence is correctly punctuated. Write *RO* if the sentence is a run-on. Correct the run-on sentences.

1. It was a cold, wet day; however, we still had our picnic at the beach.   _____

2. I plan to go to law school I hope that I am accepted.   _____

3. Mathematics is my hardest course English is my favorite course.   _____

4. Thelma will be a lawyer Thelma will be a doctor.   _____

5. Running is a good exercise; moreover, it relieves tension.   _____

6. My uncle has a cabin in Maine, and he has a cottage at Cape Cod.   _____

7. The lake was crystal clear and warm the sky was a brilliant blue.   _____

8. Cumberland's basketball team won the semifinals now the team will compete in the state finals.   _____

9. College demands quite a lot from a student; however, it offers many rewards.   _____

10. Skiing is a difficult sport moreover it can be dangerous.   _____

Check the answer key.

APPLICATION I

In the blank at the right of each sentence, write *C* if the sentence is correctly punctuated. Write *RO* if the sentence is a run-on. Correct the run-on sentences.

1. College offers many opportunities to ambitious students however each person must decide to take advantage of them. _____

2. On sunny, hot days we like to swim; the cool water is so refreshing. _____

3. Left-handed people face many obstacles few ordinary items—such as can openers and doors—are designed for them. _____

4. Tomorrow is another day, and I sure hope it's a better one. _____

5. Tryouts for the soccer team went well fifty girls qualified. _____

6. The lights in the room keep blinking I think there's a short in the wires. _____

7. The automobile industry is less successful today than in past years because new cars cost too much for most people. _____

8. There was a time when a young man held a door open for a young lady that time has passed. _____

9. Most people don't realize that the dictionary offers a plethora of valuable information they use it only to look up word definitions. _____

10. Computers are quickly replacing typewriters, yet some writers prefer their trusted manuals. _____

11. Registration is a long, boring process it is too bad that they can't shorten it somehow. _____

12. Now is the time to register to vote, for the elections are scheduled for two weeks from now. _____

13. I think clocks should be outlawed they put too much pressure on people. _____

14. East Texas offers a variety of landscapes; rice paddies flourish in the southern section, and rolling hills cover the middle section. _____

15. Whoever invented Silly Putty probably made a fortune I'd like to meet him or her. _____

16. In theory, mothers always have the best interests of their children on their minds unfortunately it isn't always like that in real life. _____

17. Children can add excitement to a family's daily life they can also add some sorrow. _____

18. The teacher said that Joey is a smart boy, but he doesn't always use his mind in a constructive manner. _____

19. Many cities are trying to revitalize deserted sections New York, Boston, and Baltimore have designed new waterfront attractions in their cities. _____

20. Wood stoves are reappearing in American homes many people find that they save money by using wood instead of oil or gas to heat their homes. _____

Check the answer key.

APPLICATION II

Each sentence in the following paragraph is numbered. Above the number at the beginning of each sentence, write *C* if the sentence is correctly punctuated or *RO* if it is a run-on. Correct all run-ons.

(1) Today's young people are blamed for a host of problems. (2) Commentators, the media, and even the older generation castigate them it seems as if youth can do nothing right. (3) The media and their commentators frequently blame the nation's crime problem on its youth they cite statistics, observations, and case studies to support their viewpoint. (4) They seem to imply that the nation would not have a crime problem if it did not have young people. (5) Would the trade-off be worth it? (6) Another problem that is attributed to today's youth is the breakdown in the nation's traditions and values. (7) American society has been changing for the past two decades during that time, a generation has been born, matured, and been assimilated into the mainstream while another generation is taking its place. (8) On which of these generations should the blame be placed? (9) Logic would seem to require placing it on the first generation, but that generation is the one that is currently complaining about young people. (10) The generation that grew to maturity and middle age during the decades of turmoil and transition not only participated in the upheaval but also precipitated it today that generation seems to

have forgotten the role it played in changing society. (11) Instead of emphasizing current problems and seeking to assign blame, it might be more useful to delineate modern advantages. (12) Due to advances in medical knowledge and technology, the nation now has a decreased infant mortality rate and an increased life span in addition, people enjoy better health for a greater percentage of their productive years. (13) Also, more people have access to an improved life style. (14) Finally, improvements in transportation and mass-marketing techniques have made a greater variety of foodstuffs available this, in turn, has improved the daily diet of a significant portion of the population. (15) Whether today's youth should be praised or punished is irrelevant; instead, let us hope they will continue the process of improving the nation.

Check the answer key.

APPLICATION III

Read the following paragraph carefully. If a sentence is correctly punctuated, write *C* above the number at the beginning of the sentence; if the group of words is a run-on, write *RO*. Correct all run-ons.

(1) Many words we use today had their origins in Greek plays, poems, or mythology. (2) A primary example is Freud's use of the term *Oedipal complex*. (3) Freud constructed the term from the name of a Greek king, Oedipus he is the central character in Sophocles' play *Oedipus Rex*. (4) In the play, Oedipus fulfilled a terrifying prophecy he unknowingly murdered his natural father and married his mother. (5) Another example is the term *Achilles' heel* this term suggests a soft spot which can easily be attacked. (6) Homer, a Greek poet, immortalized Achilles in his poem *The Iliad*. (7) According to Greek legend, Achilles' mother bathed her infant son in the river Styx; this bath was supposed to make the future warrior invulnerable. (8) However, because his mother held him by one heel, this heel was never protected Achilles met his death during the Trojan War when an arrow pierced the unprotected heel. (9) A third example is the word *narcissistic;* this word now describes someone who is in love with himself and his appearance. (10) Narcissus was a very handsome Greek youth because of his appearance, many people fell in love with him. (11) As a punishment for his callousness, a god forced the

egocentric youth to gaze forever in a pool. (12) Narcissus fell in love with his own reflection he eventually was destroyed by his obsession. (13) Finally, he was turned into a flower, which still bears his name. (14) Many other words, such as *tantalize* and *nemesis,* have their origins in Greek culture obviously, our current vocabulary owes a great debt to ancient Greek civilization. Check the answer key.

APPLICATION IV

Proofread a rough draft of a paper of your own. Check each sentence carefully. If you find any run-ons, label them *RO*. Correct all run-ons, and show your revisions to your instructor or tutor.

PART III

Sentence Choices

10

Style: Sentence Combinations

OBJECTIVES: 1. To combine ideas effectively and concisely in sentences.

2. To use knowledge of grammar and mechanics to produce effective sentences.

3. To begin sentences in an interesting manner.

KEY CONCEPT: **Sentence Combining** will help you to develop efficient and effective sentences. There are five ways to combine sentences:

1. Use adjectives and other modifiers.

2. Use appositives and relative-pronoun clauses.

3. Use participles.

4. Use coordination.

5. Use subordination to link ideas.

Consider the following paragraph:

Example: It was a hot August afternoon. The wind blew lightly and steadily. A storm cloud quickly approached. It approached from the west. The sky darkened. The thunderstorm began. It rained for one hour. Rain poured from the black sky. The storm quickly ended. The sun returned and shone brightly.

This brief paragraph is simple and, in fact, rather boring. Combining some of the sentences will add variety and interest to the paragraph.

Revision: On the hot August afternoon, a light wind blew steadily. From the west, a storm cloud quickly approached, and the sky darkened. The thunderstorm lasted an hour as rain poured from the black sky. Just as quickly as the storm cloud arrived, it departed. The bright sun returned.

The revision is more effective. Sentences move quickly, and ideas are linked by conjunctions and pronouns. Also, the sentences vary in type, length, and complexity.

Adjectives and Other Modifiers

Adjectives and other modifiers can be added to sentences in one of two ways:

1. *Create a list of adjectives joined by commas.*
   Consider the following phrase:

   Example: the quick and brown and hungry dog
   Now substitute a comma for each *and*:

Revision: the quick, brown, hungry dog
This combination is more effective than using the word *and* to join adjectives.

2. *Place two adjectives after a noun to modify it, and enclose the adjectives within commas.*

Example: The tall and handsome boy spoke to Ann.

Revision: The boy, tall and handsome, spoke to Ann.

EXERCISE   Combine the adjectives in the following group of sentences into one sentence. Include all major pieces of information.

The meadow was surrounded by oak trees.
The meadow was green.
The meadow was beautiful.

Your combination should look like one of the following sentences:

1. The beautiful, green meadow was surrounded by oak trees.

2. The meadow, beautiful and green, was surrounded by oak trees.

Have your instructor or tutor check your work.

PRACTICE 1

Combine each group of sentences into one sentence. Use one of the two methods for combining adjectives.

1. The car had plenty of chrome.
   The chrome was silvery.
   The chrome was shiny.

   _____

2. The doctor was ready to operate.
   The doctor was pale.
   The doctor was slim.
   The doctor was serious.

   _____

3. The lake was fed by a stream.
   The stream was cold.
   The stream was a mountain stream.
   The stream was clear.

   _____

4. The table was made of oak.
   The table was rickety.
   The table was old.

   _____

5. The lawyer approached the judge.
   The lawyer was bold.
   The lawyer was young.
   The judge was bald.
   The judge was old.

   _____

6. The fashion model walked into the store.
   The model was tall.
   The model was slender.

   _____

7. The sunset was spectacular.
   The sunset was red.
   The sunset was glowing.

   _____

8. A puppy makes a good companion.
   A puppy is chubby.
   A puppy is playful.

   _____

9. The spy wore a trench coat.
   The trench coat was tan.
   The trench coat was old.

   _____

10. The pudding was delicious.
    The pudding was chocolate.
    The pudding was smooth.
    The pudding was creamy.

    _____

Have your instructor or tutor check your work.

NOTE: See Chapter 14, *Commas to Separate,* for instructions on how and where to place commas.

Appositives and Relative-Pronoun Clauses

Appositives

Appositives, which are nouns or noun phrases, rename or define another noun. Consider these two sentences:

Example:	Pam is the captain of the soccer team. She led the team to the league championship.
Revision:	Pam, the captain of the soccer team, led the team to the league championship.
	The noun phrase, *the captain of the soccer team,* is an appositive. It defines Pam's position on the team. In fact, the appositive and the noun it defines or renames can be interchanged.
Alternative:	The captain of the soccer team, Pam, led the team to the league championship.
	In this sentence, *Pam* is the appositive.

PRACTICE 2

Combine each group of sentences into one sentence. Form appositives to combine the information.

1. The dog was an Irish setter.
   The dog won first prize in the annual dog show.

   _____

2. Brenda is an old friend of mine.
   Brenda is coming to visit next week.

   _____

3. The doctor is a graduate of the state university.
   The doctor is a well-known orthopedist.

   _____

4. Video games are recent inventions.
   Video games have changed American culture.

   _____

5. Harold is a Shakespearean actor.
   Harold will play the role of Romeo next season.

   _____

6. Tommy is a pinball wizard.
   Tommy now plays video games.

   _____

7. The book is a study of American literature.
   The book was written by a famous critic.

   _____

8. The dining room table is an eighteenth-century reproduction.
   The dining room table requires daily polishing.

   _____

9. The musical is a Broadway extravaganza.
   The musical will open in Las Vegas next week.

   _____

10. The car is an old station wagon.
    The car climbed its last hill.

    _____

Have your instructor or tutor check your work.

Relative-Pronoun Clauses

Relative pronouns (the words *who, which,* and *that*) take the place of nouns. Relative pronouns are used in dependent clauses (a clause with a subject and a verb that cannot stand alone). A dependent clause with a relative pronoun can act in the same manner as an appositive. It gives additional information about a noun by renaming it, defining it, or describing it.

Examples: 1. My car, *a blue Chevrolet,* needs a brake job. (*A blue Chevrolet* is an appositive for *car.*)
My car, *which is a blue Chevrolet,* needs a brake job. (*Which is a blue Chevrolet* is a dependent clause with *which* as a relative pronoun.)

2. Her father, a minister, has been a volunteer at the hospital for five years. (*Minister* is an appositive for *father.*)
Her father, who is a minister, has been a volunteer at the hospital for five years. (*Who is a minister* is a dependent clause with the relative pronoun *who.*)

3. Mr. Harmond's house, the building near the lake, is quite lovely. (*The building near the lake* is an appositive for *house.*)
Mr. Harmond's house, which is built near the lake, is quite lovely. (*Which is built near the lake* is a dependent clause with the relative pronoun *which.*)

PRACTICE 3

Combine each group of sentences into one complex sentence. Use a dependent clause that begins with a relative pronoun.

1. Jim is a lawyer.
   Jim is from England.

   _____

2. Please bring me the glass.
   The glass is on the counter.

   _____

3. The Melvins took a trip.
   The trip was very expensive.

   _____

4. The deer ran into the pine grove.
   The deer had been startled.

   _____

5. Her grandparents moved to San Antonio, Texas.
   Her grandparents had just retired.

   _____

6. The house was built in the seventeenth century.
   The house is now a historical landmark.

   _____

7. The engineer won the award.
   The engineer had worked four years to design the hundred-story building.

   _____

8. The police officer walks the beat.
   The police officer is a good family friend.

   _____

9. The rubber tree is in the corner.
   The rubber tree grows quickly.

   _____

10. The cabin is in the mountains.
    The cabin is our favorite retreat.

   _____

Have your instructor or tutor check your work.

Participles

Adding *ing* to a verb forms a present participle, and adding, usually, *ed* to a verb forms a past participle. (See Chapter 2 for irregular past-participle forms.) Participles are used as adjectives to modify nouns or pronouns. Because they are formed from verbs, they carry the actions and visual images of verbs. Consider the following sentence and the revised version of it:

Example: Admirers greeted the author, who is well known.

Revision: Admirers greeted the well-*known* author.

                This revision uses a participle, *known,* to modify the noun *author.*

NOTE: See Chapter 17, *Other Types of Punctuation,* for an explanation of compound adjectives.

Look at the following sentences and the combined version of them:

Example: We were waiting for the bus. A woman approached us. The woman was wearing a mask.

Combination: While waiting for the bus, we were approached by a masked woman.

                In this combination, there are two participles: *waiting for the bus,* which modifies *we,* and *masked,* which modifies *woman.*

NOTE: If you begin a sentence with a participle, make sure that it modifies the subject. Also, place the participle next to the noun it modifies.

Example: The child enjoyed the circus.
                The child was smiling.

Combination: The smiling child enjoyed the circus.

PRACTICE 4

Combine each pair of sentences into one sentence by forming a present or a past participle from the italicized sentence.

Example: *The fielder ran to make the catch.*
                He tripped.

                While running to make the catch, the fielder tripped.

1. We read a novel.
   The novel was written by Thomas Hardy.

   _____

2. *We watched television.*
   We ate popcorn.

   _____

3. The stream cascaded down the mountain.
   The stream tumbled and rushed.

   _____

4. The mountain goat climbed up the ridge.
   The mountain goat stumbled and tripped.

   _____

5. *The singer was performing at Lincoln Center.*
   The singer forgot the words of the song.

   _____

6. *Eileen was dancing with her fiancé.*
   Eileen saw a former boyfriend.

   _____

7. *Start the car.*
   Buckle your safety belt.

   _____

8. *We were visiting the museum.*
   We spotted a famous painter.

   _____

9. The leather jacket belonged to a World War I flying ace.
   The jacket was torn.

   _____

10. The steak made our mouths water.
    The steak was sizzling.

    _____

Have your instructor or tutor check your work.

Coordination

To add variety to sentence structure, form compound sentences. Compound sentences contain two or more independent clauses. They are formed in one of three ways:

1. Add a comma and a coordinate conjunction.
2. Add a semicolon.
3. Add a semicolon and an adverbial conjunction.

Coordinate Conjunctions

Sentences can be combined by adding a comma and a **coordinate conjunction.** There are seven coordinate conjunctions: *for, and, nor, but, or, yet,* and *so.* If you can remember the word

FANBOYS (formed from the first letters of the conjunctions), you will be able to remember all seven coordinate conjunctions.

Learn the relationships that each coordinate conjunction expresses:

1. *For* shows cause.
2. *And* shows addition.
3. *Nor* shows a negative choice.
4. *But* shows contrast or contradiction
5. *Or* shows a choice.
6. *Yet* shows contrast.
7. *So* shows effect.

PRACTICE 5

Combine each pair of sentences into one compound sentence. Use a comma and one of the coordinate conjunctions to combine the sentences.

1. Marcus will go to law school.
   He will go to medical school.

   _____

2. It was a very hot summer.
   Carlos bought an air conditioner.

   _____

3. The hundred-year-old tree was infested with gypsy moths.
   It had to be destroyed.

   _____

4. The construction on the house is not complete.
   We will move in tomorrow.

   _____

5. The California coastline is lovely.
   The Maine coastline is just as beautiful.

   _____

Semicolons

Two independent clauses can be joined by a **semicolon** (;). However, the relationship between the two clauses is only implied or suggested when you use the semicolon. The reader must determine the relationship.

Example: The captain read the latest report; he quickly called the major.

Adverbial Conjunctions

Two independent clauses can be connected by a semicolon and an **adverbial conjunction.** There are four major adverbial conjunctions: *however, therefore, nevertheless,* and *moreover.*

Example: The police officer worked a twelve-hour shift; moreover, she spent an additional four hours at work to complete her reports.

PRACTICE 6

Form a compound sentence from each of the pairs of sentences. Use a semicolon and an appropriate adverbial conjunction.

1. Founder's Day will be held on Thursday.
   The weatherman is forecasting rain.

   _____

2. The country faced an economic recession in the 1930s.
   The country faced one in the late 1970s.

   _____

3. The general ordered his troops to prepare for an attack.
   All leaves were canceled for the soldiers.

   _____

4. The sky diver broke his leg on his last jump.
   He insists that he will jump tomorrow.

   _____

5. Prior to 1950, most people did not have college degrees.
   They were able to lead successful lives.

   _____

Have your instructor or tutor check your work.

Subordination

Ideas can be joined in complex sentences. A **complex sentence** contains an **independent clause** (a group of words with a subject and a verb that can stand by itself) and one or more **dependent clauses** (a group of words with a subject and a verb that *cannot* stand by itself, because it does not express a complete thought).

Example: The harbor is beautiful at sunset. (independent clause)
         Because it is a cool evening. (dependent clause)

         The dependent clause, *Because it is a cool evening,* needs an independent clause to form a complete idea.

Example: dependent clause independent clause
Because it was a cool evening, we decided to build a fire.

Notice that the dependent clause has one word that makes it dependent—the word *because*. This word, and others like it, are called **subordinate conjunctions.**

NOTE: If a dependent clause begins the sentence, place a comma after it to separate it from the independent clause.

Here is a list of some subordinate conjunctions:

after	even though	unless
although	if	until
as	since	when
because	than	wherever
before	though	while

Placing a subordinate conjunction before a subject and a verb forms a dependent clause. You also know that relative pronouns (*who, which,* and *that*) form dependent clauses. The dependent clause can be used to modify a noun, a verb, or an adjective. It also can be used as a noun. Because independent clauses can stand by themselves, they should contain the most important information in the sentence.

Look at the two sentences below and the sentence formed by combining them.

Example: 1. The ball game was over.
2. People filed out of the stadium.

The second sentence is more important, so keep it as the independent clause. Make the first sentence a dependent clause.

Combination: After the ball game was over, people filed out of the stadium.

PRACTICE 7

Form a complex sentence from each of the pairs of sentences. Keep the most important information in the independent clause.

1. The thief ran into the alley.
   The police officer followed her.

   _____

2. The child ran a high temperature.
   His parents called his pediatrician.

   _____

3. Julio won the tennis match.
   He jumped over the net to congratulate his opponent.

   _____

4. Education is vitally important.
   All Americans must be concerned about quality education.

   _____

5. Immigrants come to America.
   Most of them become American citizens.

   _____

6. The boat was old.
   The boat was still seaworthy.

   _____

7. I could protest.
   The dentist began to drill.

   _____

8. The fog covered the area.
   The pilot did not want to land the plane.

   _____

9. He had a part-time job.
   The college student had little free time.

   _____

10. Many soap operas are aired in the afternoon.
    Some college students schedule classes before noon.

    _____

Have your instructor or tutor check your work.

Beginning Sentences

Just as sentences can be combined in different ways to vary their structure and emphasis, ideas within a sentence can be structured in a number of ways. The traditional order of a simple sentence is subject-verb-object. Because this pattern works well, beginning writers tend to belabor it; such overuse can be boring and repetitive. By varying your sentence structure, by altering the expected order of ideas, you can make your writing more interesting and enjoyable. Here are several types of sentence beginnings for you to try; their use will prevent your writing style from becoming boring and juvenile.

1. With a prepositional phrase:

   From the gloom an apparition materialized.

In a traditionally ordered sentence, the emphasis would have been on the apparition. Starting with a prepositional phrase focuses the reader's attention on a descriptive element in the sentence: *the gloom.* This shift in emphasis can enhance the overall effect of the sentence.

Usual format: An apparition materialized from the gloom.

2. **With an infinitive phrase:**

To maintain his weight, the football player ran ten miles a day.

In this sentence the infinitive phrase receives more attention than it would have in a more conventionally structured sentence.

Usual format: The football player ran ten miles a day to maintain his weight.
Here, the focus is on his running ability, rather than on the reason for his regimen.

3. **With a participial phrase:**

Hopping across the infield, the youngsters pretended they were rabbits.

Once again, this way of beginning a sentence has shifted the reader's attention from the children's pretense to a mental image of their activity.

Usual format: The youngsters pretended they were rabbits by hopping across the field.

4. **With the direct object:**

The bribe Sampson offered to the mayor.

Here the focus is on what is being offered—a bribe. Usually, the sentence's emphasis would have been on the perpetrator, Sampson.

Usual format: Sampson offered the bribe to the mayor.

5. **With a dependent clause:**

Even though he failed the test, Wilbur likes the course.

In a complex sentence, the more important idea is in the independent clause; the less important idea is relegated to the dependent clause. However, beginning the sentence with the dependent clause increases its value. The dependent clause does not attain parity with the independent clause in this format, but its value is enhanced.

Usual format: Wilbur likes the course even though he failed the test.

6. **With an adverb:**

Playfully, the chimpanzee threw the ball to his trainer.

The adverb is emphasized in this sentence. In its usual position next to the verb, the adverb is just another detail in the sentence. By starting the sentence with *playfully,* the writer requires the reader to be aware of the description.

Usual format: The chimpanzee playfully threw the ball to his trainer.

7. **With an adjective:**

Injured, the trapper nonetheless sought help for the avalanche victims.

This sentence beginning is akin to starting with an adverb. The beginning focuses the reader's attention on the descriptive element and increases the importance of that description.

Usual format: The injured trapper nonetheless sought help for the avalanche victims.

8. With a coordinate conjunction:

(*Note:* This method is usually considered to be informal usage.)

The order was not filled promptly. *For* the merchandise had not been shipped on schedule.

Most of the time, these two simple sentences would probably be joined to form a compound sentence. By leaving them as two distinct sentences, the writer emphasizes their individual meanings, yet acknowledges their relationship by using the conjunction *for*.

Usual format: The order was not filled promptly, for the merchandise had not been shipped on schedule.

9. With an absolute construction:

Book in hand, Katie returned to the classroom.

Absolute constructions are usually elliptical. In the sentence above, the phrase *book in hand* could have two possible meanings: *with her book in her hand* (a prepositional phrase), or *carrying her book in her hand* (a participial phrase). In either case, by using an absolute construction and by starting the sentence with it, the writer emphasizes that detail and helps the reader create a mental image.

Usual format: Katie returned to the classroom with her book in her hand.
Carrying her book in her hand, Katie returned to the classroom.

If you begin your sentences in an unconventional way and if you vary your sentence structure, then you catch and keep your readers' interest. This mature writing style will make it easier for your readers to comprehend your message and, thus, will ensure that they will remember it.

PRACTICE 8

Unscramble each of the following sentences. Try to begin each sentence in an interesting manner.

1. Proctored a graduate assistant the final exam.

_____

2. Sought a way jaded the jet-setter to relieve his overwhelming boredom.

_____

3. Describe dreamily the perfect wedding the young couple.

_____

4. Searched the old man grief-stricken for his lost love.

_____

5. Can do we a term project. Demonstrate or we can a new product.

_____

6. The *nouvelle-cuisine* restaurant because several cases of infectious hepatitis was closed there had been traced to its kitchen.

_____

7. Ignored the children the freezing temperatures skating around the lake.

_____

8. Jeremy Wilson at all the well-known beaches to ride the perfect wave tried surfing.

_____

9. Down Main Street gun in his holster strode the marshal.

_____

10. Faced the prizefighter belligerent his opponent.

_____

Have your instructor or tutor check your work.

A Final Word

One group of sentences can be combined in a number of ways. Each way may be technically correct, but some combinations are more effective than others. Try to combine sentences so that they are effective and concise.

Here are several sentences and some ways they can be combined:

Examples:
1. The teacher asked a question.
2. The question was complex and difficult.
3. The students did not know.
4. They did not know the answer to the question.
5. The teacher assigned work.
6. The work was additional homework.

Combinations:
1. When the teacher asked a complex and difficult question, the students did not know the answer; therefore, the teacher assigned additional homework.

2. Because the teacher had asked a complex and difficult question and the students did not know the answer, the teacher assigned additional homework.

3. Whenever the teacher asked a complex, difficult question, the students did not know the answer; the teacher assigned additional homework.

Your instructor or tutor can help you decide which is the best combination.

APPLICATION I

Combine each set of sentences into one sentence. Keep all important information.

1. The bus driver was lazy.   He took long breaks.
   He did not collect the fares.   His boss fired him.

   _____

   _____

2. The sun was setting.   The colors were very bright.
   The setting was lovely.   The colors lasted a long time.
   The colors were produced.

   _____

   _____

3. The *Titanic* was an ocean liner.   It sank on a voyage.
   The *Titanic* was luxurious.   The voyage was the maiden one.
                                        Many lives were lost.

   _____

   _____

4. The child received a bicycle.   The bicycle was blue.
   The bicycle was new.   The bicycle had ten speeds.
   The bicycle was shiny.   The child could not ride something.
                                      The something was a bike.

   _____

   _____

5. The bear was large.   The bear terrorized campers.
   The bear was a grizzly.   The campers were at a park.
   The bear was old.   The park was Yellowstone National Park.

   _____

   _____

6. Warren had a date.   Warren is a student.
   The date was last night.   Warren has a test.
   The evening was long.   The test is today.
                                      Warren did not pass.

   _____

   _____

7. The cowboy mounted his pony.   The cowboy chased a calf.
   The pony was a pinto.   The calf was a stray.
   The cowboy grabbed his rope.   The cowboy lassoed the calf.
   The rope is a lariat.

   _____

   _____

8. The restaurant was on the dock.   The restaurant was made of brick.
   The restaurant served seafood.   The restaurant had a decor.
                                          The decor was nautical.

   _____

   _____

9. We went to the movie.   We decided to go somewhere.
   We went to the ticket office.   The somewhere was to a restaurant.
   There was a line.   The restaurant was nearby.
   The line was a block long.

   _____

   _____

10. The tree was old.   The tree was in the way.
    The tree was stately.   The architect wanted to build something.
    The tree was an elm.   The something was a mall.

   _____

   _____

11. The man was a scuba diver.   The diver found a cache.
    The diver explored the wreck.   The cache had bullion.
    The wreck was sunken.   The bullion was gold.

   _____

   _____

12. We took a trip.   The castles were several.
    The trip was to England.   The castles were old.
    The trip was fascinating.   We toured a town.
    We visited castles.   The town was London.

   _____

   _____

13. There was a noise.   The noise indicated someone.
    The noise was loud.   Someone had entered.
    The noise was clanking.   The entering was into the house.

    _____

    _____

14. The biker parked a motorcycle.   A traffic officer was there.
    The motorcycle was huge.   The traffic officer gave a ticket.
    The biker parked in front of a zone.   The giving was to the biker.
    The zone was a no-parking zone.

    _____

    _____

15. The cove was sandy.   The home was to pirates.
    The cove was hidden by trees.   The pirates were many.
    The cove had been a home.   The pirates were in the Bahamas.
    The home was secret.

    _____

    _____

16. A coaster reached the top of the run.   The cars clanked.
    The coaster was a roller.   The cars plunged down the track.
    The cars swayed.   The plunging was at seventy miles
                                                  per hour.

    _____

    _____

17. The fisherman struggled with a fish.   The fisherman pulled the fish.
    The fish was a marlin.   The pulling was to the boat.
    The fisherman fought for two hours.

    _____

    _____

18. The snake slithered along a path.   The snake reached a rock.
    The snake was a garden snake.   The rock was warmed.
    The path was concrete.   The warming was by the sun.

    _____

    _____

19. The children become adolescents.
    The children go through changes.

    The changes are many.
    The changes are very rapid.

    _____

    _____

20. We have learned a great deal.
    The great deal is about science.
    The great deal is about the world.
    People are still superstitious.

    The people are many.
    The people carry a charm.
    The charm is lucky.
    For example, the charm is the foot of a
    rabbit.

    _____

    _____

21. Train stations have been turned into
    something.
    The something is houses or restaurants.
    The stations were many.
    The stations were former.

    The stations were once a crucial part of
    something.
    The something was a community.

    _____

    _____

22. One hundred years ago, toys were made of
    something.
    The toys were for children.
    The something was natural fibers or wood.

    Today, toys contain something.
    The toys are many.
    The something is microchips.

    _____

    _____

23. The grandfather clock was sold.
    The clock is an antique.

    We saw the clock at an auction.
    The selling was quick.

    _____

    _____

24. People visit national parks.
    The people are many millions.
    The visiting is annual.

    The people enjoy something in America's
    wilderness area.
    The something is backpacking.
    The something is hiking.

    _____

    _____

25. The mansion had fallen into ruins.
    The mansion was once a showcase.
    A community association decided to do
    something.

    The association was local.
    The something was to restore the mansion.

    _____

    _____

26. Writers were never able to make
    something.
    The writers were many and famous.
    The something was a living from their
    novels.

    _____

    _____

27. The town was covered by a blanket.
    The blanket was of snow.
    The town was in New England.

    The town was old.
    The town was quaint.
    The town lay quietly.

    _____

    _____

28. The two boxers glared at each other.
    One boxer was long and lean.

    One boxer was short and muscular.
    The glaring was from opposite corners of
    the ring.

    _____

    _____

29. Tourists enjoy rafting.
    The tourists are many.
    The rafting is down the Colorado River.

    The scenery and excitement make the trip
    worthwhile.
    The scenery is magnificent.
    The excitement is of the rafting.

    _____

    _____

30. The surfer grabbed his board.
    The surfer raced to the water.

    The surfer was tall.
    The surfer was tanned.

    _____

    _____

31. The mountain was once a volcano.   The once was one million years ago.
    The mountain towers.   The volcano was active.

    _____

    _____

32. Humans know more about our planet.   Humans cannot predict something.
    Humans hope to control their fate.   Humans cannot alter something.
                                              The something is the weather.

    _____

    _____

33. Writers may be prophets.   Many devices were described in novels.
    They write science fiction.   The describing was before scientists
    They are prophets of the future.   invented them.

    _____

    _____

34. The steps led to a hall.   The hall was dark.
    The steps were creaky.   The hall was silent.
    The steps were broken.

    _____

    _____

35. The circus clown wore things.   One thing was shoes.
    One thing was a dotted suit.   The shoes were yellow.
    The suit was blue and white.   The shoes were enormous.
    One thing was a baseball cap.
    The cap was red.

    _____

    _____

36. The magician pulled a rabbit.   The pulling was out of a hat.
    The magician was a master.   The magician disappeared in a puff
                                                 of smoke.

    _____

    _____

37. The pilot guided the transatlantic liner. The guiding was up the river.
    The pilot ran a tugboat.   The river was treacherous.
    The liner was large.

    _____

    _____

38. The skier was poised at the top of the jump.   The skier flew into space.
    The skier pushed forward down the ramp.

    _____

    _____

39. He believed he had seen a great play.   The play was praised later.
    The critic wrote a review.   The praising was by others.
    The review was favorable.   The praising was high.
    The review was of *Equus*.

    _____

    _____

40. Many theatergoers enjoy musicals.   The something is serious drama.
    Musicals are lighter in tone than
        something.

    _____

    _____

Have your instructor or tutor check your work.

APPLICATION II

Combine each set of sentences into one complete sentence. Make your sentences as effective and concise as possible. Do not omit any necessary information.

1. The boy grabbed a hand.   The hand belonged to his mother.
   The boy was small.   The boy glanced at his mother.
   The boy had red hair.   The glance was anxious.

   _____

   _____

2. They walked down the street.   They stopped in front of a shop.
   The walking was brisk.   The shop was small.
   The street was in a city.
   The street was crowded.

   _____

   _____

3. A pole stood outside.   The pole was white.
   The pole was red.   The pole was striped.

   _____

   _____

4. They entered the shop.   The boy began to whimper.
   The boy turned pale.

   _____

   _____

5. His mother tried to comfort him.   The chairs were against the wall.
   They sat down in chairs.

   _____

   _____

6. A man approached them.   The man wore a white coat.
   The man was older.   The man spoke to the woman.

   _____

   _____

7. The mother got up from her chair.   The chair was large.
   The mother led the boy to another chair.

   _____

   _____

8. The man placed the boy into the chair.   The man covered the boy.
   The man was older.   The covering was with a cloth.
   The boy was frightened.   The cloth was white.
   The boy was small.   The cloth covered everything except
                                                 the head.
                                              The head belonged to the boy.

   _____

   _____

9. The man turned his back on the boy.   The climbing was down from the chair.
   The boy tried to climb.   The boy's mother stopped him.

   _____

   _____

10. The man turned toward the boy.   The scissors were sharp.
    The boy saw the scissors.   The boy yelled.

   _____

   _____

11. The boy closed his eyes.   The man began to cut.

   _____

   _____

12. Hair covered the floor.   The covering was soon.
    The hair was red.   The floor was beneath the chair.

   _____

   _____

13. The man brushed the neck.   The man finished.
    The neck belonged to the boy.   The man took the cloth.
                                                The taking was off the boy.

   _____

   _____

14. The man handed a mirror.   The handing was to the boy.

   _____

   _____

15. The child sighed.   His mother beamed.
    The sighing was gentle.

   _____

   _____

16. The boy climbed.   The climbing was out of the chair.

   _____

   _____

17. The boy left the shop.   The barber handed a lollipop.
    His mother left the shop.   The handing was to the boy.

   _____

   _____

Have your instructor or tutor check your work.

APPLICATION III

Combine each set of sentences into one complete sentence. Make your sentences as effective and concise as possible. Do not omit any necessary information.

1. It is to a city's advantage to retain teams.   The teams are professional.
   The reasons are many.   The teams are sports teams.

   _____

   _____

2. The city's pride is maintained through   The something is the presence of
      something.   these teams.
   The pride is civic.

   _____

   _____

3. A sense of tradition is preserved.   A sense of continuity is preserved.

   _____

   _____

4. The citizen is better able to identify with his   The identification is when the team is
      city.   successful.
   The identification is because of the team.

   _____

   _____

5. The team receives the citizen's loyalty.   The city receives the citizen's loyalty.

   _____

   _____

6. The team helps to generate something.   The something is revenue.
   The ways are several.   The revenue is for the city.

   _____

   _____

7. For example, the city is able to tax parking   The city is able to tax concession sales.
      fees.
   The city is able to tax ticket sales.

   _____

   _____

8. The city makes money each time some-   The something is a fan buys a hot dog.
      thing occurs.
   The something is a fan buys a soda.

   _____

9. Public transportation experiences an in-
   crease in something.
   Public transportation includes buses.
   Public transportation includes taxis.

   Public transportation includes subways.
   The something is numbers of riders.

   _____

   _____

10. Fans use local businesses.
    The fans are from out of town.

    The businesses are various.

    _____

    _____

11. Hotels report patronage.
    Restaurants report patronage.
    Bars report patronage.

    The patronage is increased.
    The increasing is during the time visitors
       are in town.
    They are in town for the game.

    _____

    _____

12. The city receives coverage.
    The coverage is increased.

    The coverage is national.
    The coverage is through the media.

    _____

    _____

13. A city is written about in newspapers.
    A city is written about in magazines.

    A city is mentioned on television.
    A city is mentioned on radio.
    A city hosts a major game or series.

    _____

    _____

14. Publicity is controversial.

    Publicity helps its recipient.
    The helping is usual.

    _____

    _____

15. It is to a city's advantage to retain
       something.
    The something is its professional teams.

    The advantage is because of an increase in
       civic pride.
    The advantage is because of revenue.
    The advantage is because of coverage.

    _____

    _____

Have your instructor or tutor check your work.

APPLICATION IV

Combine each set of sentences into one complete sentence. Make your sentences as effective and concise as possible. Do not omit any necessary information.

1. Americans enjoy having something.   The something is fun.

   _____

   _____

2. A number proves this.   The parks are for amusement.
   The number is of parks.   The parks have themes.

   _____

   _____

3. Almost every state has one.   The one is a park.
   The one is at least one.   The park has a theme.

   _____

   _____

4. The parks use themes.   The themes are various.
   The themes are many.

   _____

   _____

5. Parks use themes.   The themes are historical.
   The parks are some.

   _____

   _____

6. There is an example.   The Six Flags celebrate history.
   The example is Six Flags.   The history is varied.
   The Six Flags are over Georgia.   The history belongs to Georgia.

   _____

   _____

7. Other parks use characters.   The park is famous.
   The characters are from cartoons.   The park is Disneyland.
   A park uses characters.

   _____

   _____

8. All of the characters greet visitors.   One character is Snow White.
   The characters belong to Disney.   Several characters are the Seven Dwarfs.
   One character is Goofy.

   _____

   _____

9. Some parks combine two areas.   The habitat is for animals.
   One area is amusing.   The animals are wild.
   One area is a habitat.

   _____

   _____

10. In one day, it is possible to enjoy two   One thing is a ride.
    things.   The ride is on a coaster.
    It is possible at Great Adventure.   The coaster is a roller.
    One thing is a safari.
    The safari is African.

   _____

   _____

11. All of the parks attest to needs.   The needs are for fun.
    The parks are many.   The needs are for adventure.
    The needs belong to Americans.   The needs are for excitement.

   _____

   _____

Have your instructor or tutor check your work.

APPLICATION V

Combine each set of sentences into one complete sentence. Make your sentences as effective
and concise as possible. Do not omit any necessary information.

1. Many areas underwent revitalization.   The time was during the 1970s.
   The areas were urban.

   _____

   _____

2. Years of flight left the areas in decay.   The cities were major.
   The flight was by the middle class.   The cities were American
   The flight was from cities.   The areas were urban.

   _____

   _____

3. However, people returned to the cities.   The returning was in the 1970s.
    The people were many.

    _____

    _____

4. In one city people were encouraged.   The movement was to the city.
    The city was Baltimore.   The city offered houses to the people.
    The encouragement was to move back.   The houses cost one dollar.

    _____

    _____

5. The homesteaders had to do two things.   One thing was to renovate.
    The homesteaders were urban.   The renovation was to houses.
    The doing was simple.
    One thing was to occupy.
    The occupying was within a year.

    _____

    _____

6. Cities chose programs.   The programs were different.
    The cities were other.

    _____

    _____

7. Boston chose to build an area.   The areas were on the waterfront.
    Savannah chose to build an area.   The areas were for eating.
    The areas were attractive.   The areas were for shopping.

    _____

    _____

8. New York City built an attraction.   The attraction is for tourists.
    The building was recent.   The attraction is on a river.
    The attraction is similar.   The river is the East River.

    _____

    _____

9. These projects have encouraged people.   The encouragement is to live.
    The encouragement is to enjoy.   The living is in the cities.
    The encouragement is to visit.

    _____

    _____

10. People appreciate an environment.   The environment is safe.
    The people are many.   The environment is clean.
    The appreciation is now.   The environment is attractive.
                                           The environment is urban.

    _____

    _____

Have your instructor or tutor check your work.

APPLICATION VI

Combine each set of sentences into one complete sentence. Make your sentences as effective and concise as possible. Do not omit any necessary information.

1. A date can prove to be an experience.   The date is the first.
   The date belongs to the boy.   The experience is traumatic.

   _____

   _____

2. First, he must do two things.   He must ask someone.
   He must put aside fear.   The someone is a girl.
   The fear is his.   The asking is to go out.
   The fear is of rejection.

   _____

   _____

3. Boys will do this in person.   Others find it less harrowing to use
   The boys are some.   something.
                                                  The something is the telephone.

   _____

   _____

4. The girl has accepted.   The matter is of transportation.
   The boy must handle a matter.

   _____

   _____

5. He is too young to have a license.
   The license belongs to a driver.
   His destination is a distance.
   The distance is good.
   The distance is away.

   The mother or father will have to drive.
   The mother or father belong to the boy.
   The driving happens often.

   _____

   _____

6. Then, the man must meet the parents.
   The man is young.

   The parents belong to the girl.
   He meets them when he arrives.
   The arriving is at her house.

   _____

   _____

7. Many a man has imagined the father.
   The man is young.
   The father belongs to the girl.

   The father is mild.
   The father is mannered.
   The imagining is of the father as an ogre.
   The ogre is of the worst sort.

   _____

   _____

8. The date has begun.
   The beginning is actual.
   The people can face two things.
   The people are young.
   One thing is a tendency.
   The tendency is to be uncomfortable.

   The uncomfortableness is with themselves.
   One thing is silences.
   The silences are long.
   The silences are embarrasing.

   _____

   _____

9. The boy will question.

   The question is, "Does she think I am
      stupid?"

   _____

   _____

10. The date is over.
    The boy is walking the lady.
    The lady is young.
    The walking is to her door.

    The boy wonders whether he would be
       forward.
    The forward is too.
    The forward is if he were to kiss the girl.
    The kiss is good-night.

    _____

    _____

11. Of course, the father does not make the decision easier.
The father belongs to the boy.
The father is trying to wait.
The waiting is unobtrusive.
The waiting is in the car.
The brothers and sisters do two things.
The brothers and sisters belong to the girl.

One thing is they like to peer.
The peering is from the windows.
The windows are upstairs.
One thing is they like to hide.
The hiding is in the bushes.
The decision belongs to the young man.

_____

_____

_____

12. The boy will try to make talk.
The trying is on the way home.

The talk is small.
The talk is with his father.

_____

_____

13. The boy will face that question.
The facing will be when they arrive home.
The question is from his mother.

The question is inevitable.
His mother has waited up.
The question is, "Well, dear, did you have a good time?"

_____

_____

14. Dating becomes easier.
The becoming is thankful.

The easier is as the teenager gets older.

_____

_____

Have your instructor or tutor check your work.

APPLICATION VII

Read the following paragraph carefully. It is composed of simple sentences. Rewrite the paragraph by combining sentences to make it more interesting and varied.

Vacation is a wonderful time. It is a time replete with opportunity. A range of possibilities presents itself. One can decide to explore and seek adventure. One can try overseas travel for new sights and sounds. Experiencing a different culture is a worthwhile goal. Or one can try to relax. This relaxing usually involves going to the beach, going to parties, or going to visit friends. Many people would find all that activity tiring. But while one is on vacation, this activity is relaxing and fun. Another way to spend vacation time is by preparing for the next semester. One can investigate interesting topics. Not many people read on their vacations. A final option for vacation is sleeping, trying to overcome a semester's fatigue. Many students choose this option.

Have your instructor or tutor check your work.

APPLICATION VIII

Check the sentences in a rough draft of a paper of your own. Are all sentences effective? Can some be combined? Can some sentences begin differently? If you can make the sentences more effective, then do so. Show your revisions to your instructor or tutor.

PART IV

Balanced Parts: Agreement and Reference

Subject-Verb
Agreement

OBJECTIVES:
1. To make subjects and verbs agree in number.
2. To correct problems in subject-verb agreement.
3. To use the editing symbol for subject-verb agreement (*S-V Agr*) correctly while proofreading.

KEY CONCEPT: Agreement of subjects and verbs means exactly what it says: in a sentence, the subject and verb must agree in **number.** If the subject is singular (one item), then the verb must also be singular. If the subject is plural (two or more items), then the verb must also be plural.

Singular and Plural Forms

Most singular subjects add an *s* or *es* to make a plural noun. For example, *dog* is singular, and *dogs* is plural.

PRACTICE 1

Label each of the following words either singular (*S*) or plural (*P*).

_____ 1. cat   _____ 6. miles

_____ 2. cats   _____ 7. ideas

_____ 3. he and I   _____ 8. his aunts

_____ 4. car   _____ 9. home

_____ 5. records   _____ 10. happiness

Check the answer key.

Most present-tense verbs that are singular end in *s* or *es;* most present-tense plural verbs do not end in *s.* For example, "She dan*ces*" is singular, and "They danc*e*" is plural. Look at the following chart:

Number	Subjects	Verbs
Singular	—	*es* or *s*
Plural	*s* or *es*	—

The chart provides the basic rule for subject-verb agreement. By looking at the chart, you can easily see that, in general, *either* the subject or the verb, but not *both*, will end in *s* or *es.*

Examples: The <u>cat</u> <u><u>carries</u></u> her kittens.

                Cat is singular.

                Carries is singular.

                The <u>cats</u> <u><u>carry</u></u> their kittens.

                Cats is plural.

                Carry is plural.

This chart provides a good test for subject-verb agreement. If both the subject and the verb end in *s* or *es,* check your work carefully. Usually, this will not occur.

PRACTICE 2

Revise the following sentences to make the subjects and verbs plural. The subjects have been underlined once, and the verbs twice.

Example: The <u>tree</u> <u><u>grows</u></u> straight.

The trees grow straight.

1. The <u>boy</u> <u><u>laughs</u></u> at the clown.

_____

2. The <u>mouse</u> <u><u>hides</u></u> in the pantry.

_____

3. The <u>examination</u> <u><u>seems</u></u> difficult.

_____

4. The <u>puppy</u> <u><u>nips</u></u> at my heels.

_____

5. The <u>girl</u> <u><u>dives</u></u> into the water.

_____

Check the answer key.

Verbs

There are some exceptions to the basic rule of singular and plural verb forms.

Regular Verbs

Regular verbs (most English verbs are regular) follow a pattern of conjunction in the present tense. Learn this pattern:

Singular	*Plural*
I (verb)	we (verb)
you (verb)	you (verb)
he, she, or it (verb + es or s)	they (verb)

Example: The verb *to dance* is a regular verb, and it is conjugated in the present tense as follows:

to dance

I *dance*	we *dance*
you *dance*	you *dance*
he, she, it *dances*	they *dance*

Which form of the verb changes? *he, she,* or *it* (third-person singular) *dances*
How does the third-person singular form change? It adds an *s* to the end of the verb.

Irregular Verbs

Some English verbs that we use frequently are irregular; that is, these irregular verbs do not follow the pattern of conjugation of regular verbs. For example, the verbs *to be, to have,* and *to do* are irregular verbs. Learn the present-tense and past-tense forms of these verbs.

Present-tense form of *to be:*

I *am*	we *are*
you *are*	you *are*
he, she, or it *is*	they *are*

Past-tense form of *to be:*

I *was*	we *were*
you *were*	you *were*
he, she, or it *was*	they *were*

Present-tense form of *to have:*

I *have*	we *have*
you *have*	you *have*
he, she, or it *has*	they *have*

Past-tense form of *to have:*

I *had*	we *had*
you *had*	you *had*
he, she, or it *had*	they *had*

Present-tense form of *to do:*

I *do*	we *do*
you *do*	you *do*
he, she, or it *does*	they *do*

Past-tense form of *to do:*

I *did*	we *did*
you *did*	you *did*
he, she, or it *did*	they *did*

PRACTICE 3

In the following sentences, put one line under the subject and two lines under the verb. In the blank space, write *S* if the subject is singular or *P* if the subject is plural. The first sentence is already done for you.

_S_   1. The <u>cat</u> <u>carried</u> her kittens into the next room.

_____   2. The child screamed for her mother.

_____   3. Dolphins are supposedly the most intelligent marine animals.

_____   4. Hank Thompson always answers the office phone.

_____   5. Gardens grow quickly with lots of rain and sunshine.

_____   6. A student's grades depend upon his own efforts.

_____   7. Tim works in an automobile factory.

_____   8. Chrysler was able to recover from bankruptcy.

_____   9. The dogs bark all night long.

_____ 10. They sat in the car.

_____ 11. Many millionaires own oil wells in Texas.

_____ 12. Headaches are often caused by stress.

_____ 13. The desk was in the middle of the room.

_____ 14. His favorite actor is Martin Sheen.

_____ 15. Hemingway's books make valuable reading.

_____ 16. An adolescent faces many problems.

_____ 17. The pewter bowl is on sale at the department store.

_____ 18. The reclining chair is very comfortable.

_____ 19. The bird's song was very pleasing.

_____ 20. The tennis player smashes the ball into his net.

Check the answer key.

Subjects

Always locate the subject first, because it determines whether the verb will be singular or plural. Also, remember that the noun in a prepositional phrase cannot be the subject of the sentence.

Examples: The <u>Board</u> of Directors <u>meets</u> on Thursdays.

Board is the subject of the sentence, and it controls the verb. *Directors* is the object of the preposition *of*, so it cannot be the subject.

Simple Subjects

Most subjects in sentences are usually one word. The most common type of subject is the simple subject (one noun or pronoun).

Pronouns. Pronouns can take the place of nouns. For example, in the sentence "Mary went to the store because she needed a loaf of bread," *she* is a pronoun that takes the place of *Mary*. Here is a chart of the pronouns that are most commonly used as subjects:

Singular	Plural
I	we
you	you
he, she, it	they
this	these
that	those

Examples: Those <u>doctors</u> <u>believe</u> in the holistic theory of medicine. (simple subject—plural form)

She <u>has</u> agreed to render him an apology.
(simple subject—singular form)

You should not have any problem making most simple subjects agree with their verbs.

PRACTICE 4

In each sentence, change the plural subjects to singular ones; then, make any necessary changes in the verbs.

1. Students always feel tired after exams.

2. Dogs are usually considered man's best friend.

3. Children love to receive gifts.

4. The nations have amassed a budget surplus.

5. The plants need to be repotted.

Check the answer key.

Indefinite Pronouns. However, some simple subjects do cause problems. Below is a list of indefinite pronouns. All of them take a *singular* verb.

anybody	either	nobody
anyone	everybody	no one
anything	everyone	somebody
each	neither	some one

Examples: Anybody is allowed into the school.

Each one is responsible for his own gear.

Some indefinite pronouns (for example, *all, any, more, most, none, some*) can be either singular or plural, depending on the words that modify them. This situation usually occurs when the subject is a portion or percentage.

Examples:
Most (of the swimmers) refuse to enter the water. (plural)

Most (of the summer) is gone. (singular)

Ten percent (of the money) was recovered. (singular)

Seventy percent (of all women) want equality of the sexes. (plural)

In these cases, in order to determine whether the subject is singular or plural, you must look at the modifier (usually a prepositional phrase):

- If the modifier is singular, then the subject is singular and takes a singular verb.
- If the modifier is plural, then the subject is plural and takes a plural verb.

EXERCISE Using the previous example sentences as models, change the subject in each of the sentences as indicated and make any necessary changes in the verb.

Change "of the semester" to "of my college years":

1. A quarter of the semester was spent studying Milton.

Change "of the child's day" to "of the class's time":

2. Ten percent of the child's day is devoted to art history.

Have your instructor or tutor check your work.

PRACTICE 5

Identify the subject in each sentence and indicate whether it is singular (*S*) or plural (*P*). Circle the verb that agrees with the subject.

Example: __P__ Many students (participates,(participate)) in organized sports.

_____ 1. Each person (enjoy, enjoys) the rights established by the Constitution.

_____ 2. All of the cake (was, were) eaten last night.

_____ 3. Some of the boys (has, have) decided to go camping.

_____ 4. Each of the boys (play, plays) hockey.

_____ 5. Neither of the girls (wants, want) to work tonight.

_____ 6. All of the students (enjoys, enjoy) holidays.

_____ 7. Each teenager (wants, want) his own car.

_____ 8. The horses (gallops, gallop) along the fence.

_____ 9. Most adults (enjoys, enjoy) a vacation.

_____ 10. Half of the cherry pie (was, were) gone.

Check the answer key.

Collective Nouns

A collective noun is also a simple subject, so it takes a *singular verb*. (Remember, a collective noun is one that refers to a group of individuals as a unit.) Here is a short list of collective nouns:

family	team	battalion	jury
crew	squad	company	union
herd	class	army	division
committee	crowd	quartet	mob

Examples: The class has decided to go to Central Park for a picnic.

Congress has adjourned for the Fourth of July holiday.

EXERCISE   Using the example sentences as models, make the suggested change in the subject in each of the following sentences and make any necessary changes in the verb.

Change "children" to "family":

1. The children are unhappy about foregoing a spring vacation this year.

Change "committee" to "executives":

2. The committee is undecided about the company's future plans.

Have your instructor or tutor check your work.

Titles

The title of a written work, a movie or television show, an artistic creation, or a musical composition takes a *singular* verb.

                              s   v

    Examples: "Hansel and Gretel" is a well-loved children's tale.

                                  s   v

                    The Ring and the Book presents a tangled web of lies and half-truths.

    EXERCISE   Using the above sentences as models, make the suggested change in each of the following sentences.

Change "This" to "*All the King's Men*":

1. This is my favorite book.

Change "The Kiss" to "The Destructors":

2. "The Kiss" was not a very interesting short story.

Have your instructor or tutor check your work.

Plural-Form Singular-Meaning Nouns

Some nouns are plural in form but singular in meaning; they take a singular verb. Here are some examples:

                           aerobics   calisthenics   mathematics
                           aesthetics   economics   news

                     s   v

    Example: The news is not good.

                  s   v

    Economics was not my best course.

On the other hand, "jeans," "pants," and "trousers" always take a plural verb.

    Example: Designer jeans are the hottest clothing item right now.

"Scissors" can be treated as singular or plural; base your choice on the sense of the sentence and its style. When in doubt about the number (singular or plural) of a word, consult your dictionary.

    EXERCISE   Make the suggested change in each of these sentences.

Change "history" to "physics":

1. Without a doubt, history is a boring subject.

Change "decor" to "aesthetics":

2. The decor of the room requires a restrained piece of statuary in the alcove.

Have your instructor or tutor check your work.

Nouns of Quantities. *Nouns* that refer to a *quantity* or to items that are considered a *single unit* take a *singular verb*.

Examples: Ten kilos is too much for one person to lift.

One thousand dollars was a lot to bet on the flip of a card.

EXERCISE   Make the suggested change in each of these sentences.

Change "This" to "Two miles":

1. This is too far to walk.

Change "One gallon" to "Two gallons":

2. One gallon provides about an hour's worth of motorcycle riding.

Have your instructor or tutor check your work.

PRACTICE 6

Identify the subject (S) in each sentence and indicate whether it is singular (S) or plural (P). Circle the verb that agrees in number with the subject.

Example: __S__ The flock of starlings (seems, seem) nervous.

_____ 1. This year, the gaggle of geese (has, have) stayed in this area for more than a month.
_____ 2. *The Crusaders* (is, are) a long-forgotten work by Margaret du Pleny.
_____ 3. Measles (is, are) no longer considered the scourge of mankind.
_____ 4. Trousers (has, have) made a fashion comeback.
_____ 5. One hundred pounds of potato salad (is, are) a lot to make each week.

Check the answer key.

Not all agreement problems are caused by simple subjects, however.

Compound Subjects

Whether a *compound subject* requires a singular or a plural verb depends on the sentence.

REMEMBER: A compound subject means that there is more than one subject in the sentence.

If the elements of the compound subject joined by *and* are still considered separate entities, they require a *plural* verb:

> s   v
> Examples: Tom, Harry, Joe, and Hank are in the classroom now.
>
> s   v
> Swimming and golf are my favorite sports.

However, if the nouns that are joined by *and* are considered one unit or refer to a single person, then a singular verb is required:

> s   v
> Examples: Ham and eggs is my favorite breakfast.
>
> s   v
> Meat and potatoes seems to be the only meal fit for this man.
>
> s   v
> My friend and confidante, Lucille, has been stricken by pneumonia.

EXERCISE   Following the above examples, make the suggested change in each sentence and change the verb, if necessary.

Add "and one cat":

1. One dog is about all this apartment can hold.

Add "and Susan":

2. Sally is going to the movies tonight.

Have your instructor or tutor check your work.

If the compound subject is joined by "or," "either . . . or," or "neither . . . nor," then the number of the subject that is closer to the verb determines the number of the verb.

> singular   plural   v-pl.
> Examples: Either Sally or the boys are supposed to pick your father up at the station.
>
> plural   singular   v-sing.
> Neither the teachers nor the administration wants a strike this year.

EXERCISE   Using the above sentences as models, make the suggested change in each sentence.

Change "Susan" to "the company":

1. Susan or Herman has to make a decision.

Change "media" to "*Congressional Record*":

2. Neither Congress nor the media report results accurately.

Have your instructor or tutor check your work.

PRACTICE 7

Underline the subject in each sentence. Decide whether the subject is singular (*S*) or plural (*P*), and fill in the blank at the left. Circle the correct verb.

_____ 1. Jack and Eileen (wants, want) to get married.

_____ 2. Neither the foreman nor the union representatives (wants, want) to discipline the errant worker.

_____ 3. Harold or George (swims, swim) faster than you do.

_____ 4. My friend and her husband (has, have) slipped into alcoholism. (same person)

_____ 5. Quiche and hash just (doesn't, don't) seem to complement each other.

Check the answer key.

The last two sources of confusion about subject-verb agreement stem from different types of sentences.

Relative-Pronoun Clauses

If you have a relative pronoun (*who, which,* or *that*) as the subject of the dependent clause in a complex sentence, then you must determine the noun to which it refers before you can decide whether the pronoun should be singular or plural.

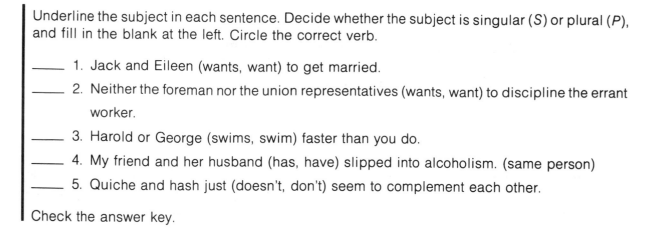

Examples: Her father, <u>who is</u> an Army major, is buying a new car. (*who* refers to *father*)

Terry's book, <u>which is</u> on the table, costs ten dollars. (*which* refers to *book*)

EXERCISE   Make the suggested change in each of the following sentences.

Make "brother" plural:

1. His brother, who is joining the Navy, likes the sea.

Make "friends" singular.

2. My friends, who are standing in the doorway, have just returned from a dance.

Have your instructor or tutor check your work.

> **NOTE:** Be careful with relative pronouns in the construction "one of." Consider the following examples:

> Examples: He is one of the men who receive their pay on Friday.
> The doctor is the only one of the staff members who understands the patient's condition.

In the first example, the relative pronoun "who" replaces the word "men"; hence, the verb must be plural. (In this sentence, the subject "he" is part of a group of men who receive their pay on Friday.)

In the second example, the relative pronoun "who" substitutes for the word "one"; thus, the verb must be singular. (In this example, the doctor is identified as the "only one" who understands the problem.) If the construction "one of" is preceded by the word "only," then the verb will be singular. However, if the construction "one of" does not have the word "only" preceding it, then you must analyze the sentence and its meaning to determine the noun or pronoun the relative pronoun replaces. Then, decide whether the verb should be singular or plural.

PRACTICE 8

Underline the relative pronoun in each sentence; then, identify the noun to which the relative pronoun refers. Decide whether the subject is singular (*S*) or plural (*P*), and fill in the blank at the left. Circle the correct verb.

_____ 1. F. Scott Fitzgerald, who (was, were) a major literary figure in the 1920s, worked in Hollywood during the late 1930s.

_____ 2. Harris is one of the lawyers who (selects, select) their cases carefully.

_____ 3. This final calculus problem is the only one that (is, are) difficult.

_____ 4. The Stonehenge monument, which (is, are) in England, served as the site of many religious ceremonies.

_____ 5. Sam is the only one of her friends who (enjoys, enjoy) tennis.

Check the answer key.

Inverted Sentences

In inverted sentences, which often begin with the adverbs *there, here,* or *where* or with prepositional phrases, the subject follows the verb. You must look for the subject after the verb before you can determine the number.

Examples: There is the book.

Here are the children.

EXERCISE Make the suggested change in each of the following sentences.

Make "outfits" singular:

1. There are the new outfits.

Change "dog" to "animals":

2. Here is the last dog.

Have your instructor or tutor check your work.

PRACTICE 9

Underline the subject of each sentence. Decide whether the subject is singular (*S*) or plural (*P*), and fill in the blank at the left. Circle the correct verb.

_____ 1. There (is, are) too many people in this elevator.

_____ 2. At the end of the shady lane (stands, stand) the county courthouse and a church.

_____ 3. Here (is, are) your letters of recommendation.

_____ 4. For each of the applicants, there (was, were) long forms to complete.

_____ 5. Behind these locked doors (lies, lie) a fortune in gold bullion.

Check the answer key.

APPLICATION I

In each of the following sentences, underline the subject of the sentence; then, choose the verb that agrees with the subject, and circle it. Enter the correct verb in the blank at the right.

Example: Today, <u>information</u> about happenings around the world (comes, come) to us through

the media.   *comes*

1. Each day several students (go, goes) to the mall after school.   _____

2. Spring and fall (is, are) my favorite seasons.   _____

3. All of her friends (was, were) at her birthday party.   _____

4. Dogs and cats (makes, make) good household pets.   _____

5. In the early days of our country, pioneer men, who (was, were) responsible for the safety of their families, defended their homes from enemies.   _____

6. Which (is, are) your books?   _____

7. She and I (is, are) going to the movies together.   _____

8. My father says that all used-car salesmen (is, are) dishonest.   _____

9. Millions of dollars were stolen from the Kansas City bank in 1920, yet
   not even one dollar (was, were) ever recovered.   _____

10. Neither James nor his teachers (has, have) a solution for his problem.   _____

11. The media (has, have) announced that the president will visit New
    Orleans this month.   _____

12. Harry, the captain of the baseball team, (is, are) going to be the starting
    pitcher.   _____

13. Half of the senior class (is, are) going on the class trip.   _____

14. Most of the cheese (was, were) eaten by a mouse.   _____

15. There (is, are) many good reasons to continue your education beyond
    high school.   _____

16. In the living room (was, were) a stereo, a television, and a radio.   _____

17. Washington, Oregon, California, and Alaska (borders, border) the Pa-
    cific Ocean.   _____

18. He and I (is, are, am) playing tennis on Friday. _____

19. Under the table (is, are) a group of kittens. _____

20. Half of the chocolate cake (is, are) gone. _____

21. Many of Roger's friends (plays, play) baseball. _____

22. The governor, as well as several state senators, (is, are) visiting our

campus. _____

23. Under the spreading chestnut tree (was, were) the village blacksmith

and his horse. _____

24. The army (is, are) on maneuvers in West Germany this summer. _____

25. The problems of transporting goods and people (is, are) compounded

by rising gasoline prices. _____

Check the answer key.

APPLICATION II

Revise the following sentences by changing all plural subjects and verbs to singular ones.

1. The records are being catalogued now.

_____

2. The cars speed down Mt. Royal Avenue each day.

_____

3. Her songs are selling quite well.

_____

4. Their children insist on staying awake until midnight.

_____

5. Our new puppies cry all night.

_____

6. Hurricanes are natural phenomena.

_____

7. The scientists declare that one day a person may live to be one hundred.

_____

8. Some statisticians have been known to manipulate data.

_____

9. Steel doors offer more protection than wooden doors.

_____

10. Swimmers exercise all the muscles in their bodies.

_____

Check the answer key.

APPLICATION III

Proofread the following paragraph carefully. Next, edit the essay for subject-verb agreement problems. If there is a problem with agreement, place the editing symbol *S-V Agr* above the error, and then correct the agreement problem.

(1) On a sports team, the coach is a leader who teach techniques, conduct practice, determines strategy, and decides who will play. (2) Many coaches use different methods of coaching and has different attitudes towards players. (3) However, these coaches have the same goal for their games and the season—to win. (4) A hard-core disciplinarian wants everything done his way, with no exceptions or excuses. (5) This type of coach stress discipline through intensive physical and fundamental training. (6) For example, every team member is required to lift weights and to run distances and sprints in a set time. (7) The disciplinarian will cut a player who fail to meet these requirements. (8) In addition, this coach does not encourage a personal relationship with his players. (9) He is their coach, not their friend. (10) In the middle are the coach who is a disciplinarian on the field, but a friend when off the field. (11) The team are required to attend very strenuous practices, but there are no set requirements about weightlifting or speed. (12) This coach produces a close-knit team that are quite well prepared. (13) The players respect and admire this type of coach. (14) On the other hand, the easygoing coach might stress the fundamentals and drills for his players, but he enjoys the role of friend. (15) This coach, who believes in a relaxed atmosphere, do expect the players to be responsible and mature. (16) As long as the team members follow his guidelines, he is willing to hear their

suggestions. (17) Each type of coach exist. (18) Their methods may be different, but they all wants to win.

Check the answer key.

APPLICATION IV

Proofread the following paragraph for subject-verb agreement errors. Place the editing symbol for subject-verb agreement over the errors. Correct any mistakes you find.

The Benefits of Being a Family

(1) Although most people don't recognize it, there are a big difference between being a "couple" and being a "family." (2) Couples are nice and are limited to two individuals, but families are better because they can include from three to ten or more people. (3) The very word "family" suggests many of the positive aspects of that lifestyle, which includes a sense of community, of being included, of being a part of a much larger whole. (4) As a family member, you always has others to rely on; you know that you do not have to be alone during troubled times. (5) In addition, you has others to share good times with, too. (6) Families provides a sense of continuity. (7) You can observe the various stages of life and see how a person change as he or she grow from childhood through adolescence and into maturity. (8) Your family help you to see that all lives are connected and that each life affect many others. (9) Overall, families are a worthwhile investment.

Check the answer key.

APPLICATION V

Proofread a rough draft of a paper of your own carefully. Edit the paper for subject-verb agreement problems. If there is a problem with agreement, write the editing symbol *S-V Agr* next to the error, and then correct the mistakes. Show the revised paper to your instructor or tutor.

Pronoun Reference

OBJECTIVES:
1. To recognize pronoun-reference problems.
2. To correct pronoun-reference problems.
3. To proofread an essay for pronoun reference. The editing symbol for pronoun reference is *pro. ref.*

KEY CONCEPT: A **pronoun** usually takes the place of a noun. The noun the pronoun replaces is called the **antecedent.** Usually, the pronoun takes the place of the closest noun.

                antecedent   pronoun
Example: *Jill* was happy; in fact, *she* was ecstatic.

Personal Pronouns and Cases

The following chart lists personal pronouns; become familiar with them.

Personal Pronouns

	Nominative Case		Objective Case		Possessive Case	
Person	Singular	Plural	Singular	Plural	Singular	Plural
First	I	we	me	us	my, mine	our, ours
Second	you	you	you	you	your, yours	your, yours
Third	he	they	him	them	his	their, theirs
	she		her		her, hers	
	it		it		its	

The **nominative** (or subjective) case is used when the pronoun is the subject of the sentence or when the pronoun is a predicate nominative.

                antecedent   pronoun
Examples: The *girls* ate lunch in a Chinese restaurant; *they* enjoyed the meal greatly.

            (In this sentence, the pronoun *they* is a subject.)

antecedent   pronoun

In last night's basketball game, *Ira* played very well. In fact, it was *he* who was

chosen the most valuable player of the game.

(In this sentence, the pronoun *he* is a predicate nominative.)

The **objective** case is used when the pronoun is a direct object, an indirect object, or the object of a preposition.

Examples: Jerry called *them* last night. (a direct object)
Time gives *us* grey hairs. (an indirect object)
Julie gave the textbook to *him*. (the object of a preposition)

To test for the objective case, place a *to* or *for* before the pronoun. If the sentence is clear, then you need to use the objective case.

Example: The teacher gave *her* the test.
The teacher gave the test to *her*.

The **possessive** case indicates ownership.

Example: The class gave *its* approval to the plan.
Mr. Mason made *his* famous chocolate cheesecake.

PRACTICE 1

Provide the correct pronoun for each of the following nouns. Pay particular attention to the case of the pronoun.

	Nominative	*Objective*	*Possessive*
1. a dock	it	it	its
2. dog	it	it	its
3. Harry and Ellen	they	them	their
4. James and I	we	us	our
5. Sara	She	her	her

Check the answer key.

Pronoun Agreement

Number Agreement

A pronoun must agree in number with its antecedent; that is, if a noun is singular, then the pronoun that replaces it must be singular. If a noun is plural, then the pronoun that replaces it must be plural.

antecedent   pronoun   pronoun

Example: The sophomore *women* decided that *they* would return to *their* rooms.

Gender Agreement

Pronouns must agree with their antecedents in gender; that is, if the noun is masculine, then the pronoun must also be masculine. If the noun is feminine, then the pronoun must be feminine. If the noun is neuter (or has no determined sex), then the pronoun must be neuter.

antecedent pronoun

Example: The little *boy* lost *his* toy. (singular, masculine)

antecedent   pronoun

The elderly *woman* dropped *her* keys. (singular, feminine)

antecedent   pronoun

The *chair* is missing one of *its* legs. (singular, neuter)

NOTE: Ships, planes, and countries are usually feminine.

Person Agreement

Pronouns must also agree with their antecedents in person. You must be able to identify the speaker (first person), the person spoken to (second person), and the person spoken about (third person).

antecedent   pronoun

Examples: *I* dropped *my* wallet. (first person, singular—the speaker)

antecedent   pronoun

Your grandfather told only *you* to stay here.
(second person, singular—the person spoken to)

antecedent   pronoun

Harold believes *he* can win a gold medal in the Olympics.
(third person, masculine, singular—the person spoken about)

PRACTICE 2

Use the pronoun chart to fill in the blanks with the correct pronoun.

1. Maria revealed that __*she*__ had been married recently.

2. The actors decided that __*they*__ did not like the script.

3. At student union meetings, only full-time students are allowed to express __*their*__ opinions.

4. I realized that I would never get __*my*__ dream car.

5. The baby waved __*her*__ tin cup at each passerby.

Check the answer key.

PRACTICE 3

In each of the following sentences, circle the pronoun and its antecedent. Write the pronoun and its antecedent in the columns to the right.

Example: We saw (The Return of the Jedi; (it)   *it*   *The Return of the Jedi*

was a marvelous film.   *Pronoun*   *Antecedent*

1. Maria gave her money to Hank.   *her*   *M.*

2. Mr. Roberts, you must do your homework.   *you*   *Mr. R—*

3. The teacher announced the test results to her class.   *her*   *teacher*

4. The radiologist completed his work.   *his*   *r—*

5. The famous trial lawyer made her opening state-

   ment to the jury.   *her*   *lawyer*

6. Steve and I decided that we had spent too much

   money on the new car.   *we*   *Steve + I*

7. The horse threw its rider.   *its*   *horse*

8. Bring the books to me; then, take them to Mr. Stone.   *them*   *books*

9. The lamp, a gift from my grandmother, had been in

   her home for years.   *her*   *g. m.*

10. The film industry caters to the public's interests;

    recently it has produced many science-fiction

    movies.   *it*   *film ind.*

11. Give the pen to me; it needs to be refilled. *it*   *pen*

12. Bonnie and Jack, will you please talk softly? *you*   *B. + J*

13. The plants need to be watered; I have not watered

    them for three weeks.   *them*   *plants*

14. The mother rushed into the house to see her child.   *her*   *mother*

15. The novel was read by many people; it sold over six

    million copies.   *it*   *novel*

Check the answer key.

PRACTICE 4

The antecedents for the pronouns in the sentences appear in parentheses. Choose the pronoun that would most logically refer to the antecedent.

Example: (Harriet) __She__ answered the phone.

1. Add some spices to the casserole; (the casserole) __it__ is bland.

2. (Paula) __She__ takes violin lessons twice a week.

3. (Mary and I) __We__ decided to take a vacation.

4. After John finished working, (John) __he__ went straight home.

5. The musician played a song that (the musician) __she__ had written.

6. The congresswoman gave (the congresswoman's) __her__ support to the loyal mayoral
   candidate.

7. Mr. Willis, my chemistry instructor, told (Mr. Willis's) __his__ students how to complete
   the experiment.

8. Martha bought a new suit. (The suit) __It__ fits her well.

9. The principal and the faculty will drive (the principal's and the faculty's) __their__ cars to
   the convention.

10. The reporter asked the president very tough questions. (The president) __He__ refused
    to comment.

11. Please check the oil in the car. (The oil) __It__ needs to be changed.

12. Whales have been hunted for many years, but now (whales) __they__ have become an
    endangered species.

13. (Samantha and Janice) __They__ plan to become vice presidents in the firm.

14. Take the meat out of the freezer. (The meat) __It__ needs to thaw.

15. (The hockey players) __they__ practice for five hours each day.

Check the answer key.

Special Problems

Split Subjects

Either . . . or and *neither . . . nor* often confuse writers. For sentences that contain *either . . . or* or *neither . . . nor,* the antecedent closer to the pronoun controls the number and gender of the pronoun.

antecedent   pronoun

Example: Neither *Tim* nor his *friends* have *their* own cars.

antecedent pronoun

Neither his *friends* nor *Tim* has *his* own car.

antecedent   pronoun

Either *Major Banks* or the *captains* will issue *their* orders.

antecedent   pronoun

Either the *captains* or *Major Banks* will issue *his* orders.

Plural Subjects

Subjects joined by *and* are usually plural, and they take a plural pronoun.

antecedent   antecedent   pronoun

Example: The *seniors* and the *juniors* will plan *their* party.

Collective Nouns

Collective nouns are words that stand for a group of members, but they are considered to be singular because the group acts as a unit. For example, the following words are collective nouns:

army	committee	trio
team	group	jury
pair	family	flock
class	herd	society

antecedent   pronoun

Example: The *army* is planning *its* practice maneuvers.

antecedent   pronoun

The Smith *family* is planning *its* vacation.

However, if the collective noun refers to a group as a number of individuals, then it may be plural and require a plural pronoun.

antecedent   pronoun

Example: The *jury* are casting *their* ballots.

However, this plural form sometimes sounds awkward. It would be better to revise the sentence: *The members of the jury are casting their ballots.*

Indefinite Pronouns

The following words are *singular* indefinite pronouns:

each	every
someone	somebody
anybody	anyone
everybody	everyone
no one	one

These singular indefinite pronouns usually take masculine, singular pronouns.

Example: Does *everyone* have *his* book?

       antecedent   pronoun

You will notice that this traditional use of masculine, singular pronouns to replace indefinite pronouns excludes the women in the audience. The same problem can occur when you want to provide a pronoun for a noun that does not identify gender, such as *student, officer, doctor,* or *athlete.* Certainly, this usage is not always appropriate, as the following sentence demonstrates:

Each *student* must register *his* car before *he* parks on campus.

This sentence, similar to many in college catalogs, is appropriate only at an all-male institution. It is inappropriate for a catalog that addresses both men and women. To avoid sexist language, you can use a number of methods.

1. Use the correct form of the expression *he or she.*

   Example: Each student must register *his or her* car before *he or she* parks on campus.

   However, if you use this alternative in a lengthy passage, you will find that the constant repetition of *he or she* is awkward and can distract your readers.

2. Alternate masculine and feminine pronouns throughout a passage.

   Example: Each student must register *his* car before *he* parks on campus. To register a car, each student must present *her* current campus identification, the car's registration, and a check for twenty dollars to the bursar.

   At best, this usage is confusing to your readers.

3. Use only nouns, instead of pronouns, in a passage.

   Example: Each student must register the student's car before the student parks on campus.

   Certainly, this method will become repetitive for your readers.

4. Use plural nouns or plural indefinite pronouns.

   Examples: Students must register *their* cars before *they* park on campus.
   All students must register *their* cars before *they* park on campus.

   This usage includes everyone, male and female, in the audience. In addition, it avoids confusion and repetition.

The following indefinite pronouns can be *singular* or *plural*: *all, some, many, most,* and *none.* The number of these pronouns is determined by the number of the noun in the prepositional phrase that follows the indefinite pronoun.

antecedent   pronoun

Examples: *All* of the police officers are required to report to *their* posts at once.

In this sentence, *all* is plural because the noun in the following prepositional phrase, *police officers,* is plural.

Some of the cake was left.

In this sentence, *some* is singular because the noun in the prepositional phrase, *cake,* is singular.

antecedent   pronoun

Some of the swimmers have completed *their* laps.

Since the word *some* is followed by the prepositional phrase *of the swimmers, some* is plural.

EXERCISE   Fill in the correct pronoun in the following sentences. Circle the antecedent.

1. Every freshman must complete ___*his*___ housing request as soon as possible.

2. Some of the sophomore women called ___*their*___ parents the first week of classes.

3. Every man and woman in the armed forces serves ___*his & her*___ country proudly.

4. Half of the seniors plan to apply to graduate school before ___*they*___ complete this semester.

5. All of the cars on this lot need repair because ___*they*___ have been driven over sixty thousand miles.

Have your instructor or tutor check your work.

Singular Pronouns

A singular pronoun is used with nouns that appear to be plural but are actually singular. For example, the nouns *news, physics, economics, mathematics,* and *genetics* are all singular and require singular pronouns.

antecedent   pronoun

Example: *Physics* operates by *its* own principles.

Mistaking the Antecedent

Sometimes prepositional phrases and relative pronouns (*who, which, that*) can cause confusion if they come between the pronoun and its antecedent.

antecedent prep phrase   pronoun

Examples: *Each* (of the dogs) buried *its* bone.

antecedent   pronoun

Jean is just one of the senior *women* who have already received *their* awards.

Ambiguous Antecedents

Be very careful not to confuse your reader by writing a sentence that has an ambiguous pronoun reference.

Example: Jim told Pablo that he should go home.

Can you tell from this sentence who should go home? Instead, use dialogue to resolve the reference problem.

Example: Jim told Pablo, "I should go home." (Jim is going home.)

Jim told Pablo, "You should go home." (Pablo is going home.)

PRACTICE 5

Fill in the correct pronoun in each sentence. Write the antecedent on the line to the right of the sentences.

Example: The jury is making *its* final decision. _jury_

1. Most societies care for _____ older people and infants. _their_

2. The herd of cattle is approaching _____ favorite watering hole. _its_

3. Everybody must bring _____ books. _his or her_

4. Neither the coach nor her players are happy about _____ loss. _their_

5. Some of the fathers are bringing _____ children. _their_

6. The company offered _____ employees a sizable raise. _its_

7. The class must learn _____ lesson. >group of individuals _it its their_

8. Neither of the two girls is capable of repairing _____ car. _her_

9. The board of trustees had _____ final meeting. _its their it_

10. She is one of the women who are making major strides in _____ fields. _their_

11. The flock of birds sighted _____ nesting ground. _their its_

12. Do all of the freshmen students have _____ registration cards? _their_

13. The dean and his associates are discussing _____ options. _their_

14. The doctor and her staff plan to present _____ research findings on Monday. _their_

15. *The New England Journal of Medicine* announced _____ new board of directors. _its_

Check the answer key.

APPLICATION I

Choose the correct pronoun and circle it. Write the pronoun on the line at the right. Underline the antecedent.

1. Each of the members of the football team took (their, his) seat on the

   bus.   _____

2. Both boys hid (his, their) report cards from the teacher.   _____

3. The moon shone (his, its, their) light on the bay.   _____

4. The company presented (their, its) new insurance program to the em-

   ployees.   _____

5. Neither the principal nor the teachers gave (his, their) approval to the

   project.   _____

6. Everyone must finish (their, his) essay within the hour.   _____

7. The jury made (its, their) decision on the murder case after ten hours of

   deliberations.   _____

8. You and I should combine (my, our, their) ideas and present (it, them) to

   the boss.   _____

9. The Joneses gave a party at (its, their) house. *not Jones family*   _____

10. Several people asked to have (his, her, their) cars insured against theft.   _____

11. Jason made a score of 100 on (his, her, its) final test.   _____

12. The chair was in (its, his, her) place by the desk.   _____

13. Henry Miller was a major American novelist; one of (his, her, its) most

    famous books is *The Tropic of Cancer.*   _____

14. One of the boys hurt (his, their) hand while playing basketball.   _____

15. Each of the women students received (their, her) diploma in engineer-

    ing.   _____

16. Either of the two girls will offer (her, their) help.   _____

17. Helga and Sean spent (his, their, her) vacation in Paris.   _____

18. A helicopter and an airplane have (their, its) advantages over land transportation.   _____

19. The mice hid from the cat in (its, their) hole.   _____

20. Loretta has a career of (his, its, her) own; she is not dependent upon (his, her) husband for money.   _____

21. He is a man who always stands by (his, their) word.   _____

22. Which one of the men had (his, their) car stolen from the parking lot?   _____

23. I must write (his, my) essay tonight.   _____

24. Neither Henry nor his teammates wanted to play (his, their) opponent, the Mercer Bulls.   _____

25. The family made (its, their) decision to move to Birmingham.   _____

Check the answer key.

APPLICATION II

Change the singular subjects, verbs, and pronouns to plural ones.

1. The dog barked at its owner.

   _____

2. The judge announced his decision on Monday.

   _____

3. Everyone told his version of the accident to the officer.

   _____

4. Neither of the boys plans to continue his education.

   _____

5. The car's engine smoked and coughed before it finally quit.

   _____

6. He told his parents that he had received a scholarship.

   _____

7. The panda ate her bamboo at the Washington Zoo.

_____

8. The crew of the space shuttle performs its duties.

_____

9. The airplane lost one of its engines.

_____

10. The referee recognized that he had made a poor call.

_____

Check the answer key.

APPLICATION III

Proofread the following paragraph for pronoun-antecedent agreement. If there is an error, circle it and place the editing symbol *pro. ref.* above it. Then, correct the error.

(1) Most of us enjoy dreaming about the future and the wonders or sorrows they hold for us. (2) Predictions about future societies have long been popular with novelists. (3) For example, in the nineteenth century, Jules Verne described submarines and underwater cities in his novel *Twenty Thousand Leagues Under the Sea.* (4) H. G. Wells predicted a devastating war between the inhabitants of the earth and Mars in its novel *The War of the Worlds.* (5) Today, film takes us beyond their galaxy. (6) Consider, for example, the television series *Star Trek,* one of the many television programs that brought to the public its vision of the future. (7) Also, George Lucas's movie trilogy, *Star Wars, The Empire Strikes Back,* and *The Return of the Jedi,* has captured the interest and devotion of a number of fans who stand in long lines to buy their movie tickets. (8) These three movies are enhanced by its amazing special visual effects. (9) Each person in the audience feels as if they are quickly traveling through the reaches of their universe. (10) People's imaginations, curiosity, and love of adventure are satisfied as they read and view science-fiction stories.

Check the answer key.

APPLICATION IV

Proofread the following paragraph for pronoun-reference errors. Place the editing symbol for pronoun reference above the error and correct any mistakes you find.

The Benefits of Being a Couple

(1) Many people pity couples without children. (2) The consensus maintains that childless couples are so by force of nature, not by choice, and so sympathy is required. (3) Such a belief is no longer valid. (4) A significant percentage of couples have chosen not to evolve into families, and he can offer reasoned arguments for this choice. (5) The first is financial. (6) Not having children enables him to spend all their income on themselves. (7) Although this may seem like a selfish act, they is actually a very generous one. (8) Unlike parents who save their discretionary income in order to assure her offspring a college education, the childless couple spends their money on vacations, entertainment, and clothes. (9) Each of this purchases generates jobs for others. (10) Similarly, without a child to demand his time and energy, the husband and wife are free to devote themselves to her careers. (11) Such self-sacrificing activity, in terms of long hours and hard work, results in productivity gains and increases in the G.N.P.; this benefits society, not the energetic individuals. (12) As can clearly be seen, those who have children are the ones who should be pitied. (13) Besides having no time or energy left for himself, they are not improving society in any way, either.

Check the answer key.

APPLICATION V

Proofread a rough draft of a paper of your own for pronoun-antecedent agreement. If there is an error, then circle it and place the editing symbol *pro. ref.* next to it. Next, correct the error. Show your revisions to your instructor or tutor.

PART V

Sentence Tools: Mechanics and Punctuation

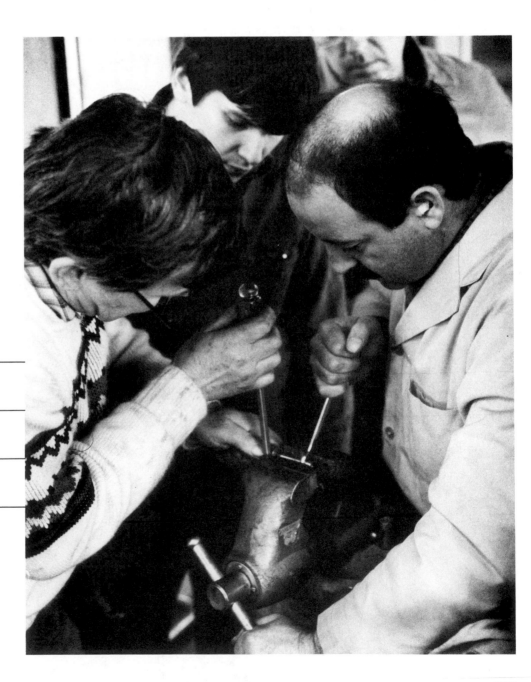

13

Capitals and End Punctuation

OBJECTIVES:	1. To recognize the need for capitals in sentences and in paragraphs.
	2. To recognize the need for end punctuation in sentences.
	3. To use capitals and end punctuation correctly.
	4. To proofread a paper for capitalization and end-punctuation mistakes, and to use correctly the editing symbols for capitals (*lc* for lower case and *cap* for upper case) and end-punctuation (*end p*) mistakes.
KEY CONCEPT:	The rules for using capitals and end punctuation help the writer to communicate effectively with the reader.

Capitals

There are seven basic rules for using capitals. You are probably familiar with some of them:

1. *Capitalize the pronoun "I" wherever it appears in a sentence.*

    Example: I told her that I had only minutes to spare. She thought that I had lied to her.

EXERCISE Following the above example, circle the first letter of any word that should be capitalized.

She replied, "(I) believe that (i) will have finished by then. At least, (i) hope so."

Have your instructor or tutor check your work.

2. *Capitalize any reference to God or any Supreme Being recognized by a religion. Also, capitalize any personal pronouns that refer to (H)im.*

    Examples: Some believe that God created His world in six days, as the Bible states.

    Many primitive peoples believed in Mother Nature and Father Sun.

EXERCISE Following the above example, circle the first letter of any word that should be capitalized.

Some feminists believe that god is female, and so they refer to her works of creation.

Have your instructor or tutor check your work.

> **NOTE:** The word *God* is capitalized only when it refers to a specific, supreme being. If the word is used in a general sense, then it is *not* capitalized.

> Example: The Romans believed in many gods. They assigned to each god a specific area of responsibility; for example, Morpheus was the god of sleep, and Eros was the god of love.

EXERCISE   Following the above example, capitalize any words that require it.

The Greeks, too, created a host of gods. In many cases, though, the Greek gods were more militant than the Roman ones.

Have your instructor or tutor check your work.

3. *Capitalize (usually) the first word of each line of poetry, and the first word of a sentence including those that are quoted or enclosed in parentheses.*

> Examples: "The gray sea and the long black land;
> And the yellow half-moon large and low;" (Robert Browning)

> Every paramedic must complete a rigorous health course in order to be certified. It's a good regulation.

> She said, "Let's go to the restaurant now."

EXERCISE   Following the above examples, circle the first letter of any word that should be capitalized.

1. psychologists have studied weather patterns for years. they think the patterns provide clues to man's behavior.

2. The instructor demanded, "whose spy are you?" *if broken, don't cap 2nd*

3. "busy, curious thirsty fly!
   drink with me, and drink as I:" (William Oldys)

Have your instructor or tutor check your work.

> **NOTE:** When part of a poem is set horizontally instead of vertically, then slashes divide the lines of poetry. (Usually, you would incorporate no more than three lines of poetry, or a stanza if the poem is short, into a sentence. Indent longer passages.)

> Example: One of William Blake's most famous poems, "The Tyger," begins dramatically: "Tyger! Tyger! burning bright / In the forests of the night, / What immortal hand or eye / Could frame thy fearful symmetry?"

You were probably already familiar with rules 1, 2, and 3 for capitalization. Now, review them in the following practice.

PRACTICE 1

Capitalize any word that requires it by circling its first letter.

1. (t)here is one major difference between monotheistic and polytheistic religions. The former recognize only one (g)od, while the latter worship many gods.

2. "(i) insist upon seeing the manager," she said. "(i)n fact, (i) demand it."

3. "(y)e gods!" he cried. "(i) can't stand it anymore."

4. (a)ccording to one theory, sunny days invigorate people, and rainy days enervate them. *def

5. "(h)e clasps the crag with crooked hands; / (c)lose to the sun in lonely lands, / (r)inged with the azure world, he stands."   (Alfred Lord Tennyson)

Check the answer key.

The following rules for using capitals may be less familiar to you.

4. *Capitalize all the important words in the titles of books, magazines, newspapers, plays, poems, articles, and songs.*

Examples: *Tender Is the Night* (novel)	*U.S.A. Today* (newspaper)
The New York Times (newspaper)	*Antony and Cleopatra* (play)
The Ring and the Book (poem)	*Ebony* (magazine)
Ordinary People (movie)	*The King and I* (play)

NOTE: Nouns, verbs, adjectives, and adverbs are usually considered important words, so they would be capitalized. Articles, prepositions, and conjunctions are usually considered unimportant, so they are not capitalized. However, if they are more than five letters long, or if they are the first or last word in the title, they are capitalized.

Examples: "As Time Goes By"
In Search of History
Through the Looking-Glass

EXERCISE   Following the above examples, circle the first letter of any word that should be capitalized.

1. (p)aper (m)oney

2. (t)he (v)alley of the (h)orses

3. (t)he (r)eturn of the (j)edi

4. (h)ow to (s)ucceed in (b)usiness (w)ithout (r)eally (t)rying

Have your instructor or tutor check your work.

5. *Capitalize people's names, titles, and family names.*

Examples: Aunt Teresa   Governor Edwards
Grandpa Smith   Reverend Milton
Captain La Rue   Lawrence Sandringham

NOTES: 1. The title should be capitalized when it refers to a specific person, even if that person's name is not given.

Examples: Thank you, Mr. President.
Right away, Senator.
I'll be glad to get it for you, Uncle.

2. The title should *not* be capitalized if it is preceded by a possessive pronoun (*my, our, their*, etc.).

Examples: My company's president had just filed for personal bankruptcy.
Our grandmother refuses to live in a nursing home.
Their senator ignored their requests for help.

EXERCISE Following the above examples, circle the first letter of any word that should be capitalized.

1. History will show that chairman mao changed his country's destiny.
2. The surgery will be performed by doctor cooley, the famous heart surgeon.
3. After we gave the gift to our grandfather, he thanked us all.

Have your instructor or tutor check your work.

6. *Capitalize all important words in the names of organizations, institutions, and brand names.*

Examples: The Elks   Mid-Manhattan
The Chamber of Commerce   General Motors
National Association of Manufacturers   Betty Crocker
Parkland Memorial Hospital

EXERCISE Following the above examples, circle the first letter of any word that should be capitalized.

1. The moose club decided to hold its annual convention at walt whitman high school.
2. The unfortunate old woman was rushed to sloan-kettering memorial hospital.
3. I buy only ford trucks.

Have your instructor or tutor check your work.

Review rules 4, 5, and 6 before completing the following practice exercise.

PRACTICE 2

Capitalize any words that require it.

1. Abraham Lincoln, the president, was shot while watching a play at ford's theater.
2. That was such a spectacle that even the mountain eagle ran a front-page story on it.
3. The local chapter of the american workers association wants to unionize the kitchen staff at tall oaks community hospital.
4. The one drawback is that our family doctor is not affiliated with any hospital.
5. I prefer wheaties to rice krispies.

Check the answer key.

The last rule encompasses the greatest amount of material.

7. *Capitalize proper nouns, their abbreviations, and adjectives derived from them.*

NOTE: A proper noun gives the name of a specific person, place, or thing; a common noun gives a general word for persons, places, or things.

Examples:	*Common Noun*	*Proper Noun*	*Abbreviation*	*Adjective*
	country	France	Fr.	French
	man	Karl Marx		Marxist
	manufacturer	General Motors	G.M.	
	region	South	So.	Southern
	city	New York	N.Y.	New Yorker
	day	Friday	Fri.	
	people	Africans		African
	document	the Constitution		Constitutional
	decade	the Twenties		

NOTE: Designations of time, *ante meridiem* and *post meridiem,* are abbreviated A.M. and P.M. Current usage, however, suggests that the abbreviations do not need to be capitalized.

EXERCISE Following the above examples, circle the first letter of any word that should be capitalized.

1. For my honeymoon, I'd like to go to acapulco, cape cod, or tahiti.
2. My girlfriend is a francophile. she eats french cheese, uses french perfume, wears french clothes, and plans to marry a frenchman.
3. Businesses generally agree that december and august are lost months; the former is too hectic for production work, the latter too hot.

Have your instructor or tutor check your work.

NOTE: Do not capitalize the seasons of the year (winter, spring, summer, autumn) or the points of the compass (north, south, east, west) unless they appear as the first word in a sentence. Occasionally, poets will capitalize the seasons of the year as part of a personification of the season. In addition, make sure that you distinguish between the points of the compass and the regions of a country. Regions designated by location (the North, the South, the East, the West) are capitalized.

Examples: Many senior citizens like to go south to Florida for the winter and then north to the Catskills for the summer.
Although Robert E. Lee had served in the U.S. Army during the Mexican War, he fought for the South in the Civil War.

PRACTICE 3

After reviewing the rules for capitalization, capitalize any words that may require it.

1. I think midwinter recess is a waste; however, spring vacation is great.
2. Many psychiatrists discount freud's theories, so they try to apply jungian principles to psychoanalysis.
3. Although we are taught that the middle ages was quickly followed by the renaissance, in reality there was quite an overlapping of the two eras.
4. napoleonic france and regency england were bitter enemies.   *no rule given for regency*
5. the declaration of independence led to the revolution.   *no rule given for (revolution*
6. even though she's a good teacher, i think it's ridiculous to have a person who doesn't believe in god teach a theology course.
7. Every spring, our grandparents travel east to missouri.
8. although he appears pompous, judge White actually is a decent fellow.
9. Before the child left for school, he kissed his mother.
10. Businesses are rejoicing because christmas sales have increased by 40 percent this year compared to last year.

Check the answer key.

End Punctuation

End punctuation has a very practical purpose; it lets the reader know where each thought ends, and, thus, makes reading an easier task.

Example: The day was bright and sunny, a relief after the weeks of rain however, the weather forecast was dismal it suggested that this was just a brief interlude before another storm what can be done to change the weather.

Obviously, reading that paragraph presents difficulties. It is much simpler to read with the appropriate end punctuation.

Revision: The day was bright and sunny, a relief after the weeks of rain. However, the weather forecast was dismal. It suggested that this was just a brief interlude before another storm. What can be done to change the weather?

There are three marks of end punctuation, or end stops, as they are sometimes called:

- the period (.)
- the question mark (?)
- the exclamation point (!)

Each end stop performs a different task. The end stops replace the inflection, stress, and pitch of our voices, the clues we use in conversation to help our listener understand our thoughts.

Examples: It's two down and ten to go.   (merely a statement of fact)
It's two down and ten to go?   (asking for information)
It's two down and ten to go!   (an expression of strong emotion)

In each instance, the words are the same, but the intentions are changed by the end stops.

The Period (.)

The period ends statements, requests, or indirect questions.

Examples: *Statements*

This year, classes will end ten days later than last year.
In fact, blue is a terrible color for her.

Requests

Please turn down the radio.
Kindly hold the elevator door for me.
Mow the lawn today.

Indirect Questions

Please tell me when the spring semester begins.
Let me know whether the item is in stock.
I wonder whether they're going to the show on Thursday.

NOTES: 1. A request does not anticipate a reply. It is assumed that the listener will comply with the request.

2. An indirect question is a tactful way of asking for information; it implies a request for information. It is not as straightforward as a direct question, and in conversation we would not raise the pitch of our voice at the end of the thought, as we do with a direct question.

EXERCISE Following the above examples, correctly punctuate these sentences.

1. Although this may be hard to believe, soon there will be a glut of lawyers

2. Rather than learning a new trade, he preferred to retire

Have your instructor or tutor check your work.

The Question Mark (?)

The question mark ends sentences asking for information, that is, direct questions.

Examples: What schedule did you choose?
When do you expect to graduate?

NOTE: Direct questions assume that the listener will make a response; the question is a blunt way of seeking information. Usually, a direct question begins with an interrogative pronoun (*who, which, what*) or adverb (*when, where,* etc.), and its sentence order is inverted; in other words, the verb precedes the subject.

EXERCISE Following the above examples, correctly punctuate these sentences.

1. Do you think the conglomerate should make a bid for that company

2. Have her motives been determined

Have your instructor or tutor check your work.

The Exclamation Point (!)

The exclamation point is used to indicate commands, strong emotions, surprise, or, in general, to emphasize thoughts.

Examples: Stop! (command)
My son is wounded! (emotion)
Oh, my goodness! (surprise)
She won't do it! (emphasis)

NOTE: Exclamation points are rarely used in expository writing; they are more suited to dialogue and stories. Therefore, use them carefully and with forethought.

EXERCISE Following the above examples, correctly punctuate these thoughts.

1. What a horrible day

2. Watch out

Have your instructor or tutor check your work.

PRACTICE 4

Correctly punctuate the following thoughts.

1. Since the beginning of time, man has tried to change his environment

2. Where is the seminar being held

3. Are you suggesting that a take-over may be pending

4. Go away

5. Have you found a solution to the problem

6. As you all remember, geometry requires you to memorize proofs

7. Interplanetary space travel is a possibility; one wonders if interstellar space travel can be far behind

8. Most new cars are quite expensive

9. Look out below

10. Some experts maintain that diamonds have lost one-third of their value Is that so

Check the answer key.

APPLICATION I

Proofread the following paragraph for capitalization and end-punctuation errors. Use the correct editing symbol to indicate the type of error—that is, use *end p* for end-punctuation errors; use *cap* for lower-case letters that should be capitalized, and use *lc* for upper-case letters that should not be capitalized. Circle the points that require correction. Then, correct the errors.

Example: (there were many(P)roblems at the store today○The first was Tony.

(1) There were many problems at the store today. (2) the first was Tony; He thinks he owns the place Rather than that, he just works there Sometimes his behavior is so high-handed that It's incredible. (3) he treats the other workers not like peers, not even like employees, but like machines. (4) In fact, Tony even tried to give Me an order Well, i let him know a thing or two. (5) Now, I'll bet he's wondering why he's out of a job can you beat that (6) Another problem was inventory because of the recession, We did not stock a great variety of items. (7) Now, people are feeling confident about the economy, so they are spending money. (8) however, they have become smart shoppers before they spend their money, the Customers want to check out all the possibilities and decide on the best buy for their hard-earned dollars. (9) that means the store had better have a whole range of similar items. (10) we'll have to start rebuilding our Inventory (11) The last Problem was me today I just wasn't in the mood for work. (12) I wanted to be at the beach, so my mind kept drifting there Whenever someone asked me about a problem, i had to force myself to return from the sand, sun and surf (such inattention can cause problems in a business establishment) (13) Finally, i decided that since today had been an unproductive one, the Solution was to admit it and give in at three o'clock, I left and went to the shore. Check the answer key.

APPLICATION II

Proofread the following essay for capitalization and end-punctuation errors. Use the correct editing symbol to indicate the type of error. Use *end p* for end punctuation, use *lc* for lower-case and *cap* for upper-case letters. Then, correct the errors.

(1) Nearly everyone has heard of The Preakness, the Second race of the Triple Crown. (2) Another Maryland race is equally as important. (3) The maryland Hunt Cup is an annual event; riders and horses from all parts of the state are present for the four-hour race. (4) Although

owners and riders focus all of their attention upon the race, some spectators prefer to spend their time enjoying the warm Spring weather, good food and drink, pleasant friends, and new acquaintances. (5) A spectator must be able to handle two situations: the pre–hunt cup preparations and his Social interactions.

(6) Preparation often takes days It covers everything from enough food and drink for the tailgate party to appropriate clothing. (7) When preparing for the biggest Preppie event of the spring, one must also try to follow the old adage, "Eat, Drink, and Be Merry." (8) To begin, one needs plenty of soft drinks on hand? (9) Hamburgers and Hot Dogs are necessary to quell the appetites of starving spectators. (10) Also required are the normal Tailgate party items: different salads, sandwich items, cups and napkins, Lawn chairs, and a Golden Retriever named macDuff. (11) All of this, of course, follows the basic outlines set forth in *the Preppie handbook*.

(12) However, all of this preparation will be useless unless a spectator presents himself properly to friends, acquaintances, and strangers! (13) After one has eaten, it is important to tour the Grounds and say hello to everyone. (14) Social interaction is most important when a spectator visits other groups. (15) One must make it a point to talk to everyone he knows Even the most obscure acquaintance deserves a "How are you!" (16) While learning the status of the harvard Crew Team, or the Hopkins Lacrosse Team, one must make sure that the conversation does not last more than five minutes. (17) After all, a spectator attends the Hunt cup to see the race!

(18) Preparation and social interaction are the keys to a successful, fun-filled Afternoon. (19) I hope that this Spring it will be a date to see you there. (20) I will be the one sitting in a lawn chair at the back of the dark-green station wagon My trusty companion MacDuff will be by my side.

Check the answer key.

APPLICATION III

Proofread a rough draft of a paper of your own. Check carefully for errors in capitalization and end punctuation. Correct all errors that you find, and show your revisions to your instructor or tutor.

Commas to Separate

OBJECTIVES:
1. To recognize the need for commas in sentences and in paragraphs.

2. To use commas correctly.

3. To proofread a paper for comma mistakes, and to use correctly the editing symbol for comma mistakes (*P*).

KEY CONCEPT: Commas are used to separate six different parts or elements in a sentence:

1. Independent clauses joined by coordinate conjunctions,

2. Items in a series,

3. Coordinate adjectives,

4. Long introductory elements,

5. Dates and addresses, and

6. Any elements that might be misread and misunderstood if they were not separated by commas.

Independent Clauses

An independent clause is a group of words that contains a subject and a verb and can stand alone. In other words, it is a simple sentence and may be punctuated as such. However, you may want to join two independent clauses and write them as one compound sentence; in that case, you must use one of two methods:

1. *Join two independent clauses with a* **semicolon.**

Examples: The teachers elect their representatives. (independent clause)
The administration approves them. (independent clause)

The teachers elect their representatives; the administration approves them. (compound sentence)

The children decided to buy their parents a gift. (independent clause)
They raided their piggy banks. (independent clause)

The children decided to buy their parents a gift; they raided their piggy banks. (compound sentence)

2. *Join two independent clauses by adding a* **comma** *and a* **coordinate conjunction.**

Examples: The teachers elect their representatives, but the administration approves them.

The children decided to buy their parents a gift, so they raided their piggy banks.

NOTE: The comma comes before the coordinate conjunction. There are only seven coordinate conjunctions: *and, but, for, so, or, yet,* and *nor.* (See "Compound Sentences" in Chapter 6.)

EXERCISE Join the following independent clauses to form a compound sentence by using a comma and a coordinate conjunction.

Independent clauses: Susan cooked an elaborate dinner.
                        John washed the dishes afterwards.

Compound sentence:

_____

Independent clauses: The manager reviewed the sales figures.
                        He was not happy with what he saw.

Compound sentence:

_____

Have your instructor or tutor check your work.

NOTE: Remember that the comma precedes the coordinate conjunction only when it is joining two independent clauses, but usually not when the conjunction is joining words, phrases, or dependent clauses.

Examples: The boys decided to swim and fish. (joins prepositional words)

             The girls are either at the beach or at the pool. (joins phrases)

             A child must know that his parents love him and that they will care for him. (joins dependent clauses)

PRACTICE 1

If there is a comma error in a sentence, write *P* in the blank, and then correct the sentence by inserting a comma wherever necessary. If a sentence is correctly punctuated, write *C* in the blank.

1. The boys and girls could not decide whether to swim or fish. _____

2. On Thursday the governing board will decide on next year's budget and this year's dues obligation. _____

3. The children played in the schoolyard for the teachers were attending a faculty conference. _____

4. The bride wanted to party for another hour but the groom was anxious to begin the honeymoon. _____

5. The cake must bake for an hour and the cookies have to bake for forty minutes. _____

Check the answer key.

Items in a Series

Commas are used to separate each item in a series from the preceding item. Remember that a series is a group of three or more items having the same function and form in the sentence.

Examples: Sara, Mike, and Elton are good friends. (series of words)

In the living room, in the playroom, and in the basement are radios. (series of phrases)

Mary Jean promised that she would be a good girl, that she would not bite her brother, and that she would not climb onto the television. (series of clauses)

EXERCISE Add commas wherever necessary in the following sentences.

1. We bought apples peaches and bananas at the fruit store today.
2. The instructor looked through his briefcase through his desk and around the office for the lost grade book.
3. Despite the facts that she was only 5′2″ tall that she weighed 180 pounds and that she had dyed her hair green, Marcie believed she could get a job as a high-fashion model.

Have your instructor or tutor check your work.

PRACTICE 2

If there is a comma error in a sentence, write *P* in the blank and then correct the sentence by inserting a comma wherever necessary. If a sentence is correctly punctuated, write *C* in the blank.

1. People who want to buy a foreign car have a wide range of choices: Datsuns Toyotas and Volkswagens. _____
2. Milky Ways M&Ms and Mounds are my favorite candies. _____
3. I bought a dress and a coat the other day. _____
4. She buys gifts for Christmas Thanksgiving and Easter. _____
5. I have to stop at the cleaner's buy some milk and pick up the twins at school. _____

Check the answer key.

Coordinate Adjectives

Commas are used to separate coordinate adjectives. Coordinate adjectives are two or more adjectives that modify a noun or pronoun and that have equal value in modifying the noun or pronoun.

Examples: happy, lively children
beautiful, sophisticated woman

To test whether two adjectives are coordinate, reverse the order of the adjectives and insert *and* between them. If the phrase still makes sense, then the adjectives *must* be separated by a comma.

Examples: happy, lively children
lively and happy children

beautiful, sophisticated woman
sophisticated and beautiful woman

wholesome Italian food
Italian and wholesome food

> **NOTE:** Obviously, the last phrase does not contain coordinate adjectives; therefore, it should not contain a comma.

EXCEPTIONS: Adjectives that describe size, age, or color generally are not separated by a comma.

Examples: big black Cadillac
little old lady

EXERCISE Follow the above examples, and insert a comma where necessary in the following sentences.

1. He acted the part of the charming convivial host.
2. That fancy expensive sports car has too many gadgets for my taste.

Have your instructor or tutor check your work.

PRACTICE 3

Insert a comma wherever necessary in the following sentences. If a sentence is correctly punctuated, mark it *C*.

1. The little old woman seemed to shrink even more under her son's harsh impersonal gaze.
2. The yellow foreign roadster sped from the scene of the accident.
3. A dirty dingy file cabinet creates a bad impression in an executive's office.
4. The short blond-haired youngster was the prime troublemaker in the group.
5. The Irish setter with the long red hair seemed out of place among the poodles.

Check the answer key.

Long Introductory Elements

These must be separated from the rest of the sentence by a comma. The key words here are *long* and *introductory*. If the element is short, or if it is not at the beginning of the sentence, no comma is needed.

Examples: On Tuesday we went to the movies. (short prepositional phrase)
On that fateful and fear-filled Tuesday, we went to the movies. (long prepositional phrase)

People feel guilty when they reject another's plea for help. (clause at end of sentence)
When they reject another's plea for help, people feel guilty. (introductory clause)

EXERCISE   Correct these sentences by following the above examples.

1. Before going home the man decided to play one last game of pool.
2. After Susan decided to sue for divorce she moved out of the apartment.

Have your instructor or tutor check your work.

PRACTICE 4

If there is a comma error in a sentence, write *P* in the blank, and then insert a comma wherever necessary. If a sentence is correctly punctuated, write *C* in the blank.

1. Having been introduced to the star once before Harry felt at ease in her presence.   _____

2. Tonight I want to go straight home.   _____

3. Before the group moved down the road each member checked his equipment.   _____

4. In the total darkness with only the ticking of the clock to guide him the burglar stumbled on the carpet.   _____

5. Because the tests are machine-graded it is unlikely that there would be an error.   _____

Check the answer key.

Dates and Addresses

Commas are used to separate individual items in a date or an address.

Examples: Ty Cobb hit his last home run on September 11, 1927, at Wrigley Field.
The new Regency House is at 42 Marston Lane, Ridgefield, Ohio, a major metropolis.

NOTE: The comma is optional when only the month and year are given.

Example: Most people believe the Great Depression began in October 1929 and ended with the advent of World War II.

EXERCISE Correct the following sentences by inserting a comma where necessary.

1. My parents were married on August 14 1975 and divorced in May 1985.
2. Their first home was at 1225 Elm Street Florham Station Arizona.

Have your instructor or tutor check your work.

PRACTICE 5

If there is a comma error in a sentence, write *P* in the blank and then correct the error. If a sentence is correctly punctuated, write *C* in the blank.

1. December 7 1941 is a date few people will ever forget. _____
2. One famous address for Americans is 1600 Pennsylvania Avenue Washington D.C. _____
3. The real-estate broker just mentioned that the house at 27-01 32nd Avenue, Flushing, is for sale. _____
4. Before you leave, let me remind you that the term project is due November 2, and not a day later. _____
5. Even though you prefer the apartment at 227 Oak Crest Drive, it will not be available until July 1988. _____

Check the answer key.

Elements That Might Be Misread or Misunderstood

The reason for a comma in this situation is obvious. Some sentences might be easily understood when you hear them but misunderstood when you read them. In order to prevent this, separate any phrases that might cause confusion by inserting a comma.

Example: Before eating the children washed their hands.

Correction: Before eating, the children washed their hands.

The sentence should be punctuated with a comma; otherwise, your reader might assume that you eat children.

Example: Although we were expecting only three fifty guests arrived.

Correction: Although we were expecting only three, fifty guests arrived.

The above sentence needs a comma to prevent a misunderstanding about the number of guests.

EXERCISE   Correct the following sentences by inserting a comma where necessary.

1. At eleven fifty Boy Scouts began the hike up Stone Face Mountain.
2. After mile twenty five more people dropped out of the race.

Have your instructor or tutor check your work.

PRACTICE 6

If there is a comma error in a sentence, write P in the blank, and then correct the error. If a sentence is correctly punctuated, write C in the blank.

1. After jumping the dog raced toward the cat.   _____
2. Exactly at nine thirty men raced home.   _____
3. When old horses should be put out to pasture.   _____
4. Before Byron was thirty one masterpiece had been published.   _____
5. Precisely at twelve o'clock four blasts were sounded on the horn.   _____

Check the answer key.

APPLICATION I

If there is a comma error in the sentences, write *P* in the blank to the right and correct the error. If the sentence is correctly punctuated, write *C*.

1. Jerome began his graduate studies in September 1971, and he received his degree on January 23 1981. _____

2. She said she wasn't too uncomfortable although she looked funny. _____

3. The baby was turning blue and seemed very cold so we rushed her to the hospital. _____

4. After hitting the batter raced towards first base. _____

5. Within the warm confines of the womb the embryo is protected from most hazards. _____

6. The young woman locked herself behind the safe secure steel doors. _____

7. Staples seem to be trivial items yet much work depends on them. _____

8. The students enjoyed the senior prom; they danced and ate until three o'clock in the morning. _____

9. That tall oak tree has provided shelter to many children for decades. _____

10. The cat cannot sleep on the bureau jump on the bed or eat on the table. _____

11. The governor's mansion requires a large, housekeeping staff. _____

12. The puppy's short, spindly legs made him a comical figure. _____

13. After falling into the lake, losing his wallet, and injuring his hand, Poindexter decided to forego trout fishing. _____

14. At first George wanted to be an architect but then he decided to be a nurse. _____

15. The tall lean basketball player attracted attention. _____

16. Even though it was raining the children wanted to go to the zoo. _____

17. At the end of every day, I hope for a quiet evening. _____

18. Each child's Christmas list included a toy a book and an item of clothing. _____

19. The old dilapidated chair did not look like an antique to me. _____

20. The company moved its warehouse from 3307 Underhill Lane, Tacoman Mississippi to 29 First Place, Finleyburg Missouri because of rising rent costs. _____

Check the answer key.

APPLICATION II

Proofread the following paragraph carefully. Place a *P* above any sentence that contains a comma error, and correct the error by adding the necessary commas.

(1) In his freshman year a college student can encounter many problems. (2) First of all, if he is living on campus then the student must adjust to dorm life. (3) Sometimes sharing a room

with another person—or even two or three—can be frustrating. (4) The different schedules different tastes and different goals of roommates can complicate a student's life. (5) Second each freshman must be responsible for his own time. (6) College professors usually require more homework and independent study than high school teachers do so a student must devise good study plans attend classes and budget his time. (7) In addition, a student's social life can interfere with his academic progress. (8) For example away from watchful parental eyes many students enjoy great freedom; some enjoy it too much. (9) In fact, many students neglect their work because they want to socialize with their friends. (10) Finally, freshmen tend to question themselves and their world more than they did before. (11) However these potential problems can be overcome if a student knows what to expect when he enters college. (12) The first year of college can be a rewarding exciting and valuable experience.

Check the answer key.

APPLICATION III

Proofread the following essay carefully. Place a *P* beside any sentence that contains a comma error, and correct the error by adding the necessary commas.

(1) The summer is over. (2) Yes, school has arrived. (3) When the ocean the crab feasts and the baseball games fade into chaotic dreams, two kinds of people face the reality of school. (4) On the one hand, the scholarly student has already purchased all of his books and has gone to Rite-Aid for such utensils as a protractor, a ruler, and a gum eraser. (5) On the other hand, the lackadaisical student has lost his book-sale notice with the rest of his mail and has decided to spend the remainder of his summer money on new records. (6) One student sees summer as a restful time and heads eagerly to school. (7) The other considers the summer a long party and staggers into school for the nine-month sentence. (8) Neither of the two, however, has any advantage over the other: both usually pass.

(9) Nevertheless, the scholarly fellow seems more productive. (10) When the teacher returns a test he taps three holes through the paper with his handy hole-puncher. (11) He then files the test in his binder. (12) The scholar perfects all his homework days before deadlines. (13) He

rushes to class five minutes early opens his briefcase and pulls out a pen from a plastic case with a convenient sliding cover. (14) Then, he waits.

(15) Ten minutes later the slothful student straggles into class. (16) He flounders upon a desk falls into it and scratches his head for he is ready to learn. (17) The listless fellow borrows a piece of paper from some generous classmate and pulls a pen from his pocket. (18) He flicks the pen, licks it, and then flicks it again. (19) The pen, however, will not write: its ink has splotched his pocket. (20) The teacher returns a test and watches the student gaze at it crumple it and then casually toss it into the trash can. (21) He never takes notes; however, he occasionally bothers to copy homework.

(22) When it comes to testing however, they both seem to have learned the same amount. (23) An organized student always has his work done; therefore, he does not have to study long before a test. (24) Yet, he does not feel that he has studied enough for on the weekends the scholarly fellow remains at home to do work rather than going out to relax. (25) The other type of student tends to cram before tests and to take the life between them easily. (26) He contents himself with getting by. (27) All of this is nice in school but when it comes to the real world the organized student will receive big money and buy plush homes. (28) He will retire earlier and live longer than the slacker.

(29) Perhaps all of this says something about school. (30) Education offers an opportunity to learn. (31) Some take advantage of this; others do not. (32) But, what is always true is that students take from school what they want. (33) Those who work in school live hard childhoods and easy adulthoods but those who do not work live long childhoods. (34) They never pay their dues; when the time comes for benefits there are none. (35) Neither student has the advantage over the other. (36) There is, however, a medium and the students who have sufficient organization and not too much relaxation are the ones who will succeed the most.

Check the answer key.

APPLICATION IV

Proofread a rough draft of a paper of your own. Check carefully for comma errors, and mark those you find with a *P*. Correct all the errors, and show your revisions to your instructor or tutor.

15

Commas to Enclose

OBJECTIVES:
1. To recognize poorly punctuated sentences, in isolation and in paragraphs.
2. To use commas to enclose or set off words, phrases, and clauses correctly.
3. To proofread a paper for comma errors and to use the editing symbol for a comma error (*P*).

KEY CONCEPT: Commas are used to enclose or set off six major elements that interrupt sentences:
1. Direct address,
2. Speaker in a dialogue,
3. Apposition,
4. Out-of-place adjectives,
5. Nonrestrictive clauses and phrases, and
6. Parenthetical expressions.

Interrupters are extra words or ideas added to the basic thought of a sentence. Because they are not necessary to the basic sentence, interrupters must be enclosed or set off by commas. Depending on its placement in the sentence, the interrupter will require either one or two commas to isolate it.

Examples: If I'm not mistaken, his pay averages about $200 per week. (beginning of the sentence—one comma)

His pay, if I'm not mistaken, averages about $200 per week. (middle of the sentence—two commas)

His pay averages about $200 per week, if I'm not mistaken. (end of the sentence—one comma)

Commas in Direct Address

When the speaker in a sentence talks to another person and names that person, the process is called *direct address* because the speaker is addressing his audience directly.

Example: I think, dear, you're wrong.

The speaker is talking to a person whom he calls "dear." Therefore, "dear" must be enclosed within commas. Because the interrupter is placed in the middle of the sentence, two commas are used to enclose it.

Example: Your performance is poor, Nancy.

The speaker is talking to a person, and that person is named at the end of the sentence. Therefore, one comma is used to set off the noun in direct address, "Nancy."

Example: You poor little waif, you seem frozen.

The speaker is addressing a person whom he calls "you poor little waif." Because that direct-address interrupter is placed at the beginning of the sentence, one comma is used to isolate it.

EXERCISE   Correct the following sentences by inserting the necessary commas.

1. The children don't trust any authority figure sir.
2. Let me assure you boss there's a reason for my tardiness.

Have your instructor or tutor check your work.

PRACTICE 1

Correctly punctuate the following sentences.

1. Professor MacBride may I ask a question?
2. He really thinks Charles that he has grounds for a lawsuit.
3. Your Honor I object to the tone of his question.
4. Tomorrow you will go to the parade children.
5. Let's go to the game tonight Mary.

Check the answer key.

Commas in Dialogue

A dialogue is a conversation between two or more people. If the speaker (not the listener) in the conversation is identified, his name (or the noun or pronoun used to refer to the speaker) and the verb that refers to his speaking are enclosed within commas.

Examples: Mary said, "I dislike concerts because the music is too loud."

"I dislike concerts because the music is too loud," said the girl.

"I dislike concerts," proclaimed the teenager, "because the music is too loud."

In each of these sentences, the speaker is identified. Therefore, in the first sentence the phrase "Mary said," which is at the beginning of the sentence, is set off by one comma. The phrase "said the girl" is at the end of the second sentence, so one comma is used. Finally, the phrase "proclaimed the teenager" is in the middle of the last sentence, so it is enclosed by two commas.

NOTE: Dialogue is usually punctuated by quotation marks. So, if you see quotation marks, check to see whether there is a speaker stated in the sentence, and, if so, enclose the speaker and the verb within commas.

EXERCISE   Correct the following sentences by inserting a comma where necessary.

"I'm as happy as a lark" yelled George.

She screamed "Don't you say another word."

Have your instructor or tutor check your work.

PRACTICE 2

Correctly punctuate the following sentences.

1. "Teachers don't understand" screamed the disgusted student.
2. "Bugs" said the little girl quite primly "are dirty creatures."
3. Before he left home, six-year-old John stated very emphatically "I will not return."
4. "I am not at all interested" said Mother to the salesrepresentative.
5. The proud owner of a prize-winning Persian unequivocally declared "Cats are much smarter than dogs."

Check the answer key.

Commas with Appositives

When a noun is immediately followed by a group of words that explain or rename it, the group of words is called an appositive and must be enclosed within commas.

Example:	Alexander Pope, the Neo-Classic poet, is famous for his monologues.
	Alexander Pope is famous for his monologues.
	"The Neo-Classic poet" gives additional information about Pope; therefore, it is in apposition and is enclosed within commas. The appositive could be omitted, and the sentence would still make sense and provide enough information to be understood.
Example:	The New York Jets, the underdogs, surprised everyone by winning the Super Bowl.
	The New York Jets surprised everyone by winning the Super Bowl.
	"The underdogs" gives the reader additional information about the football team, but the phrase is not necessary for comprehending the sentence. Thus, "the underdogs" is in apposition and is enclosed by commas.

NOTE: When an appositive offers additional, *nonessential* information about the noun, it is enclosed in commas. However, some appositives are necessary to identify the noun. In this case, the appositive is not enclosed in commas. Consider the differences in meaning between these examples.

Examples:	The poet Dryden is famous for his satire.
	My neighbor Mr. Taracks is the neighborhood busybody.
	Neither of the above sentences could be rewritten without losing the sense of the sentence.

Examples: The poet is famous for his satire. *Which poet?*

My neighbor is the neighborhood busybody. *Which neighbor?*

The sense of the sentences has been lost. The information was necessary to identify the noun; therefore, no commas were used to enclose the information.

EXERCISE   Using the example sentences as models, insert commas wherever necessary in the following sentences.

1. My only sister Sue is studying engineering.
2. *Childe Roland to the Dark Tower Came* an epic poem was written by Robert Browning.
3. Sally the class busybody loves to take charge of every project.

Have your instructor or tutor check your work.

PRACTICE 3

In the blank to the right of each sentence, write *C* if the sentence is correctly punctuated or *P* if there is a comma error. Correct the comma errors.

1. My history teacher Professor Jones gives difficult tests.   _____
2. Mrs. Smith Sally's neighbor likes to wear hot-pink shorts in the summer.   _____
3. Old Lyin' George a famous panhandler died peacefully last night in a nursing home.   _____
4. President Carter the nation's thirty-ninth chief executive refused to return to the peanut business.   _____
5. My only brother Harry wants to join the Peace Corps.   _____

Check the answer key.

Commas with Out-of-Place Adjectives

Because adjectives usually precede the nouns they modify, any deviation from that usual pattern catches the reader's attention and interrupts the flow of thought. When that happens, the out-of-place adjective(s) must be enclosed by commas.

Examples: 1. The tall, slender girl attracted everyone's attention. (usual pattern)

2. The girl, tall and slender, attracted everyone's attention. (out-of-place)

3. The grand, imposing house required a large housekeeping staff. (usual pattern)

4. The house, grand and imposing, required a large housekeeping staff. (out-of-place)

EXERCISE   Using the example sentences as models, correctly punctuate these sentences.

1. The woman witty and sophisticated charmed her hostile audience.
2. The toddler sturdy and daring was determined to climb out of the crib.

Have your instructor or tutor check your work.

PRACTICE 4

In the blank to the right of each sentence, write *C* if the sentence is correctly punctuated or *P* if there is a comma error. Correct the comma errors.

1. My child bright and witty will be famous some day.   _____

2. The old man tired but undaunted faced his accusers.   _____

3. The fresh air of spring exhilarating and uplifting should be packaged and sold
   for use during the winter.   _____

4. The young boy senile before his time was a victim of a dreaded disease.   _____

5. The beautiful and happy baby laughed at the puppy's antics.   _____

Check the answer key.

Commas with Nonrestrictive Clauses and Phrases

A nonrestrictive clause or phrase gives extra information about the word it modifies, so it is not essential to the sentence and is enclosed by commas.

Example: My brother, who has a weak knee, should not play football.

The basic thought of this sentence is that the speaker's brother should not play football. Because the speaker obviously knows his brother, he is able to offer the reason for that prohibition, but that reason is not essential to the sentence. Therefore, because the clause acts as an interrupter, stopping the flow of the sentence, it must be punctuated as one. Enclose it within commas.

Example: Steven Stomes, whose show you like, will host a party next week for disabled vets.

EXERCISE   Using the example sentence as a model, correctly punctuate the following sentences.

1. Mary who is a great athlete is also an outstanding scholar.
2. King George III who lost the American colonies is not considered an outstanding monarch.

Have your instructor or tutor check your work.

NOTE: Remember, *non*restrictive clauses and phrases are enclosed within commas. Anything that is essential to the meaning of the sentence should be left as an integral part of the sentence and *not* enclosed.

Example: The man who is standing by the door is a security policeman.

"Who is standing by the door" is essential for identifying the man; without this clause, the reader would have no means of identifying the security policeman. Consequently, no commas are used in the sentence.

Now, note the effect commas can have on the meaning of a sentence.

Example: Journalists, who write well about crucial issues, are rewarded with a large audience.

The basic thought of the sentence is that journalists have large audiences; the nonrestrictive clause (which has been enclosed by commas) merely gives the reason for the large audiences. It provides extra information to the reader.

Example: Journalists who write well about crucial issues are rewarded with a large audience.

The meaning has changed. Now, it is only proficient journalists who reach large audiences. The clause is essential to the sentence because it identifies the journalists. Therefore, no commas are used.

PRACTICE 5

In the blank to the right of each sentence, write C if the sentence is correctly punctuated or P if there is a comma error. Correct the comma errors.

1. Parrots although notorious for their ability to mimic speech are really shy birds. _____

2. Puppies while amusing you with their tricks can turn a house upside-down. _____

3. Fashionable dress because the criteria change so often should not be used to judge another person's worth. _____

4. The parishioners who often leave early disrupt the service. _____

5. The gentleman who is standing by the fireplace is a well-known composer. _____

Check the answer key.

Commas with Parenthetical Expressions

When a word or phrase is inserted into a sentence to explain or comment on that sentence, it is called a parenthetical expression. Because the word or phrase is not essential to the sentence (it is merely providing additional information), it is enclosed by commas.

Example: The dean, on the other hand, believes in vigorously recruiting students.

The basic thought of this sentence is the dean's desire to seek students actively. The phrase "on the other hand" serves as a *transition*; it helps to move the reader from one idea to another, in this case contrasting, idea. Because it acts as an interrupter in the middle of the sentence, it is enclosed by two commas.

EXERCISE   Following the above examples, correctly punctuate these sentences.

1. In fact the author believes his works were plagiarized.
2. The original cowboy to tell the truth would not match today's idealized version of a cowpuncher.

Have your instructor or tutor check your work.

Following is a discussion of the two most common types of parenthetical expressions.

Transitional Expressions

In general, transitional expressions help give unity and coherence to an essay or paragraph. They influence the style of the writing, so they are enclosed by commas.

Below is a chart of some commonly used transitions and the type of relationship each one indicates.

Type of Relationship	*Transition*
Cause and Effect	consequently, hence, therefore, thus
Chronological	first, second, third, last, finally, later
Comparison/Contrast	similarly, however, nevertheless, on the other hand, in contrast, on the contrary
Example	for example, to illustrate, for instance
Importance/Repetition	as a matter of fact, generally speaking, in addition, in fact, on the whole, to say the least, to tell the truth, moreover
Summary/Conclusion	in brief, in short, to conclude, to summarize, therefore

Note that these expressions require the reader to pause while reading the sentence, so they are enclosed by commas.

On the other hand, some short parenthetical expressions of one or two words do *not* force the reader to pause; therefore, they would not be enclosed by commas. Here are some examples:

actually	at worst	perhaps
also	if any	then
at best	indeed	too
at least	of course	

Examples: Then everyone decided to leave the dance hall.

Of course the inflation rate had also climbed to 20 percent by that time.

EXERCISE   Correctly punctuate these sentences.

1. Perhaps the hospital expects too much from its volunteers.
2. Actually they have always expected too much.

Have your instructor or tutor check your work.

Mild Interjections

Mild interjections are words such as *oh, wow,* and *ah*. They are usually placed at the beginning of a sentence to comment on it. Again, because they are not essential to the sentence and because they interrupt its thought, they are considered parenthetical elements and are enclosed by commas.

Examples: Oh, I didn't know you were here.

Wow, that's some black eye!

EXERCISE   Correctly punctuate these sentences.

1. Ah how I appreciate a fine cigar.
2. Oh that was an unexpected move.

Have your instructor or tutor check your work.

PRACTICE 6

In the blank to the right of each sentence, write C if the sentence is correctly punctuated or P if there is a comma error. Correct the comma errors.

1. In fact she is quite a good cook.   _____
2. He is, I believe, determined to ascend the corporate ladder.   _____
3. Surprisingly Calhoun's Clogs won the steeplechase easily.   _____
4. To conclude productivity has improved, but not by as great a percentage as we
   had hoped.   _____
5. John Darlingston believe it or not is an accomplished pianist.   _____

Check the answer key.

APPLICATION I

In the blank to the right of each sentence, write *C* if the sentence is correctly punctuated or *P* if there is a comma error. Correct the comma errors.

1. The unfortunate graduate student on the other hand was dismissed from the course.   _____

2. My prize-winning dog a long-haired Pomeranian almost died from exposure.   _____

3. The jockey young and alert was nervous about her first race.   _____

4. The police officer said "Before you go, I must have a word with you."   _____

5. You have not answered my question honestly sir.   _____

6. Oh it is a beautiful evening!   _____

7. "Indeed I do," declared Jose with vehemence.   _____

8. College students generally speaking earn more money over the course of a lifetime than high-school graduates earn.   _____

9. "Then the best course of action" she stated "is to forget the whole enterprise."   _____

10. Andy I can neither condone nor support your proposed course of action.   _____

11. The football player muscular and tanned seemed out of place in the aerobics class.   _____

12. She truly believes, Mona, that hypnosis is the best solution.   _____

13. The telephone, which was invented by A. G. Bell, is about to be transformed by modern technology.   _____

14. Ann D'Arcy the Dean of the College participated in last week's financial seminar.   _____

15. Every child who is born with a handicap deserves special attention.   _____

16. My mother's award-winning recipe for apple pie, a family secret, is credited with saving many a marriage.   _____

17. My oldest brother who loves to play golf has just retired.   _____

18. Plants not dogs should be considered man's best friend.   _____

19. The management has decided young man that the staff must be trimmed.   _____

20. Trust, on the other hand, is essential in marriage.   _____

Check the answer key.

APPLICATION II

Proofread the following passage, in which each sentence is numbered. If the sentence is correctly punctuated, write *C* above its number. If the sentence contains a comma error, write *P* next to its number and correct the error.

(1) Many journalism students who all hope to become great writers try their hand at writing dialogue. (2) Usually, the result is stilted and boring. (3) The following is an example:

(4) "Hello dear" said Nancy. (5) "How was work today?"

(6) "Terrible Nancy terrible. (7) The boss that idiot demoted me and promoted Harry the sweet-talking imbecile" replied her disgruntled husband. (8) "Can you believe that darling?"

(9) The young wife confused and upset looked to her husband for support. (10) "Can't you do something about it? (11) Can't you do something to get your job interesting and well-paying back? (12) You must do something" she cried.

(13) Most readers even though they may not be trained literary critics would immediately label such writing "juvenile." (14) They would be correct. (15) Indeed writing an interesting and profitable task is not an easy one.

Check the answer key.

APPLICATION III

Proofread the following paragraph carefully. If the sentence is correctly punctuated, write *C* above its number. If there is a comma error, write *P* next to the number of the sentence and correct the error.

(1) One football game my most memorable was on November 13, 1982, a cold Friday night against Howard High School our main rival. (2) On that unforgettable night, I scored three touchdowns and one extra point, gained two hundred and four yards, and intercepted two passes. (3) Of all these accomplishments, I will never forget my ninety-five-yard touchdown reception. (4) My team the Mt. Hebron Vikings was huddled in our own end zone; the ball was placed ninety-five yards from Howard's end zone. (5) John Fleming our quarterback announced the play to the huddle; suddenly my heart seemed to pound through my chest. (6) The thrill of excitement entered me, and the anticipation of a successful play filled my head. (7) We broke the huddle; then, trying to hide my excitement, I casually trotted toward my spot on the field. (8)

As I reached my position, sweat ran down my face, and I began to shake. (9) As the pressure mounted, I told myself "No matter what happens, just catch the ball!" (10) As the center snapped the ball, I broke slowly in order to disguise my pattern. (11) Then, as my defender relaxed, I exploded by him with a sudden burst of speed. (12) As he realized my intentions, he tried to regain his strategic position between me and the end zone; however it was too late. (13) I was gone out of his reach. (14) My outstretched hands caught the ball around our forty-yard line, and I danced sixty yards down the sideline to a celebration by fans, teammates, and me. (15) As I turned to look down the field at my ecstatic teammates, I saw the defeat and humiliation of my defender who was lying face down on the field. (16) I knew that the rest of the game was mine!

Check the answer key.

APPLICATION IV

Proofread a rough draft of a paper of your own for comma errors. Place a *P* beside each error. Correct all errors, and show your revisions to your instructor or tutor.

Apostrophes

OBJECTIVES: 1. To recognize the need for apostrophes.

2. To use apostrophes correctly.

3. To proofread a paper for apostrophe errors. The editing symbol for apostrophes is *apos*.

KEY CONCEPT: Apostrophes are used for three purposes:

1. To indicate possession,

2. To form contractions, and

3. To form plurals of certain words.

Use of Apostrophes to Indicate Possession

An apostrophe is used to demonstrate possession. The apostrophe takes the place of omitted words of ownership. If you can reverse the order of the words and use *of* or *for,* then you need an apostrophe. For example, *child's book* becomes *the book of the child.*

Examples: son's chores (the chores of the son)
sons' chores (the chores of more than one son)
Octavia's cake (the cake of Octavia)
Nelson's journey (the journey of Nelson)

NOTE: An apostrophe is not required for possessive pronouns. The pronouns *my, mine, your, yours, his, her, hers, its, our, ours, their,* and *theirs* do not need apostrophes to make them possessive.

Examples: *His* car is not here. Shall we take *yours* or *mine?*
Each cat had *its* favorite spot in the house.

Rules for Forming the Possessive

1. *Add the apostrophe plus an* s *('s) to show possession in these cases:*

a. a singular noun—

Examples: a cat's cry
the astronaut's suit

b. an indefinite pronoun—

 Examples: someone's keys
      everyone's answers

c. plural nouns that do not end in *s*—

 Examples: children's coats
      women's responsibilities
      men's roles

d. compound (more than one word) expressions used as a singular noun—

 Examples: her father-in-law's chair
      the chief-of-police's gun

e. joint possession and separate possession—

 Examples: Libby and Cindy's rooms (same rooms)
      Libby's and Cindy's rooms (different rooms)

PRACTICE 1   *write on board*

Make the following items possessive.

1. the rules of the school _____

2. the idea of someone _____

3. the responses of some people _____

4. the regulations of the agency _____

5. the child whose parents are Thelma and Gene _____

6. the families of Mr. Grant and Mr. Stone _____

7. the quilt of my mother-in-law _____

8. the motives of the thief _____

9. the responses of the congregation _____

10. the insults of the crowd _____

Check the answer key.

2. *Add an apostrophe (') or an apostrophe plus an* s *('s) to* singular *words ending in* s.

a. Add the apostrophe plus the *s* to singular words of one syllable.

 Examples: my boss's schedule
      the bus's tires

b. Add an apostrophe plus an *s* or an apostrophe only to singular words of two syllables. Your choice depends upon sound.

Examples: Thomas's or Thomas' dog
discus' flight or discus's flight

c. Singular words of three or more syllables use only an apostrophe to make them possessive.

Examples: Martinkus' book
Pythagoras' theory

EXERCISE Make the following proper nouns possessive.

the inhabitants of the Ozarks _____

the boat of Ross _____

Have your instructor or tutor check your work.

3. *Add only an apostrophe (') to plural nouns ending in* s.

Examples: goats' pasture
bridges' supports

EXERCISE Make the following words possessive.

the engines of the tractors _____

the caps of the swimmers _____

Have your instructor or tutor check your work.

Use of Apostrophes to Form Contractions

Use apostrophes in place of some letters to form contracted words or numbers. Make sure that the apostrophe is in the same place as the omitted letters or numbers.

Examples:

of the clock	o'clock
he did not	he didn't
she will	she'll
Kim will not	Kim won't
he is	he's
I am	I'm
they are	they're
1965	'65

Usually, except for a contraction like *o'clock,* you should not use contractions in formal writing.

Use of Apostrophes to Form Plurals

Use apostrophes to form plurals of letters, numbers, abbreviations, and words referred to as words.

Examples: Please distinguish between your *i*'s and your *t*'s.
Nathan's 7's often look like 9's.
The VIP's arrived at the gala opening of the new play.
You used too many *and*'s in your last paper.

EXERCISE Make the following words and letters plural.

1. the letters *t* and *b* _____

2. the abbreviations IBM PC (Personal Computer) and MP (Military Police) _____

3. the numbers 17 and 1,000 _____

4. the words *make* and *sing* _____

Have your instructor or tutor check your work.

NOTE: In current usage, the plurals of this century's decades—the '20's, for example—are written without the apostrophe plus *s*. Instead, these decades appear with only the initial apostrophe to indicate that the first numbers are absent and the *s* to indicate plural. The Sixties are now written numerically as the '60s.

PRACTICE 2 *write on board*

Use an apostrophe to make the following sets of words possessive, contractions, or plurals.

1. the ball of the team _____

2. the work of a rabbi _____

3. the passengers of the bus _____

4. the passengers of the buses _____

5. the record of someone _____

6. the credit cards of Ms. Jones _____

7. the racquet of the tennis pro _____

8. the weather conditions of today _____

9. the motto of the Marines _____

10. the national anthem of America _____

11. the responsibilities of the commander-in-chief   _____

12. the refrigerator of his grandparents   _____

13. the restaurants of Jack and Tony (same restaurants)   _____

14. the restaurants of Jack and Tony (different restaurants)   _____

15. the special effects of the movie   _____

16. the concern of the people   _____

17. I will not   _____

18. he cannot   _____

19. they have   _____

20. the plural of the word *several*   _____

21. the plural of the word *yet*   _____

22. the jungles of Brazil   _____

23. the wares of the salespeople   _____

24. the uniform of the soldier   _____

25. the plural of the letter *z*   _____

Check the answer key.

APPLICATION I

Find the apostrophe error in each of the following sentences and write the correct form of the word in the space at the right. Some sentences may contain more than one error.

1. Her familys mansion is a lovely one; its between Southampton and Easton. _____

2. Its a good idea to buckle ones seat belt before driving the car. _____

3. Professor Harvey's course isnt too difficult. _____

4. Everyones invited to Sam's party at his fathers house. _____

5. Women's clothes always seem to cost more than mens. _____

6. Please sign this paper if youre going to the teams game on Friday. _____

7. Taylor sorted his money into piles of 10s, 20s, and 100s. _____

8. Have you noticed that the defense lawyer uses too many *ahs* and *okays*? _____

9. Theyre very superstitious people; they have twenty lucky rabbits feet. _____

10. During the 20s, many Americans enjoyed jazz. _____

11. Hanks teacher told him that there are two *rs* in *occurrence*. _____

12. Its true that a womans career is as important as a man's. _____

13. The childrens bicycles were ruined by the rain. _____

14. Ricks Place is a very popular night club. _____

15. Smith and Sons pizza isnt the best in town. _____

16. For heavens sake, please lower the volume of that radio! _____

17. Four new Beatles' songs have been found; theyll be released later this year. _____

18. This year, twenty-one candidates will participate in New Hampshires presidential primary. _____

19. *The Electric Company* is a very popular childrens program.   _____

20. Police officers duties are numerous.   _____

Check the answer key.

APPLICATION II

Proofread the entire paragraph below for apostrophe errors. Circle any apostrophe error. Write the editing symbol *apos* in the margin next to a sentence in which an apostrophe should be included or deleted. Correct the errors.

(1) The instructor sighed as he sat down to review his students grades. (2) According to the principal, he had given too many Fs. (3) But what could he do? (4) The students' essays were appalling; they wrote as if this were still the 1960s. (5) They couldnt see that the times had changed and that colloquialisms were no longer acceptable. (6) In addition, their vocabularies were terrible; *but*s, *sure*s and *okay*s riddled their papers. (7) "My mother-in-laws vocabulary is better," he thought. (8) "And their diction—there are so many *gonna go*s and *should of*s. (9) You would think that they were speaking another language." (10) So what was he going to do? (11) The principal had been adamant; he wanted to see a precise distribution of grades: 10 percent As, 15 percent Bs, 50 percent Cs, 15 percent Ds and 10 percent Fs. (12) That meant he had to upgrade about fifty mark's. (13) "Oh, well, I guess I'd better get to work," he muttered. Check the answer key.

APPLICATION III

Proofread the entire paragraph below for apostrophe errors. Circle any apostrophe error. Write the editing symbol *apos* in the margin next to a sentence in which an apostrophe should be included or deleted. Correct the errors.

(1) My ideal job has a lot of *don't*'s associated with it. (2) Dont hassle me. (3) Dont be petty about punctuality. (4) Don't be stingy about pay. (5) Of course, there are also a lot of *do*s associated with it, too. (6) Do be kind. (7) Do understand my need for several coffee break's throughout the day. (8) Do praise me for a job well done or for one even half well done. (9) Why, you may ask, do I have such standard's? (10) Are they really necessary? (11) Well, I might respond, the standard's are mine, not your's. (12) Ive been in too many jobs where Ive had to

abide by other people's rule's, and I can't stand it anymore. (13) Ive had to react to their job

ratings of 60s and 65s when I know I deserve much higher. (14) So I'm finished with all that. (15)

From now on, Ill set my job requirements high, and I won't accept a job until it fit's me like a

glove.

APPLICATION IV

Proofread a rough draft of a paper of your own for apostrophe errors. Place the editing symbol *apos* wherever an apostrophe should be included or deleted. Correct the errors and show the edited essay to your instructor or tutor.

Other Types of Punctuation

OBJECTIVES:

1. To learn how to use various types of punctuation correctly.

2. To learn to proofread for punctuation errors and to correct them.

3. To learn to use the editing symbol (*P*).

KEY CONCEPT:

You should become familiar with a few other types of punctuation:

1. Quotation marks (" "),

2. Colons (:),

3. Ellipsis points (. . .),

4. Dashes (—) and hyphens (-), and

5. Parentheses ( ) and brackets [ ].

You will use some of these marks more often than others, but you should be familiar with all of them.

Quotation Marks (" ")

Quotation marks are always used in pairs. The first one is called the opening quote; the second one, the closing quote. At some time, you may also use single quotation marks (') to indicate a quotation within a quotation. Quotation marks are used with four types of material:

1. Verbatim material,
2. Titles,
3. Words used in a special sense, and
4. Dialogue.

In expository writing, you probably will not use dialogue; nonetheless, you should know how to punctuate direct speech correctly.

Verbatim Material

Verbatim material is that which you are copying word-for-word from a source, either a writer or a speaker. All of the copied material must be enclosed by quotation marks to indicate to the reader that you are quoting material that is not your own original work. If the quoted material is interrupted by explanatory words, you must begin and end the quotation marks twice.

Examples: "Many others maintain," according to the prestigious *Journal of Contemporary Clichés*, "that literacy will become a lost art."

The little-known Institute of Public Prohibitions believes that "mankind has allowed itself to be overwhelmed by taboos."

If the quoted material is long (more than five lines), it is correct to indent from the left and right margins and to single-space, rather than to use quotation marks, to indicate that the material is a quotation.

Example: The general's famous speech is usually credited with turning the tide of the battle:

> This day we must all give of ourselves; we must give to the fullest extent possible. There must be no holding back, no looking over our shoulders. We must fight as if our lives, our dreams, our very civilization depend upon us, for, in truth, they do.

There's another side to military speeches, though; for instance, Lieutenant Lewis is remembered for a speech that lost the battle:

> Well, men, we're supposed to go out there now and face those 16-inch guns. I'm not quite sure why we're supposed to do that, but I know I've received my orders. So here goes! Let's go out there and show them what we're made of. And if the generals don't like it, they can find someone else to fight this war.

If you are quoting someone who has quoted another source, then you must use single quotation marks to indicate a quote within a quote.

Examples: Joe turned to his buddy and said, "Remember the drill sergeant's warning, 'Don't shoot 'til you see their baby blues.' "

As Joe muttered, "Susan always said, 'I'll see you there first,' " he threw a guarded look over his shoulder.

EXERCISE Following the above examples, correctly punctuate these sentences.

1. I think I lost my mittens the little girl said mournfully.

2. Complete liquidation of assets, according to *Crimes Cost Money,* is not a wise course.

3. *Television Tonight* states, The modern audience is more aware, more discerning. One viewer even told us, I use Dan Rather as my voice coach; I try to model my intonations and inflections on his.

Have your instructor or tutor check your work.

Titles

Titles of works that are too short to be published as one volume, (for example, short poems, one-act plays, magazine articles, songs, short stories, and book chapters) should be enclosed in quotation marks.

Example: "I Could Have Danced All Night" (song)
"The Lottery" (short story)
"The Second Coming" (poem)

EXERCISE   Following the above examples, correctly punctuate these sentences.

1. Tennyson's The Charge of the Light Brigade is one of my favorite poems.
2. I still think America, The Beautiful would be a better national anthem than The Star-Spangled Banner.

Have your instructor or tutor check your work.

Titles of books, magazines, newspapers, plays, television series, and films are italicized when they are printed. If you are typing or writing those titles, you can underline them.

Examples: *Tender Is the Night* (book)
Through the Looking-Glass (book)
Newsweek (magazine)

EXERCISE   Following the above examples, correctly punctuate these sentences.

1. The Castle of Otranto is generally considered to be the first Gothic novel.
2. The Sound of Music was first a successful play and then a successful movie.

Have your instructor or tutor check your work.

Words Used in a Special Sense

If you are qualifying a term or using a word ironically, you should use quotation marks. (If you are referring to a word as a word, use quotation marks, italics, or underlining.)

Examples: For the movie *Mary Poppins,* Disney's people made up "supercalifragilisticexpialidocious" and gave it meaning.

Today's students have trouble using the words "affect" and "effect" correctly. (You may also use *affect* or *effect*—italics for words used as words.)

Most Americans don't realize that "chips" means french fries to a Londoner.

EXERCISE   Following the above examples, correctly punctuate these sentences.

1. Run has multiple meanings; forty-seven, I think.
2. Asking a secretary to xerox may infringe on Xerox's patent; the correct term is photocopy.

Have your instructor or tutor check your work.

Dialogue

Dialogue is the spoken conversation between people; it should always be quoted. To make the reader's task easier, begin a new paragraph every time you change speakers.

Example: Hepsabah was ecstatic.
"Why?" asked Susan. "You look as if you've won the lottery."

"Oh no! It's even better than that."

"Well? I'm waiting for your explanation," Susan said impatiently.

To repeat, dialogue usually belongs in fictional writing, not expository essays; however, dialogue does require quotation marks, and so it is offered to you.

EXERCISE   Following the above example, correctly punctuate these sentences.

1. Mother always liked you better, the elder brother whined.

2. Maybe so, cried the exasperated forty-year-old, but don't you think it's time to forget that and begin living our own lives?

3. Never! I'm scarred for life.

Have your instructor or tutor check your work.

Quotation Marks and Other Punctuation

There are a few simple rules governing quotation marks and other marks of punctuation.

1. A comma or a period always goes *inside* the quotes. There is no exception.

   Examples: "I believe in magic," sighed the young girl.

   In fact, the magazine tried and convicted the pair: "There can be no doubt of their guilt, no question about their dishonesty."

2. A colon or semicolon goes *outside* the quotes.

   Examples: "Run" can mean "a tear in a stocking" or "a type of fast movement"; indeed, it can have multiple meanings.

   The "Gettysburg Address" probably has one of the most-often-quoted opening lines: "Four score and seven years ago. . . ."

3. A question mark, exclamation point, or dash goes *inside* the quotes only when it is part of the material being quoted. If it applies to the whole sentence, then it goes *outside* the quotation marks.

   Examples: Why did he shout, "I hate you!"?

   "I think—," he hesitated and began again, "I think she said, 'Am I late?' "

NOTE: The end punctuation of the material enclosed in single quotes is also the end punctuation for the whole sentence.

PRACTICE 1

After reviewing the rules for using quotation marks, correctly punctuate these sentences.

1. The author could barely hide his disdain, I never write soap operas.

2. The poem Sailing to Byzantium is by William Butler Yeats.

3. Once again, the herd is crying for blood: He has dishonored the office; such transgressions cannot go unpunished.

4. Emily Dickinson had a realistic view of marriage, which she expressed in the following lines: I gave myself to him/And took himself for pay. . . .

5. Nerd, turkey and buster are not flattering terms.

Check the answer key.

Colons (:)

Colons inform the reader that the material following the colon is an explanation, illustration, or example of the material that preceded the colon.

Examples: Please buy me some fruit: apples, peaches, pears, and bananas.

She has all the qualities necessary to be a captain: knowledge of navigation, ability to lead and command, and love of the sea.

The American Short Story: An Intriguing Analysis

NOTE: In the last example, the title and subtitle of a book are separated by a colon, because the subtitle provides additional information about the title.

EXERCISE   Following the above examples, correctly punctuate these sentences.

1. The bargaining team suggested some novel demands paid paternity leave, on-site day care, and time off for excellent attendance.

2. To bake a great cake, do as he suggested 1) buy a box of cake mix, 2) read the directions carefully, 3) follow them, and 4) nap while the cake is baking.

Have your instructor or tutor check your work.

NOTE: Never use a colon to separate a verb from its object or its predicate nominative, or a preposition from its object.

Examples:

Incorrect: For his birthday the toddler wanted: a doll house, a doll carriage, and a wagon.

Correct: For his birthday the toddler wanted a doll house, a doll carriage, and a wagon.

or: For his birthday, the toddler wanted some expensive gifts: a doll house, a doll carriage, and a wagon.

Incorrect: For the position of nursing supervisor, he had interviews with: the nursing staff, the nursing director, the chief of the medical staff, and the board of directors.

Correct: For the position of nursing supervisor, he had interviews with the nursing staff, the nursing director, the chief of the medical staff, and the board of directors.

or: For the position of nursing supervisor, he had interviews with the following: the nursing staff, the nursing director, the chief of the medical staff, and the board of directors.

PRACTICE 2

Correctly punctuate the following sentences.

1. You must always remember one thing how to whistle.

2. *How to Succeed in Bankruptcy A Primer for the Overextended* has already sold over 500,000 copies.

3. The list of demands is never-ending a color television in the staff lounge, free parking spaces, birthdays and anniversaries off, six weeks of paid vacation, a low-cost lunch program, etc.

Check the answer key.

Ellipsis Points

Ellipsis points (or ellipses) indicate to the reader that you have deliberately omitted some part or parts of the material you have quoted. The three spaced periods tell the reader that you did not think it was necessary to quote the material in its entirety.

Examples: 1. "Time and time again . . . one begins to make a profound comment only to realize that the idea is best expressed by a familiar adage."

(This is the complete quote: "Time and time again in conversation—usually boring conversations, I might add—one begins to make a profound comment only to realize that the idea is best expressed by a familiar adage.")

2. "With this excellent resolve for the future, Goodman Brown felt himself justified. . . ." ("Young Goodman Brown" by Nathaniel Hawthorne)

(The complete sentence is "With this excellent resolve for the future, Goodman Brown felt himself justified in making more haste on his present evil purpose.")

NOTE: If the material that has been omitted ends in a period (that is, if nothing further is quoted from the sentence), then the quote will end with four dots—one for the period at the end of the sentence and three for the ellipses.

Hyphens (-) and Dashes (—)

Hyphens and dashes are frequently confused and misused.

- A **hyphen** (a one-space line) is used to separate elements within a *word*.
- A **dash** (a two-space line) is used to separate elements within a *sentence*.

The Hyphen

The hyphen has several uses:

1. *To indicate that a word has been continued from one written line to the next.* When you are writing, it is not always possible to fit a whole word on the end of the typed line. In such a case, it is acceptable to break the word with a hyphen and to continue writing it on the next line.

   Examples: grada-   humani-   super-   in-   unim-
                   tion   tarian   fluous   active peachable

In such a case, however, you must follow the rules for syllabication:

- Never divide a one-syllable word.

   Examples: three, night, clock

- Never leave a one-letter syllable alone on a line.

Incorrect	*Correct*
a-/lone	alone
i-/deal	ideal
i-/conoclast	icono-/clast

If in doubt about correct syllabication, check your dictionary.

2. *To form compound words.* A compound word is composed of two separate words that have been joined to form a new word.

   Examples: steady-state   mother-in-law   rock-ribbed

The process of forming compound words is not rigid. Frequently, the words are initially written as separate words; then, they are hyphenated, and, finally, common usage suggests that they be written as one word.

   Examples: steam ship   steam-ship   steamship
                  home sickness   home-sickness   homesickness

During the intermediate stage, the words should be hyphenated to form one word. If you are unsure whether a compound word is currently hyphenated, check your dictionary.

EXERCISE Following the above examples, correctly punctuate these sentences.

1. The vice principal issued his orders; the man at arms jumped.
2. In Biblical times, each family prayed for a man child.

   Have your instructor or tutor check your work.

3. *To join two words that become a* **compound modifier** *and function as a single adjective does to describe a noun.*

   Examples: gray-green eyes   wind-blown hair   water-logged motor

EXERCISE   Following the above examples, correctly punctuate these sentences.

1. The jewel like colors of his evening clothes have made Charles a name to be reckoned with in the fashion world.
2. Bell bottom trousers made the transition from naval uniform to high fashion.

Have your instructor or tutor check your work.

4. *To join the prefixes* self-, all-, ex-, *and the suffix* -elect *to root words.*

   Examples: ex-spouse   self-control   all-important

5. *To join the elements of an improvised compound word.*

   Examples: smarty-pants   fantasy-land   know-it-all

EXERCISE   Following the above examples, correctly punctuate these sentences.

1. Many Japanese designers are breaking into the ready to wear market.
2. At home wear has captured a large percentage of the suburban retail clothing market.

Have your instructor or tutor check your work.

6. *To join the numerator and the denominator in written fractions, and to join the elements in compound numbers.*

   Examples: nine-tenths   one-fifth   twenty-eight

EXERCISE   Following the above examples, correctly punctuate these sentences.

1. Two thirds of the population owns one quarter of the VCRs.
2. Estimates suggest that seventy eight percent of Americans believe in the institution of marriage.

EXERCISE   Remembering all the rules for using hyphens, correctly punctuate these words.

father in law   _____

well known   _____

four eighths   _____

commander in chief   _____

swept back   _____

governor elect   _____

Have your instructor or tutor check your work.

The Dash

The dash is used in three specific cases:

1. *To indicate a sudden break in thought.*

   Examples: He is the world's worst—no, I won't continue.

   Maybe you're right—but I want to try this first.

2. *To emphasize a parenthetical element.* (Remember: a parenthetical element is an inserted expression that interrupts the thought of the sentence to explain or comment on it.)

   Examples: She was—I thought—a very good chief executive officer.

   It is alleged that he knew—that he *must* have known—that his subordinates were breaking the law.

NOTE: It is also possible to separate parenthetical elements from the rest of the sentence by using commas or parentheses; dashes are sometimes preferred, because they add vigor and emphasis to the interruption.

3. *To set off an appositive or brief summary.*

   Examples: He has everything he needs—except money.

   After a month of bone-chilling cold and mind-rattling wind, our destination was in sight—the tribesmen's camp.

EXERCISE   Following the above examples, correctly punctuate these sentences.

1. After the dance it was such a nice one I thought we could go to the club for drinks.
2. She has vision, competence, and the ability to inspire people everything a CEO should have.

Have your instructor or tutor check your work.

PRACTICE 3

After reviewing the rules for using dashes and hyphens, correctly punctuate these sentences.

1. My brother the one who's the doctor is very soft hearted.
2. I wish I could tell you but I promised!
3. The well known opera star she drinks two thirds of the time has gained weight recently.
4. Thirty two thousand dollars! for a broken finger?
5. The heir apparent has little use for old fashioned conventions.

Check the answer key.

Parentheses () and Brackets []

Parentheses and brackets are both used to enclose material that you are inserting into writing, but there is one important difference between their uses.

Parentheses

Parentheses are used to enclose parenthetical material that is connected in only an indirect way to the sentence in which it is inserted.

Examples: She is (I don't think this can be called gossiping) a terrible cook.

Five or six lights after that (I never was good about directions) you make a left turn.

EXERCISE   Following the above examples, correctly punctuate this sentence.

Water-skiing not my favorite sport is becoming less popular in this area.

Have your instructor or tutor check your work.

Brackets

Brackets, on the other hand, are used to enclose material that you are inserting into a quotation. Their purpose is to decrease your reader's confusion.

Example: "Behind the General [John Smithstone] came his battle-weary men."

In this sentence, the writer seems to be quoting a newspaper report. Because the sentence has been taken out of context, the writer's audience does not know to which general the report was referring. Therefore, the writer included the general's name, but enclosed it in brackets because he or she was inserting the name into quoted material.

Example: "In the fourth year of the High One's reign [1042 B.C.], there came a terrible drought."

In this sentence also, the original reader of the report probably knew during which year there was a drought, but a modern reader of the quoted material would not even know who the "High One" was. So, to lessen the modern reader's confusion, the writer inserted the date and enclosed it in brackets.

Example: "They [the ancient Greeks] believed," continued the speaker, "in a form of life-after-death."

Again, in order to avoid confusing the reader, who was not present at the lecture and so does not know the speaker's topic, the writer inserted the topic into the quote.

Example: Mr. Campbell the noted historian, concurred with the archeologist's findings: "[H]e has established the location of the Temple of Arac beyond a doubt."

In this example, the quote was taken from the last part of a longer sentence, so the first letter of the first word of the sentence was not capitalized in the original quote. However, in the example above, the partial quotation is a complete sentence, and the first letter of the first word must be capitalized. To indicate that the writer altered the original quote, the change is enclosed in brackets.

EXERCISE   Following the above examples, punctuate this sentence.

"These dresses Aran knit and Fair Isles generally cost 2,000 francs $750 each," explained the designer.

Have your instructor or tutor check your work.

PRACTICE 4

Correctly punctuate these sentences, inserting brackets and parentheses where necessary.

1. Since the beginning of the Civil War which should never have been fought, both parties have sought outside help.
2. "When do you plan to go public?" she asked. "Next year 1989?"
3. They decided to operate because the calcification process which still isn't understood had already begun.
4. "Each bushel basket ten pounds costs fifteen dollars," he replied.
5. Henry VIII of England he had six wives was nicknamed "Good King Hal."

Check the answer key.

APPLICATION I

In the blank to the right of each sentence, write *C* if the sentence is correctly punctuated or *P* if there is a punctuation error. Then correct the errors.

1. The Road Not Taken is one of Robert Frost's best known poems.   _____

2. Few people remember its opening lines, though.   _____

3. Had we but world enough, and time . . . was an intriguing introduction to the seminar "Nuclear Freeze."   _____

4. Do you know what the word manatee means? he asked.   _____

5. The corporate board demanded many changes revised travel allowance, increased fees, and more input into scheduling.   _____

6. Supply side economics contends that supply governs the marketplace.   _____

7. Mr. Jackson decided to forego his well paid consulting job and concentrate on counseling drug addicts.   _____

8. "Four score . . . our forefathers . . ." are words that should be recognized by most people.   _____

9. Diagnosing the problem is quite difficult; one must consider every aspect of the situation.   _____

10. Warren G. Harding most people don't recognize the name was once president of the United States.   _____

11. "That year 1660 proved to be a momentous one for England."   _____

12. I believe I must believe that everything will turn out all right.   _____

13. The ad stated several qualifications literacy, driver's license, and a respectable appearance.   _____

14. My ex spouse we're not on speaking terms is quite a swinger, I understand.   _____

15. Time will tell is a favorite saying of my mother's.   _____

16. "Ten years ago 1928 Americans were generally optimistic about the future."   _____

17. Tyger! Tyger! burning bright/In the forests of the night are the first lines of a poem by William Blake.   _____

18. Tomorrow or is it the next day? she's supposed to enter the hospital.   _____

19. "I do so love to listen to you play," the young lady murmured.   _____

20. The prize-winning Belgian shepherd soon sickened and died.   _____

Check the answer key.

APPLICATION II

Read the following paragraph carefully and proofread it for punctuation errors. Write the editing symbol *P* above sentences with punctuation errors, and then correct the errors.

(1) Few people realize how proverb ridden our lives are. (2) Time and time again in conversations usually boring conversations, I might add one begins to make a profound comment only to realize that the idea is best expressed by a familiar adage. (3) Then, insult is added to injury with the realization that the proverb need not be completely stated; simply saying the first few words generally suffices because, in all probability, the listener can supply the omitted words. (4) Here are some examples When in Rome, A stitch in time, and Don't count your chickens (5) These examples support the thesis very well indeed because of their familiarity. (6) No one has to think twice before responding. (7) Why even on Mr. Reginald Dunsworthy's award winning game show Choose Your Mate! a contestant could feel confident and answer immediately.

Check the answer key.

APPLICATION III

Read the essay carefully and proofread it for punctuation errors. Write the editing symbol *P* above sentences with punctuation errors, and then correct the errors.

(1) "if I were a rich man . . ." begins the famous song, but money is money. (2) No matter who you are, it never hurts to have a little extra around. (3) The problem is how to make that extra money. (4) Unless you are an expert counterfeiter in which case you, literally, would be making money or a safe-cracker which is as is the previously mentioned occupation illegal, there are basically only two ways of acquiring that elusive green. (5) One of the two ways is far less demanding than the other, but it does not provide rewards or benefits outside those of a financial nature. (6) The less demanding of these money-making systems is through inheritance; for the rest of the world, there is always the working profession, the job. (7) To inherit or to earn these are the possibilities.

(8) Contrary to what Smith-Barney might advertise We make money the old-fashioned way

we earn it the old fashioned way of making money is to inherit it. (9) It is really a simple matter. (10) One day, you have your hand in your father's pocket; the next day, you find his hand in yours. (11) One day you are poor; the next day, the Porsche arrives. (12) The only criterion for this type of work is a rich parent, or two rich parents who have willed to you the entire family fortune and estate. (13) The inheritor inherits and becomes instantly independent and wealthy.

(14) On the other hand, the worker, from a traditional family, must struggle to provide for himself. (15) He must create his own wealth and declare his own independence. (16) He may receive help from his parents, but they are not the source of his money. (17) He is given neither estate nor fortune. (18) He must earn all that he needs and learn the ways of the world.

(19) The inheritor is surely contented, but, as is the case with all things, there are disadvantages to even his way of life. (20) In all the splendor of a regal existence, the inheritor misses life's simple pleasures. (21) He does not need to worry about mundane matters mortgages, bills, debts, tax forms, pay cuts, or layoffs. (22) He must stomach total relaxation, because he cannot enjoy a forty hour week. (23) The heir's life must be empty without the need to clean the house, cook meals, or do the food shopping. (24) Servants are such an encumbrance to his life, because they prevent him from doing any number of these exciting tasks. (25) How one must pity the inheritor's existence, and praise the worker's life, for the worker alone experiences all of these things on a regular basis.

(26) On a more serious level, the worker's life is undoubtedly the more difficult of the two. (27) Yet, hardship produces certain characteristics a sense of accomplishment, confidence, and self-respect. (28) The inheritor has the ability to acquire more money through the use of his money, and, although this may appear to be a step forward, it is simply the increasing of the family's accounts. (29) It is not a personal achievement. (30) The inheritor does nothing; therefore, he must lack a sense of accomplishment his accountants are the force behind his wealth. (31) The worker can see what he has done and can prosper intellectually and emotionally.

(32) Thus, though the inheritor may have considerably more funds than the worker, he is very much the less wealthy of the two. (33) He does not experience the hardships of the working man, and without struggle, there can be no gain. (34) The inheritor comes to know only money,

while the worker knows himself and others. (35) Both seek the green of their goals, but the worker is far richer by virtue of his having worked for position, salary, and family. (36) To be given everything is to lose a sense of value; to gain a sense of value is to be richer than even the richest man.

Check the answer key.

APPLICATION IV

Proofread a rough draft of a paper of your own. Check carefully for punctuation errors. Place a *P* beside any error, and correct all errors. Show your revisions to your instructor or tutor.

PART VI

The Correct Forms

Misplaced and Dangling Modifiers

OBJECTIVES:

1. To recognize words or phrases that are misplaced in a sentence.

2. To recognize dangling participles and other dangling modifiers.

3. To recognize split infinitives.

4. To correct misplaced modifiers, dangling modifiers, and split infinitives.

5. To proofread a paper for misplaced modifiers, dangling modifiers, and split infinitives. The editing symbols are *mm* for misplaced modifier and *dm* for dangling modifier.

KEY CONCEPT: Misplaced and dangling modifiers are words or phrases that confuse the meaning of a sentence. They are easily recognized, because their position in the sentence makes the sentence seem meaningless or unclear.

Misplaced Modifiers

Some words, particularly adverbs that modify (describe) the verb, work well wherever they are placed in a sentence. Consider the following sentences:

> Jerry *happily* looked at Tina.
> *Happily,* Jerry looked at Tina.
> Jerry looked *happily* at Tina.
> Jerry looked at Tina *happily*.

Although the word *happily* changes its position in the sentence, the meaning is the same in each sentence.

However, this is not the case with other words and phrases. There are three major types of misplaced modifiers:

1. Single words in a sentence.
2. Phrases or clauses in a sentence.
3. Split word order in a sentence.

Each of these problems needs to be corrected.

Single-Word Misplaced Modifiers

Unlike the previous example, some words must have an exact place in a sentence. The words *only,* *nearly,* and *almost* can change their places in a sentence, but the meaning of the sentence changes, also.

286

Examples: *Only* Harold received a score of 70 on the test.
Harold received *only* a score of 70 on the test.
Harold received a score of *only* 70 on the test.
Harold received a score of 70 *only* on the test.

In the first sentence, *Only Harold received a score of 70 on the test*, the meaning is clear: one person in the class scored 70, and Harold was the person.

In the second sentence, *Harold received only a score of 70 on the test*, the meaning is clear; Harold did not receive any comments other than his score.

In the third sentence, *Harold received a score of only 70 on the test*, poor Harold should have done better.

In the fourth sentence, *Harold received a score of 70 only on the test*, it seems that Harold has not studied for this particular test; on others, he has done better.

Obviously, the placement of the word *only* is critical to the meaning of the sentence.

EXERCISE Correct the following sentences. Use the meaning indicated in parentheses to determine the position of the word.

1. Jane paid nearly a thousand dollars for a new couch. (You want to say that Jane came close to buying a new couch but didn't.)

_____

_____

2. Christopher almost played a perfect game. (You want to say that Christopher's game was not quite perfect.)

_____

_____

Have your instructor or tutor check your work.

Phrase and Clause Misplaced Modifiers

Phrases and clauses should be placed next to the word that they modify. When they are placed in another position in the sentence, the sentence becomes confused and often ludicrous.

Examples: 1. The new book was read by every student *on the second shelf*.

Explanation: Were the students on the second shelf? One hopes that they were not; it would be quite crowded. Consider what was on the second shelf.

Correction: The new book *on the second shelf* was read by every student.

2. The cowboy was thrown by the bull *with a leather vest*.

Explanation: A bull would look rather ridiculous with a vest, so the phrase *with a leather vest* is misplaced.

Correction: The cowboy *with a leather vest* was thrown by the bull.

3. The train station was located by a river *which was made of red brick.*

   Explanation: Most rivers are not made of red brick, so the clause *which was made of red brick* must modify the station.

   Correction: The train station, *which was made of red brick,* was located by a river.

EXERCISE Correct the misplaced modifiers in the following sentences.

1. The lamp shone brightly through the window with the ceramic base.

   _____

   _____

2. The opera singer was upstaged by the mime with the robust voice.

   _____

   _____

Have your instructor or tutor check your work.

Unnecessary Splitting of Word Order

Do not split subjects from verbs, verb phrases, and verbs and their modifiers, unless there is a good reason for doing so.

Examples: 1. You would have, if you had listened to me, finished hours ago.

   In this sentence, the verb phrase *would have finished* is interrupted by the clause.

   Correction: If you had listened to me, you *would have finished* your paper two hours ago.

   2. She, in my opinion, is a good doctor.

   In this sentence, the subject *she* is separated from the verb *is.*

   Correction: In my opinion, she is a good doctor.

EXERCISE Correct the following sentences.

1. Jason was, if I remember correctly, made valedictorian of our class.

   _____

2. Jean, during the test, changed her answer four times.

   _____

Have your instructor or tutor check your work.

The following sentences demonstrate correctly split word order:

Examples: 1. He has already finished his paper.

In this sentence, the adverb *already* splits the verb phrase *has finished*.

2. The engineers have often been told not to drink on the job.

In this sentence, the adverb *often* divides the verb phrase *have been told*.

These sentences would sound awkward and overly formal if the adverbs were placed after the verb phrases.

Dangling Participles and Dangling Modifiers

A misplaced modifier can be corrected merely by changing the word order of the sentence. On the other hand, a dangling modifier is a more serious error. Since the dangling modifier does not describe any noun or pronoun, the entire sentence must be revised.

Dangling Participles

A **participle** is formed in one of two ways:

1. a verb + *ing* (a present participle)
2. a verb + *ed,* or another past-tense form (a past participle)

Participles are used as adjectives. (See Chapters 2 and 3.)

Examples: bake + d = baked
The apple pie, baked by my mother, won first prize.

write + ing = writing
Susan, writing in her diary, lost track of time.

A participle is "dangling" if, for example, it comes at the beginning of the sentence and does not modify the subject of the sentence. *A participle at the beginning of a sentence must modify the subject of the sentence.* To correct dangling participles, make certain that the participle modifies the correct noun or pronoun.

Examples: 1. Riding his bicycle down the road, a dog attacked Bill.

Did a dog ride his bicycle? Or did Bill?

Correction: Riding his bicycle down the road, Bill was attacked by a dog.

2. Written by Faulkner, we have been reading the novel *Go Down, Moses.*

Needless to say, *we,* the subject, was not written by Faulkner.

Correction: We have been reading the novel *Go Down, Moses,* written by Faulkner.

Other Dangling Modifiers

If an **infinitive** (*to* + a verb; for example, *to run, to jump*) or an infinitive phrase begins the sentence, it must modify the subject. It acts in the same manner as a participial phrase. (See Chapters 2 and 3.) To correct the dangling infinitive, make sure that the subject performs the action of the infinitive.

Examples: 1. To join the service, a test had to be passed by Helen.

Tests do not join the service, so you must choose another subject. In this case, use *Helen* as the subject of the sentence.

Correction: To join the service, Helen had to pass a test.

2. To party all night, much stamina is needed.

Obviously, stamina does not party; people do.

Correction: To party all night, one needs much stamina.

Prepositional phrases can also be dangling modifiers if their placement in the sentence is confusing. To correct such a problem, make sure that the prepositional phrase is next to the word it modifies.

Examples: 1. At the age of sixteen, the birthday present was a Mustang convertible.

A birthday present is not sixteen, and the phrase *at the age of sixteen* does not modify any word in the sentence.

Correction: At the age of sixteen, she received a Mustang convertible from her father.

2. As a college freshman, the role of Othello was challenging.

The phrase *As a college freshman* does not modify any word in the sentence.

Correction: As a college freshman, Steve found the role of Othello challenging.

PRACTICE 1

Rewrite the following sentences to eliminate the dangling participles or misplaced modifiers. In the blank at the right, identify whether the error is a dangling modifier (*dm*) or a misplaced modifier (*mm*).

1. To run in the Boston Marathon, many hours of practice were needed by Beth.

_____   _____

2. Dancing all night, the dawn was seen.

_____   _____

3. To earn an *A*, many hours of study are needed.

_____   _____

4. Written by Jan, the teacher received her report.

_____   _____

5. At the age of six, our family moved to Colorado.

_____   _____

Have your instructor or tutor check your work.

Split Infinitives

Usually, the parts of an infinitive (*to* + a verb) should not be split.

Examples: 1. To quickly run away from the kidnappers was his goal.

   Correction: To run quickly away from the kidnappers was his goal.

2. To quietly leave was the young girl's objective.

   Correction: To leave quietly was the young girl's objective.

There are some cases in which splitting an infinitive is permissible; sometimes the sentence may sound overly formal if the infinitive is not split. However, you might decide to reword the sentence.

EXERCISE   Rewrite the following sentences to correct the split infinitives.

1. The instructor told the class to carefully read the assignment.

_____

_____

2. The purpose of this exercise is to quickly identify your mistakes.

_____

_____

Have your instructor or tutor check your work.

APPLICATION I

If the sentence contains a misplaced modifier or split infinitive, put *mm* in the blank, and correct the sentence. If the sentence contains a dangling modifier, put *dm* in the blank, and correct the sentence. If the sentence is correct, place a *C* in the blank.

1. There are two weeks only left before summer vacation. _____

2. Margaret nearly fainted when she saw the phone bill. _____

3. The athletes frequently were told to practice and to lift weights. _____

4. While hanging by a thread, the fly was attacked by the spider. _____

5. In order to join the army, Ted had to take a physical and get his parents'

   permission. _____

6. The lecture on world health problems was held on Tuesday night. _____

7. Al wants to, if at all possible, pass his economics examination. _____

8. I told him on Friday to meet me at the train station. _____

9. My car was towed to the gas station which had a flat tire. _____

10. The house destroyed by the hurricane had been my great-grandmother's. _____

11. The bright light was reflected in the mirror hanging from the ceiling. _____

12. Mr. Smythe with a cane bottom sat in a chair. _____

13. Students succeed in college who study diligently. _____

14. When judging other people, Agatha is always fair. _____

15. The robber mugged the old lady with a masked face. _____

16. To completely fulfill the requirements, you must submit a twenty-page report. _____

17. After studying all day, the party was attended by the girls. _____

18. In her opinion, all teachers are demanding. _____

19. The vagrant with his police dog was approached by the officer. _____

20. The horse was ridden by the best jockey with the star on his forehead. _____

Check the answer key.

APPLICATION II

If a sentence in the following passage contains a misplaced modifier or split infinitive, place *mm* beside the error, and correct it. If a sentence has a dangling participle or dangling modifier, place a *dm* above the sentence, and correct the error. If a sentence is correct, mark it *C*.

(1) Shaking with a tremendous jolt and finally stopping, the middle-aged man only could push the car to the curb. (2) He recognized that it was time to buy an obviously new car. (3) Fortunately, his car had rolled to a halt just in front of a car dealership. (4) The man, unfortunately, had a hundred dollars nearly in his wallet. (5) He knew he would have trouble trading his rusty wreck of a car for a newer automobile. (6) A dealer approached him with shifty eyes.

(7) "Interested in a slightly used car?" the man queried.

(8) "Sure, we are," responded the salesman, "if it's still running, or if we can sell it for junk."

(9) "Okay—take a look at my car," the owner replied.

(10) The car looked to the dealer with a rusty fender like a mammoth pile of glass and twisted metal. (11) Hanging by a bolt, the man gazed at the car. (12) The yellow left fender chose that moment to fall from the body of the car. (13) And, kicked once too often, a back tire emitted a dying sound.

(14) With his loud tie flapping in the breeze, the salesman turned to his customer and said, "I'm sorry. (15) There is nothing we can do for you unless you want to only see a new car with all the accessories."

Check the answer key.

APPLICATION III

Read the following passage carefully. If a sentence contains a misplaced modifier or split infinitive, put *mm* beside the error, and correct the sentence. If a sentence contains a dangling modifier, place *dm* above the error, and correct the sentence. If a sentence is correct, mark it *C*.

(1) A few days ago, I decided to visit the stream where I played as a child. (2) I remembered the summer excursions to the stream. (3) I went with a friend usually. (4) We descended the embankment on all fours because it was steep. (5) It then only took us a while to get used to stream-walking. (6) To be avoided at all costs, this walking consisted of leaping and bounding from rock to rock in the stream. (7) Even though it would have been much faster to walk beside

the stream, stream-walking gave one a sense of accomplishment. (8) Each new step was a hurdle to be cleared; each yard gained was a victory. (9) Where the banks narrowed from fifteen to five feet, jumping and bounding, we eventually arrived at our favorite part of the stream. (10) Here, the banks that could be moistened and molded were made of clay. (11) We lingered at that spot. (12) Here, we tried to dam often the creek. (13) Never were we successful. (14) By the time we left the clay banks, our faces were dirty, and we looked like little men with beards. (15) Soon afterward, we found walking sticks to help us, and we completed our journey on three legs instead of two. (16) I would arrive home from the stream with a pail of crayfish in tow cold and wet. (17) I would dry off and eat a hot meal. (18) Just returned from fabulous lands, I felt like a famous explorer. (19) The daydream evaporated. (20) It has been ten years since I last walked on the rocks and explored the stream. (21) However, I have now new challenges, new places to explore.

Check the answer key.

APPLICATION IV

Proofread a paper of your own for misplaced and dangling modifiers. Place the editing symbols *mm* and *dm* next to any errors. Correct any errors. Show your revisions to your instructor or tutor.

Adjectives and Adverbs

OBJECTIVES:

1. To be able to define, identify, and use adjectives correctly.

2. To be able to define, identify, and use adverbs correctly.

3. To be able to use the editing symbol for adjectives and adverbs (*Ad*) when proofreading.

KEY CONCEPT:

Both adjectives and adverbs are *descriptive* words. They tell more about the words they describe, without changing the essence of the word.

Functions of Adjectives and Adverbs

Adjectives. An **adjective** describes a noun or a pronoun.

Examples: The *blue* dress is mine.
She seems *distraught*.

Blue tells you the color of my dress; it provides you with more specific information about my dress.

Distraught tells you about the person's state of mind; again, it provides more specific information.

Adverbs. An **adverb** describes a verb, an adjective, or another adverb.

Examples: The child cried *loudly*.
The octogenarian looked *very* tired.
Please drive my new car *really carefully*.

Loudly tells you *how* the baby cried; it describes the verb.

Very tells you *how* tired the person looked; it describes the adjective.

Really tells you *how* carefully the new car should be driven; it describes the adverb *carefully*, which tells *how* the new car should be driven.

In other words, adverbs frequently answer the question "How?"

- How did the baby cry?   (*loudly*)
- How tired was the person?   (*very*)
- How should the car be driven?   (*carefully*)
- How carefully should the new car be driven?   (*really*)

Notice that adjectives and adverbs usually are placed near the words they describe.

EXERCISE   In each sentence, add an appropriate adjective or adverb.

1. The horse pranced ————————— .

2. The matron ————————— shook her head.

3. Each spring, ————————— flowers carpet this meadow.

4. At just that moment, she appeared and ————————— surveyed the room.

Have your instructor or tutor check your work.

Although the process of adding adjectives and adverbs to a sentence seems easy, the writer will sometimes encounter problems. There are some important rules to remember in using adjectives and adverbs; we will discuss these one at a time.

1. *Use an adverb to describe a verb.*

   Examples: 1. The teacher questioned me harsh.

   Harsh is an adjective; an adverb is needed here to describe *how* the teacher questioned.

   Correction: The teacher questioned me harshly.

   Harshly is an adverb describing the verb *questioned.*

   2. The dog growled fierce at the postman.

   Fierce is an adjective; an adverb is needed here to describe *how* the dog growled.

   Correction: The dog growled fiercely at the postman.

   Fiercely is an adverb describing the verb *growled.*

EXERCISE   Using the above sentences as models, insert the adverbial form of the word given in parentheses into the blank.

1. He annoyed everyone by talking ————————— throughout the exam. (loud)

2. She dresses ————————— . (careless)

Have your instructor or tutor check your work.

2. *Use an adverb to modify an adjective or another adverb.*

   Examples: 1. The bad injured lion was tormented by the hyena.

   Bad is an adjective; an adverb is needed here to describe the adjective *injured.*

   Correction: The badly injured lion was tormented by the hyena.

   Badly is an adverb describing how injured the lion was.

2. The class worked real hard to finish the project on time.

   Real is an adjective; an adverb is needed here to describe the adverb *hard*.

   Correction: The class worked really hard to finish the project on time.

   Really describes how hard the class worked.

EXERCISE   Using the above sentences as models, insert the adverbial form of the word given in parentheses into the blank.

1. The broker promised to call his elderly client _____ soon. (real)

2. The toddler was _____ adamant about eating the brussel sprouts. (vehement)

Have your instructor or tutor check your work.

3. *Use an adjective to modify the subject* in Sentence Format 4. (See Chapter 5.)

   Examples: 1. Many citizens in totalitarian countries are unhappy with their governments.

   In this sentence, the predicate adjective, *unhappy*, tells the reader more about the subject, *citizens*.

   2. The giraffe was ill because he had eaten too many different kinds of grasses.

   Likewise, in this sentence *ill* describes the animal.

The most frequent source of problems is confusion over such verbs as *appear, become, be, feel, look, seem, smell, sound,* and *taste*. The verbs *become, be,* and *seem* are always linking verbs, and these other verbs (*appear, feel, look, smell, sound,* and *taste*) sometimes act as linking verbs.

Examples: Susan looked tired.

   Susan appeared angry.

In this example, *looked* is functioning as a linking verb, so it is followed by the predicate adjective *tired*.

Examples: Harold became angry after he learned the truth.

   Harold was angry after he learned the truth.

When these verbs act as linking verbs, they may be followed by a predicate adjective. However, sometimes *appear, feel, look, smell, sound,* and *taste* express action.

Examples: The little girl felt ill.

S   V   ADV
The little <u>girl</u> <u><u>felt</u></u> carefully under the pillow for the gift left by the tooth fairy.

In the first sentence, *felt* is a linking verb followed by a predicate adjective. In the second sentence, *felt* is an action verb followed by the adverb *carefully*.

                             S   LV   PA
Examples: That <u>pastry</u> <u><u>tasted</u></u> good.

                                  S   V
That pastry <u>chef</u> <u><u>tasted</u></u> every one of his creations.

Consequently, to avoid misusing adjectives and adverbs, you should analyze the word's function in the sentence and then decide which form of the word to use.

EXERCISE Using the above sentences as models, insert the correct form of the word given in parentheses into the blank.

1. The derelict looked _____ (weary).

2. The derelict looked _____ at me. (weary)

3. The baby smelled _____ after her bath. (fresh)

4. The baby smelled the pungent fruit _____ . (wary)

Have your instructor or tutor check your work.

In many cases, you can form adverbs from adjectives simply by adding *-ly* to the adjective.

Examples: *Adjective*   *Adverb*

                constant   constantly
                happy   happily
                loud   loudly
                sad   sadly

EXERCISE Write the adverbial form for each of the adjectives.

     Adjective   *Adverb*

1. sorrowful   _____

2. broad   _____

3. careful   _____

4. suspicious   _____

5. pretty   _____

6. penitent   _____

7. wary   _____

8. precise   _____

9. quaint   _____

10. morose   _____

Have your instructor or tutor check your work.

However, it is not that simple in all cases. In some instances, the *-ly* form is the adjectival form.

Examples: She is a *friendly* child.

The defendant answered the question in a *gentlemanly* way.

In other cases, the adjective and adverb have the same form.

Examples: The *barefoot* boy seemed unaware of his poverty. (adjective)

They enjoyed walking *barefoot* through the sand. (adverb)

When in doubt about the correct form of a word, consult your dictionary.

PRACTICE 1

In Column A, list each word that is used as an adjective or adverb in the following paragraph. Do not list the articles *a, an,* or *the.* Label each word *Adj.* for adjective or *Adv.* for adverb. Then, in Column B, list the word that each adjective and adverb describes.

The Fourth of July is really a great holiday. Nationalistic fervor and historic patriotism combine perfectly with warm summer weather to produce a day that everyone fully enjoys. There is hardly any dissension with regard to this holiday. Most people willingly and joyfully participate in the celebration of our national heritage.

Column A   *Column B*

Column A	*Column B*
_____	_____
_____	_____

Check the answer key.

Descriptive modifiers change their form to indicate their function as either adjectives or adverbs. In addition, adjectives change their form to indicate degrees of quantity or quality.

Examples: She is a *smart* girl. (Positive form.)

She is the *smarter* girl. (Comparative form; two girls are being compared; one is judged to be smarter than the other.)

She is the *smartest* girl. (Superlative form; three or more girls are being compared; one is judged to be the smartest of them all.)

The *positive* form is simply the basic adjective.

The *comparative* form compares two persons or items. You either add *-er* to the positive adjective or place the word *more* before it.

Examples:

Positive	*Comparative*
tall	taller
big	bigger
fat	fatter
beautiful	more beautiful
handsome	more handsome
wicked	more wicked

In general, words of one syllable add *-er* to form the comparative, and words of two or more syllables add the word *more*. However, there are exceptions which are listed below.

The *superlative* form compares three or more persons or items. You either add *-est* to the positive adjective or place the word *most* before it.

Examples:

Positive	*Comparative*	*Superlative*
slow	slower	slowest
small	smaller	smallest
thin	thinner	thinnest
foolish	more foolish	most foolish
interesting	more interesting	most interesting
hideous	more hideous	most hideous

Again, the general rule applies for deciding which format to use when indicating the superlative. Some words have irregular forms:

Exceptions:

Positive	*Comparative*	*Superlative*
bad	worse	worst
good	better	best
little	less	least

Try to remember them.

PRACTICE 2

Write the comparative and superlative forms for each of the adjectives.

Positive	Comparative	Superlative
1. gaunt	_____	_____
2. tiny	_____	_____
3. high-minded	_____	_____
4. flexible	_____	_____
5. shrewd	_____	_____
6. sleepy	_____	_____
7. obvious	_____	_____
8. crazy	_____	_____
9. gaudy	_____	_____
10. vivid	_____	_____

Check the answer key.

Because adjectives and adverbs are *descriptive* words, they are also *limiting* words; another way to say this is that adjectives and adverbs make the words they modify more specific and concrete.

Examples:		
dress (general noun)	If you try to imagine the concept "dress," there are many different fashions, colors, etc., that you might consider.
blue dress (modified noun)	The adjective "blue" limits the "dress" and eliminates some choices.
cornflower blue silk dress (limited noun)	The noun is limited even more. You now know the specific shade of blue and the type of material the dress is made of.
cornflower blue silk shirtwaist dress (specific noun)	By adding another adjective, you are telling your reader the style of the dress you are describing. Obviously, it will be much easier for the reader to imagine "a cornflower blue silk shirtwaist dress" than it will be for him or her to imagine "a dress."

The same is true for adverbs. By adding them to verbs, you can make the action more specific and concrete.

Examples: speaks (general verb)
speaks slowly (modified verb)
speaks slowly and distinctly (limited verb)
speaks slowly, distinctly, and defiantly (specific verb)

You should also notice that when you *limit* a noun or a verb (when you add *specific* adjectives and adverbs), you control the writing process and, thus, prevent any misunderstanding on the part of your reader. For example, if you provide your reader with a general word (such as *dress*), he or she may think of the style, color, and material that he or she is most familiar with; that may not be what you, the writer, had in mind. However, because you did not provide specific details, the reader is entitled to use his or her own imagination. Therefore, to prevent any misunderstandings, be as *concrete and specific* as you can.

EXERCISE   Limit each of the given nouns and verbs by adding adjectives and adverbs to them.

1. general noun   child

   modified noun   _____

   limited noun   _____

   specific noun   _____

2. general noun   evening

   modified noun   _____

   limited noun   _____

   specific noun   _____

3. general verb   plays

   modified verb   _____

   limited verb   _____

   specific verb   _____

4. general verb   drives

   modified verb   _____

   limited verb   _____

   specific verb   _____

5. general verb   dances

   modified verb   _____

   limited verb   _____

   specific verb   _____

Have your instructor or tutor check your work.

APPLICATION I

In the blank to the right of each sentence, write *C* if all the adjectives and adverbs are correctly used. Write *Ad* if there is an error; then, correct the error.

1. The new ambassador behaved very foolish the other night. _____

2. She always tries to act proper. _____

3. After all that, he developed into a very prim person. _____

4. Although the play seemed interesting, the audience acted boringly. _____

5. Jennifer is cutest than Samantha. _____

6. Of all my acquaintances, he is the wiser. _____

7. Christopher was voted "More Likely to Succeed" for the Class of '64. _____

8. Because the child was upset, she ran directly to her mother. _____

9. He dresses carelessly. _____

10. Politicians should take their responsibilities serious. _____

11. The child danced a happily little jig around the room. _____

12. This foul weather tempers my normal optimistic outlook on life. _____

13. The child greeted his new teacher guardedly. _____

14. Lately, interior decorators seem to prefer exotic plants for their clients' offices. _____

15. His boldly plaid tie clashed with his sombre suit. _____

16. The supervisor looked suspicious at her wayward employee. _____

17. The injured beagle snapped savagely at the extended hand of mercy. _____

18. The bigger Christmas gift arrived after the other four had been opened. _____

19. This year's inflation rate is the lower of the last decade. _____

20. Fortunately, the young man decided that the salary increase was sufficiently

    high to justify his staying with the company. _____

Check the answer key.

APPLICATION II

Rewrite each sentence to make it as specific and concrete as possible by adding adjectives and adverbs.

1. The dog growled at the person.

_____

2. The cost of housing has risen lately.

_____

3. The parcel arrived a while ago.

_____

4. She is such a bad driver that terrible things will probably happen to her.

_____

_____

5. Cigarettes may be bad for you, according to some reports.

_____

Have your instructor or tutor check your work.

APPLICATION III

Proofread the following paragraph for adjectival and adverbial errors. If the sentence is correct, write *C* in the margin. Circle the errors and write *Ad* in the margin. Then correct all the mistakes.

(1) Writing good is a lost art. (2) Many people nowadays think that only cranky and crotchety old English professors are worried about the written word. (3) The vastly majority of the populace stout and adamant maintains an attitude of studied indifference to the basic principles of writing; few people express any interest in the elements of fine writing. (4) This attitude is evidently everywhere. (5) Television and radio commercials persistent and consistent abuse grammar and syntax in the more shameful manner. (6) When taken to task public for their incorrect usage, most copywriters claim "poetic license." (7) Even journalists have fallen prey to the modern disregard for the elements of style. (8) Despite the obviously fact that the written word provides their livelihood, some newspaper writers and columnists seem to adhere to the belief that "The message is all-important—never mind spelling correct." (9) Such an

attitude represents a dramatic shift from the days when Marshall McLuhan proclaimed "The medium is the message." (10) Although some people in public relations still seem to think that style counts and they package their products very careful, most people would prefer to dispense with writing altogether and just talk on the phone.

Check the answer key.

APPLICATION IV

Proofread the following paragraph for adjectival and adverbial errors. If a sentence is correct, write *C* in the margin next to it. Circle the errors and write *Ad* in the margin. Then correct all the mistakes.

(1) If my fairy godmother came up to me and granted me my choice of a lifelong companion, I have a well idea of what qualifications are required to fill the position. (2) I can visualize her face now: longer brown hair falling to the center of her back, brightly blue eyes enhanced by perfect-applied make-up, and a nicely proportioned heart-shaped face. (3) In addition, her body has eye-catching curves, which are accented by her longer legs. (4) All in all, her physical appearance seems pleasant. (5) My companion's gorgeous face complements her perfect-formed body, but these are just the surface attributes of the most wonderful woman alive. (6) Beneath the high-polished looks lie the effervescent personality, consisting of a great sense of humor, a kind heart, and the most generousest soul. (7) Furthermore, her witty and refreshing humor goes hand-in-hand with her exceptional intelligence. (8) I must be able to converse serious with her one minute and then be able to giggle and play the next. (9) Indeed, if I were granted a woman such as this, I would be the happier man in the world. (10) True, I would have a dream companion.

Check the answer key.

APPLICATION V

Proofread a paper of your own carefully for adjectival and adverbial errors. When you find a mistake, circle it and write *Ad* in the margin. Then correct the error. Finally, show the revised essay to your instructor or tutor.

20

Diction

OBJECTIVES: 1. To learn to choose the words used in an essay carefully, in order to express your precise meaning.

2. To learn to edit your essays for poor word choice.

3. To learn to use the correct editing symbol (*D*) for word choice.

KEY CONCEPT: When you think, you use words; likewise, in writing and in speech, you express your thoughts by using words. Therefore, your choice of words is very important. If you choose inappropriate or inexact words, your meaning may get lost, and you may confuse the reader. So you must use correct diction (word choice) when you are writing.

Vocabularies

Everyone has *three vocabulary levels*: speaking, writing, and reading.

Speaking Vocabulary

Your speaking vocabulary contains the fewest words. Most people tend to use the same words over and over again, because they can rely on additional aspects of the communication process, not just their diction, to convey their meaning to their audience. For example, they can use voice intonations and inflections, facial expressions, and hand gestures. In addition, if speakers are not communicating successfully with their audience, they can expect some reaction from their listeners. This reaction will tell them that they are not conveying their messages, and they then have another chance to reword their thoughts.

Writing Vocabulary

Your writing vocabulary contains your speaking vocabulary, plus some additional words to add style and a formal tone to your writing.

Examples: We had a *good* vacation. (speaking)
We had an *interesting* vacation. (writing)

He's an *okay boss*. (speaking)
He's an *effective supervisor*. (writing)

Reading Vocabulary

Your reading vocabulary is the largest because, in addition to encompassing your speaking and writing vocabularies, it also contains your recognition vocabulary. Your **recognition vocabulary** is all the words that you recognize when you read and that you can understand in a general way, because you are able to use context clues to decipher their meanings. However, you are not familiar enough with these words and their meanings to be able to use them confidently in your writing and speaking.

Examples: We had an *interesting* vacation. (writing)
This year, our vacation was an *edifying* experience. (reading)

He's an *effective* supervisor. (writing)
He's an *assiduous* worker and an *effective, solicitous supervisor*. (reading)

Obviously, your goal should be to increase your reading vocabulary, to incorporate your reading vocabulary into your writing, and to upgrade your speaking vocabulary by including some of your writing vocabulary in it.

EXERCISE   Improve each of the following sentences by substituting more precise words for the italicized ones.

1. According to the critics, this play is *nice*.

   _____

   _____

2. The letter of recommendation states that Marsha Gerard is a *good* worker.

   _____

   _____

3. Joe labored long and hard and finally produced a *fine* dinner.

   _____

   _____

4. Yesterday, Hal and Susan *made* a new video game.

   _____

   _____

5. We all decided that it would be fun to *go* to New Orleans.

   _____

   _____

   Have your instructor or tutor check your work.

Using Appropriate Language

Besides trying to improve and upgrade your vocabulary level, you must also choose *appropriate language* when you are writing. However, a writer sometimes forgets to target his word choice to his audience and, therefore, his message is lost. This usually happens if you use the following words:

- jargon
- slang
- obsolete and archaic words
- pompous language

Jargon

Jargon, or technical language, is appropriate diction in a particular situation. However, once you leave the specific environment in which the language functions effectively, jargon becomes incomprehensible.

> **Examples:** "Stat. Code 99. Bring cart and I-V pole."
> This is appropriate in a hospital setting.
>
> "The tranny, the cams, and the PCV all need replacing."
> This is appropriate in an automobile repair shop.

Therefore, restrict your use of jargon to its natural setting. When writing for a general audience, do not use jargon.

Slang

Slang should not be used in expository writing. Frequently, the precise meaning of a slang word is unclear, so its use contributes to confusion and imprecise thinking. Also, slang words vary from place to place and from time to time. Therefore, by using slang, you lose control of your written thoughts and risk your reader's misunderstanding your ideas.

> **Examples:** What was once "swell" became "boss" and was transformed into "bad."
> (All of these words express approval and delight.)
>
> Similarly, "aced out" and "lucked out" both mean that one was fortunate.

Obsolete and Archaic Words

Obsolete words are those that are no longer used.

> **Examples:** *baseborn,* meaning "illegitimate"
> *begat,* meaning "conceived"

Archaic words are old-fashioned words that are rarely used now.

> **Examples:** *thou   thine   aeroplane*

It is best not to use obsolete and archaic words in your writing for two reasons:

1. Your reader may not understand the word.
2. Such wording calls attention to itself and, thereby, distracts the reader from your message.

Pompous Language

Pompous, or artificial, language usually occurs when you are trying to make your writing sound impressive. Sometimes, it results from an attempt to introduce your reading vocabulary into your writing, without a corresponding attempt to determine the exact definition of a word. Like obsolete words, unnecessarily formal words call attention to themselves and distract the reader from your message.

> **Examples:** *masticate* for *chew*
> *ratiocination* for *thinking*
> *perambulation* for *walking*
> *proboscis* for *nose*

It is readily apparent that incorrect usage could result in some embarrassment and ridicule; therefore, *choose and use your words carefully.*

PRACTICE 1

Rewrite the following sentences to eliminate jargon, slang, obsolete, and pompous words. Stay as close to the original meaning as possible.

1. Every night at ten o'clock we get the munchies and head for the refrigerator.

   _____

   _____

2. Despite the deleterious climactic conditions, the team reaffirmed its decision to ascend the steep slope.

   _____

   _____

3. Joining the rat race in the central city is a real downer each day.

   _____

   _____

4. A stitch punctually applied conserves multiple efforts.

   _____

   _____

5. Rudimentary mathematical principles are easy to ascertain.

_____

_____

Have your instructor or tutor check your work.

Denotation and Connotation

Another facet of precise wording that you should be aware of is the denotation and connotation of words. In effect, the **denotation** is the dictionary definition of the word, its literal meaning. The **connotation** is the word's associated or implied meaning; it is the literal meaning, plus all of the ideas that your mind conjures up when it hears the word.

Examples: *Denotation*

picnic—a meal eaten outdoors on an excursion.

Connotation

picnic—lots of food, games, friends, fun time
or
picnic—heat, bugs, spoiled food, noise, commotion.

As you can see, everyone agrees with the *denotation* of a word. However, everyone does not necessarily agree about the *connotation,* because that is based on personal experience. One person may love the excitement of a picnic; another may abhor the confusion and discomfort. So, when you are choosing a word, think of the connotation and choose carefully.

Examples: She is a *skinny* woman.   That man is *corpulent.*
She is a *lithe* woman.   That man is *obese.*
She is a *lean* woman.   That man is *fat.*
She is a *thin* woman.   That man is *rotund.*

A word's connotation calls to mind a host of associated ideas and emotions. Consequently, when you are writing, you should be aware of the emotional overtones of your chosen words.

Strive for objectivity and neutrality, but not colorlessness. Use connotations to suit your purposes, but remember that, to some extent, word connotation is subjective and beyond your control.

EXERCISE   Next to each word, try to list some implied or suggested emotions and ideas associated with it, and their positive or negative impact.

	Associations	*Impact*
1. country	_____	_____
	_____	_____
2. mother	_____	_____
	_____	_____

3. detention _____   _____

_____   _____

4. foreigner _____   _____

_____   _____

5. failure _____   _____

_____   _____

Have your instructor or tutor check your work.

PRACTICE 2

Rewrite the following sentences by choosing words whose connotations match the tone of the sentence.

1. The young man turned to his date and said, "Just sniff the beautiful night air."

_____

2. We watched the group of toddlers strolling across the street in a double file and holding

hands.

_____

3. The job-seeker decided to cogitate about the salary before accepting the position.

_____

4. The usual funeral obsequies must be observed in this instance.

_____

5. You are prevaricating, my dear.

_____

Have your instructor or tutor check your work.

Because many people's writing vocabularies are mediocre, most of the words in the English language are rarely used; writers seem stuck on the same old words.

Examples: We had a *good* time. (boring!)
It was an *interesting* discussion. (ambiguous)
He talks so *slowly*. (vague)
She dresses *nicely*. (says nothing)

It is not incorrect to use those words, but it is certainly uninteresting. *General* words and *abstract* words are intangible; they are useful when classifying material, but they can be deadly in expository writing. *Specific* and *concrete* words are tangible; they usually refer to at least one of the senses. They make the writing more interesting, colorful, and vivid for the reader, which makes it easier for the reader to form a mental image of the topic.

Examples: *Poor*:

The person conveyed his thoughts to the hostess. (general and abstract)

Better:

Her guest thanked her for her thoughtfulness and generosity. (concrete and specific)

Poor:

The entertainment was interesting. (general and abstract)

Better:

The children's dance routine was well choreographed and competently executed. (concrete and specific)

Remember, you want to control the communication process as well as you can. Choose the word that best expresses your thought in order to avoid any misunderstandings on the reader's part. Do not take a chance on an overused, imprecise word.

EXERCISE   Write three words that are more concrete and specific than the italicized word(s) in each sentence.

1. Hal *ate a lot*.

   _____

   _____

   _____

2. Susan *did* all her work *on time*.

   _____

   _____

   _____

Have your instructor or tutor check your work.

NOTE: For a more detailed discussion of general/specific, abstract/concrete, see Chapter 4.

Euphemisms and Neologisms (Invented Words or Meanings)

There are two types of problems associated with diction. You should try to avoid both of them.

1. **Euphemisms** are words or phrases that are substituted for other words or phrases that might offend a reader's sensibilities. Euphemisms attempt to soften the impact of the message they are intended to convey.

   Examples: *gone to his reward* substitutes for *die*
   terminated substitutes for *fired*
   sanitation engineer substitutes for *garbage man*

   Because the concept remains the same, it is better to use the more direct expression. Never take a chance that your reader may misunderstand your message.

2. **Neologisms,** or **invented words,** are just what the words state: words that have been made up or invented, or legitimate words for which new meanings have been invented.

   Examples: traffic-wise
   weather-wise } unnecessarily vague in meaning
   to conference
   to impact } verbs illegitimately made from nouns

   There are too many words in the English language, most of them unused, for it to be necessary to invent words. Instead, try to improve your vocabulary in order to be able to use the precise word to express your meaning.

EXERCISE   Revise the following sentences, by correcting any diction problem.

1. After hauling fifty-pound bags of sand across the field, the construction worker perspired profusely.

   _____

   _____

2. Because he acted probityly, the supervisor was promoted by the corporation.

   _____

   _____

Have your instructor or tutor check your work.

PRACTICE 3

Rewrite the following sentences by making them more specific and concrete if necessary or by removing euphemisms and invented words.

1. The production supervisor was excessed by the new managing agent.

   _____

   _____

2. The principal decided to allow the student to remain a year in grade for the student's own benefit.

   _____

   _____

3. I hate it when she tries to be officious and act executively.

   _____

   _____

4. Grade-wise, my son did well this year.

   _____

   _____

5. Because of her very premature birth, this child was handicapped intellect-wise.

   _____

   _____

Have your instructor or tutor check your work.

Wordiness and Redundancy (Unnecessary Repetition)

Finally, there is one more aspect of word choice that you must be aware of: when you write, avoid wordiness and needless repetition.

Examples: Because Howie was illiterate and could neither read nor write, the other students ridiculed him.

The professor fully intended and carefully planned to terminate his lecture with a concluding story.

Such poor sentences as these usually result from an attempt to lengthen a written sentence and to make it sound "better." However, as you can see, the finished product does not fulfill its writer's wishes. Therefore, when you are writing, *write briefly and concisely*. Choose your words carefully so that your thought is presented in a grammatically correct and stylistically appealing manner.

EXERCISE   Revise the following sentences, by correcting any diction problems.

1. All the children, toddlers, preschoolers and school-aged, were directed to proceed all the way down the hall to the end of the corridor.

2. Believing that fraternity parties were primarily devoted to drinking, boozing, and imbibing, Susan declined to attend and decided not to go on Saturday night.

Have your instructor or tutor check your work.

APPLICATION I

Write *C* in the blank if the sentence's diction is correct. Write *D* if there is a diction problem, and then revise the sentence.

1. The intended victim seized the andiron and bopped the burglar on the head.   _____

2. His bum advice made me lose five hundred dollars at the track.   _____

3. Radiation sometimes has an enhancing effect when it is used in conjunction with chemotherapy.   _____

4. The board wanted to gain an overview of the cash-flow problem.   _____

5. It was decided that the best course to follow was for everyone—management, workers, and even the chief executive officer—to conference about the new pay guidelines.   _____

6. The couch should be placed over yond against the blue wall.   _____

7. Each floppy disk should be categorized according to its most-frequent user.   _____

8. Currently, Mr. J. Doe is pushing up daisies.   _____

9. As a young man, he was so in love with Stacey that he practically placed her on a pedestal.   _____

10. The gang decided to oblivie the stool pigeon.   _____

11. By the third week of each month, my income becomes outgo, and my budget is in a state of imbalance.   _____

12. Each day, my attitude becomes more and more positive.   _____

13. On the other hand, each week my finances become negativer and negativer.   _____

14. This was a very pleasant discussion.   _____

15. That dress looks real nice on you.   _____

16. After adapting to their new environment, the snail darters began to reproduce rapidly.   _____

17. Hamilton believes in working prodigiously.   _____

18. Supposedly, this movie is the cat's pajamas.   _____

19. Because my grandson is only five months old but weighs twenty-three pounds,

    I consider him portly.   _____

20. Inspiration frequently deserts those who act under pressure.   _____

Check the answer key.

APPLICATION II

Proofread the following paragraph carefully. Place the editing symbol *D* next to any diction errors. Correct any diction errors that you find. Show the revised essay to your instructor or tutor.

(1) Once upon a time, a long, long time ago, in the older days when kings were kingly-like and queens were feminine, a baby was born. (2) This baby had a lot going for her. (3) She was pretty and sweet, full of sugar and spice, in addition to having a millionaire-type father. (4) Unfortunately, her patriarch and matriarch could not be considered vivacious, garrulous, or even talkative. (5) They seemed to adhere to the maxim, proverb, or cliché of "The less said, the better." (6) Her parental guardians rarely communicated orally with her. (7) The vast majority of the time, in fact most of the time, they would deign only to nod their heads in agreement or disagreement. (8) The monarchs would never express their emotions openly and overtly. (9) Now, to a great many of you out there this may sound like an optimal and ideal situation, but, I assure you, it was not. (10) The poor child longed to hear the sound of a human voice talking and speaking. (11) She wanted and desired to be cooed to, babbled with, or even yelled at. (12) Alas and alack, her parents were psychologically incapable of responding to her elemental, primal, and deep-seated needs. (13) Thus, her only interaction with her parents consisted of the mutual nodding and shaking of heads. (14) And so, this offspring who should have been sitting on top of the world with the universe on a string instead faced a life of silence and reticentcy. (15) This is not your usual happy ending.

Check the answer key.

APPLICATION III

Proofread the following paragraph carefully. Place the editing symbol *D* next to any diction errors, and correct the errors you find. Show the revised essay to your instructor or tutor.

(1) The young man responded very disgraciously. (2) "I think we need to provide more articulation with them. (3) Such occasional and infrequent input is very unbeneficial to the situation. (4) In fact, it may even deleteriate the problem more by simply institutionalizing it." (5) To me, that seemed to be a very impactful pronouncement. (6) How could I reactivate? (7) What should I do? (8) I decided the optimum approach was to be very down-keyed and merely wait for more verbiage from him. (9) My method worked. (10) Soon the young protagonist was expounding, proparounding, and exhorting me anew. (11) "Fie, fie on an accursed and ill-starred venture. (12) Your mechanized household engineer will probably go the way of the Edsel and rightly so! (13) It should definitely be deep-sixed." (14) Then I eyed him with hostility and hatred. (15) No one, especially not a young pup and upstart like him, was granted permission to speak to me like that.

Check the answer key.

APPLICATION IV

Proofread a paper of your own carefully for diction errors. Place the editing symbol *D* next to any diction errors. Correct any errors you find and then show the revised version to your instructor or tutor.

21

Confusing and Often Misused Words

OBJECTIVES: 1. To recognize words whose spelling and usage are frequently confused.

2. To use these words correctly.

3. To proofread a paper for errors in the use of these words and to use the editing symbol (*ww*) correctly.

KEY CONCEPT: Some words are frequently misread and misused because the words are confused with similar-sounding and/or similar-looking words. Sometimes, the confusing words even have similar meanings, but are different parts of speech. The following list defines each word and uses it correctly in a sentence. Study the list carefully.

√ 1.

a — is used before a word that begins with a consonant sound.
He owns *a* horse, *a* car, and *a* boat.

an — is used before a word that begins with a vowel sound.
In *an* hour, Sue will eat *an* egg for breakfast. (The *h* is silent in *hour,* so the first sound you hear is a vowel.)

and — joins ideas, words, or phrases of equal worth.
John *and* Mary went for a ride in a buggy.

These words are frequently confused because of poor pronunciation.

√ 2.

accept — means "to receive" or "to get." It is a *verb.*
She *accepted* his token of appreciation.

except — means "not included" or "excluded"; it is a *preposition.*
Everyone went skiing *except* Bertha.

These words are frequently confused because of poor pronunciation.

√ 3.

advice — means "counsel" or "opinion"; it is a *noun.*
Don't accept your mother-in-law's *advice.*

advise — means "to offer an opinion" or "to offer counsel"; it is a *verb.*
In-laws often try to *advise* newlyweds.

4.

affect — means "to influence"; it is a *verb.*
Children can be deeply *affected* by the death of a pet.

effect — as a *noun* means "result" or "consequence."
There are many unfortunate *effects* of inflation.

as a *verb* means "to cause" or "to bring about."

The negotiators labored all night to *effect* a compromise between the opposing unions.

Again, confusion results from poor pronunciation.

5.	all ready	means "everyone (or everything) is ready."
		The foreman told the judge, "We're *all ready* to give our verdict, sir."
	already	means "previously, before, or by a specific time"; it is an *adverb*.
		The paramedics were *already* at the scene of the accident.

6.	allot	means "to distribute, assign, or give"; it is a *verb*.
		The camp director *allotted* one bowl of rice and one cup of milk to each refugee.
	a lot	means "plenty of, much of."
		NOTE: It is *never* spelled as one word.
		He received *a lot* of money for his birthday.

7.	among	is used when discussing *at least three* ideas or concepts; it is a *preposition*.
		The budget is divided *among* many competing claimants.
	between	is used when discussing *two* concepts or ideas; it is a *preposition*.
		Let's decide *between* the movie and the party.

8.	borrow	means "to take something with the intention of returning it"; it is a *verb*.
		Right now, it is hard to *borrow* money for home improvements.
	lend	means "to allow someone to use something, on the condition that it is returned"; it is a *verb*.
		Many parents *lend* their children the down payment for their first house.

9.	bought	means "purchased"; it is the past tense of the verb *to buy*.
		They *bought* a new house.
	brought	means "taken from there to here"; it is the past tense of the verb *to bring*.
		They *brought* a quiche back from the party.

10.	break	means "to crack" or "to destroy"; it is a *verb*.
		Please be careful with that Ming vase; please do not *break* it.
	brake	as a *verb*, it means "to stop."
		To avoid hitting the child who had dashed into the street, the bus driver *braked* quickly.
		as a *noun*, it means "the mechanical device for slowing the speed of a vehicle or machine."
		Our *brakes* squeaked as we slowed for the stop sign.

11.	breath	is the *noun* form.
		Halitosis is a fancy word for bad *breath*.
	breathe	is the *verb* form.
		When she has an asthma attack, she can't *breathe*.

12.	bring	means "to cause to come here by carrying or leading"; it is a *verb*. "You may *bring* a friend with you," said the hostess, "provided he *brings* his own food."
	take	means "to grasp or get possession of" and "to carry from here to there"; it is a *verb*. Mothers always admonish their children "to *take* my hand when we cross the street."

13.	burst	means "to explode"; it is a *verb*. In early spring, the forsythia's yellow buds *burst* into bloom.
	bust	as a *verb*, it means "to destroy." (NOTE: The verb *bust* is actually slang; as such it rarely belongs in academic writing.) The fragile vase was *busted*. as a *noun*, it means "a sculpture of an individual's head and shoulders." A magnificent *bust* of Abraham Lincoln was placed in the Lincoln Monument yesterday.

14.	buy	means "to purchase"; it is a *verb*. She wants to *buy* a new dress for the party.
	by	means "next to, near, or according to"; it is a *preposition*. This article was written *by* a cub reporter.

15.	capital	means "chief, most important," or "money"; it is a *noun*. Business needs *capital* to create jobs.
	capitol	means "the building in which a *state* legislature meets"; it is a *noun*. The legislators burned the midnight oil at the *capitol* last night. When the word is *capitalized*, it refers to the building in Washington in which Congress meets. The president delivered his State of the Union address at the *Capitol* last night.

16.	choose	means "to make a choice"; it is the present-tense form of the verb *to choose*. She must *choose* a major.
	chose	has the same meaning, but is the past-tense form. She finally *chose* architectural engineering.

√ 17.	cite	means "to quote from another source"; it is a *verb*. He *cited* passages from Thoreau's "Civil Disobedience" as his defense.
	site	means "a location for a building or activity"; it is a *noun*. They chose Carmel, California, for the *site* of their vacation home.
	sight	as a *verb*, it means "to get a glimpse of, to see, or to observe." As the weary sailors nearly abandoned hope, they *sighted* land. as a *noun*, it means "vision, the ability to see, or something worth seeing." We plan to see the *sights* of Paris this fall.

18.	complement	as a *verb*, it means "to complete or bring to perfection." A good wine *complements* the meal.
	compliment	as a *verb*, it means "to praise." She *complimented* him on his perspicacity. as a *noun*, it means "praise." Chefs love to receive *compliments*.
19.	desert	as a *verb*, it means "to abandon." Soldiers are trained never to *desert* their unit. as a *noun*, it means "arid land." The *desert* is considered inhospitable to life.
	dessert	means "a sweet dish at the end of a meal"; it is a *noun*. I prefer ice cream for *dessert*.
20.	fewer	means "a smaller number of, not so many as"; it is an *adjective*. Because she became so cranky, she has *fewer* friends than she used to have.
	less	means "a smaller portion or quantity"; it is an *adjective*. Nowadays, I have *less* trouble meeting people than I used to have.
21.	hear	means "to listen"; it is a *verb*. She never *hears* her mother.
	here	means "a specific place nearby"; it is an *adverb*. Many people claim that George Washington slept *here* in this very bed.
✓ 22.	its	shows ownership. It is the *possessive* form, meaning "belonging to it." The boat lost *its* motor.
	it's	is a shortened form of "it is" or "it has." *It's* a nice day today. *It's* been a long time since I last saw you.
✓ 23.	lead	as a *verb*, it means "to direct, to guide." The concertmaster will *lead* the orchestra tonight. as a *noun*, it means "the heavy gray metal." There is a high *lead* content in this old paint; it must be removed.
	led	is the past-tense form of "to lead"; it is a *verb*. The hikers were *led* to safety by the park ranger.
24.	learn	means "to gain knowledge or understanding"; it is a *verb*. Each person must *learn* from his or her own mistakes.
	teach	means "to instruct, to assist in the learning process"; it is a *verb*. I can *teach* you how to tie your shoelaces, but you must practice it yourself.
25.	leave	means "to cause to remain behind, to go away from"; it is a *verb*. He must *leave* his teddy bear home when he *leaves* for camp.
	let	means "to cause to, to allow to"; it is a *verb*. The stuck valve *let* the water pour through the broken water main.

26.   loose   means "not tight"; it is an *adjective*.
               Babies should wear *loose* clothing.

       lose   means "misplaced or lost"; it is a *verb*.
               Johnny frequently *loses* his money on his way to school.

27.   passed   means "went by"; it is the past-tense form of the verb *to pass*.
                 The parade *passed* this way an hour ago.

       past   as a *noun*, it means "in former times."
               History teaches us about the *past*.

               as a *preposition*, it means to "go beyond."
               We drove *past* the haunted house.

               as an *adjective*, it means "belonging to previous times."
               The *past* decade brought many changes to America.

28.   precede   means "to come before"; it is a *verb*.
                  The seniors will *precede* the juniors in the ceremony.

       proceed   means "to go on" and "to continue"; it is a *verb*.
                  Proceed with your implausible story.

29.   principal   as an *adjective*, it means "chief, main, or most important."
                    He is the union's *principal* negotiator.

                    as a *noun*, it means "the head of a school."
                    The *principal* sets school policy.

       principle   means "a fundamental truth or rule"; it is a *noun*.
                    You must study geometric *principles* if you want to be an architect.

30.   quiet   is a *noun* that means "peace and calm."
                Libraries are *quiet* places.

       quite   is an *adverb* meaning "positively or really."
                She is *quite* an aristocrat.

31.   raise   means "to increase in height" and "to obtain"; it is a *verb*.
                Please *raise* the window; this room is stuffy.

       rise   means "to get up" and "to move upward"; it is a *verb*.
               The stock market's value is *rising*.

32.   right   as a *noun*, it means "privilege or claim."
                Our *rights* as American citizens are protected by the Constitution.

                as an *adjective*, it means "correct."
                Terrance gave the *right* answer to the calculus problem.

       rite   means "a ceremony, often religious"; it is a *noun*.
               There are few formal *rites* of passage for today's youth.

       write   means "to form letters on a surface, usually by means of a pen and paper"; it is
                a *verb*.
                Please *write* your address on your application.

33. stationary   means "not moving"; it is an *adjective*.
                       Mountains are usually *stationary* objects.

      stationery   means "writing paper"; it is a *noun*.
                       Some correspondents try to get attention by using lilac *stationery*.

34. suppose   means "to guess or assume"; it is a *verb*.
                       I *suppose* he is coming to the wedding.

      supposed   implies an obligation; it means "should"; it is the past tense of the verb *suppose*.
                       She was *supposed* to babysit for me tonight.

√35. than   is used when comparing two items; it is a *subordinate conjunction*.
                       She is taller *than* her brother.

      then   refers to time; it is an *adverb*.
                       Then the dog began chasing the cat.

√ 36. their   is the *possessive* form meaning "belonging to them."
                       Those poor people lost *their* homes.

      there   is an *adverb* that refers to a place.
                       I distinctly remember putting the keys right *there*.

      they're   is a *contraction*, a shortened form of "they are."
                       They're going on a long vacation to New Zealand.

37. thorough   means "complete"; it is an *adjective*.
                       Hallie made a *thorough* search of the house for the missing car keys.

      through   means "to pass between or to move from one end to the other"; it is a *preposition*.
                       On her way from New York to Florida, Janice will pass *through* seven states.

√38. to   means "toward or in the direction of"; it is a *preposition*.
                       They are going *to* the movies.

      too   means "also" or "more than enough"; it is an *adverb*.
                       I ate *too* much cake yesterday.

      two   refers to the number that is the sum of one plus one; it is an *adjective*.
                       The child has *two* dollars to spend on a gift for his mother.

√39. weather   refers to the climate; it is a *noun*.
                       The *weather* report for today is sunny.

      whether   indicates that one must make a decision; it is a *conjunction*.
                       She doesn't know *whether* to go to law school or graduate school.

40. who's   is a *contraction*, a shortened form of "who is."
                       The police don't know *who's* the burglar.

      whose   is the *possessive* form meaning "belonging to whom."
                       Whose hat is this?

41.   use   means "to make use of, or to employ"; it is a *verb*.
                Do you know how to *use* a dictionary?

        used   means "was accustomed to or was in the habit of "; it is the past tense of the
                verb *use*.
                I *used* to like pizza until I developed an allergy to cheese.

✓ 42.   your   is the *possessive* form meaning "belonging to you."
                Where is *your* warm-up suit?

        you're   is a *contraction*, a shortened form of "you are."
                You're a big bore!

APPLICATION I

Underline the word that best fits the meaning of the sentence.

1. Because (its, it's) (a, an, and) beautiful day, I've decided to (accept, except) (your, you're) invitation.

2. (To, Two, Too) days before, he decided that (to, too, two) many people were involved.

3. George, Tom (a, an, and) Harry were gravely (affected, effected) by (their, there, they're) first-grade teachers.

4. She (use, used) to go swimming every day.

5. (Hear, Here) are the books, and (their, there, they're) are the students.

6. If you climb four flights of stairs, (your, you're) likely to (loose, lose) (your, you're) (breath, breathe).

7. First, you must (choose, chose) (among, between) French, German, and Italian for (your, you're) language requirement.

8. You weren't (suppose, supposed) to do that!

9. Have you (passed, past) any course yet?

10. On his (advice, advise) she (bought, brought) some stock with all her available (capital, capitol).

11. (Who's, whose) to say that sunny (weather, whether) is the best?

12. Are you (quiet, quite) sure he meant to (complement, compliment) her on the (dessert, desert)?

13. I (adviced, advised) him to quit his job (quiet, quite) a long time ago.

14. (Weather, Whether) or not you (use, used) to eat strawberries is not important.

15. The (passed, past) few weeks have been (quiet, quite) hard on her.

16. The millionaire couldn't decide whether to (leave, let) his money to charity or to his wastrel nephew.

17. Light beer, which is really just a watered-down product, has (fewer, less) calories (than, then) regular beer.

18. Ever since she was a child, that girl has had (allot, a lot) of problems.

19. If the school goes to Washington, D. C., will the students visit the (capital, capitol, Capitol)?

20. Many people misunderstood (a, an, and) instructor's function: it is to (learn, teach). Only the student himself can (learn, teach).

21. The (break, brake) on the winch failed; our piano crashed to the ground.

22. As the bombs (bust, burst) around him, Francis Scott Key thought of the (rites, rights, writes) the new country had fought for in the Revolution.

23. On what (cite, sight, site) do you plan to build your new house?

24. The Christmas choir was (lead, led) by a rotund man in a red suit.

25. In the class (preceding, proceeding) lunch, we will discuss Plato's *Republic*.

26. As the reluctant private (raised, rose) his hand to volunteer for the dangerous mission, the captain knew that her squad members would cooperate with one another.

27. Henry David Thoreau liked to joke that he was a (thorough, through) man.

28. On our next trip to Europe, we plan to see the (sights, sites, cites) of Rome and Athens.

29. In your research paper, how many authors did you (cite, site, sight)?

30. Many primitive cultures have strict initiation (rights, rites, writes) for adolescents.

Check the answer key.

APPLICATION II

Each sentence in the following paragraph is numbered. If all the words in the sentence are correctly used, write *C* next to the number of the sentence. If one or more words are misused, write *ww* above the number. Then, correct all errors.

(1) I said I was going too the store to buy ice cream, an Mary said she'd come along to. (2) As we passed the Victorian mansion, she began to complement me on my outfit; she liked the jogging shorts with the tuxedo shirt. (3) Then Mary embarrassed me again buy asking whether I would except a small gift from her. (4) What was I supposed too do? (5) I had to explain that I was use to acting on principal and so I could not accept the gift. (6) Furthermore, I offered her some unsolicited advise, which she wasn't too happy to hear. (7) I told her to save her money until she had accumulated two hundred dollars. (8) At that time, she should invest her capitol in a blue-chip stock portfolio. (9) The last time I heard from Mary, she was doing quiet well. (10) She was deciding which suitor to accept; her choices were the man who brought her to ten-carat diamond rings or the other man. (11) She wasn't sure weather she'd be happy with the rich man or the poor man.

Check the answer key.

APPLICATION III

Proofread the following paragraph carefully for confused and misused words. If there is a problem, write the editing symbol *ww* above the number of the sentence, and then correct the error. If all the words in the sentence are correctly used, write *C* next to the number of the sentence.

(1) The principle's advise was not easy to except. (2) I had to decide between college, an job, and my own goals. (3) This meant I had to chose weather to please myself or a authority

figure. (4) What a dilemma this was! (5) Ultimately, I opted for a cop-out. (6) Because I couldn't lend enough capitol too start a business, I was forced to put my dreams on hold. (7) On the other hand, college just wasn't a viable option; I would have had to a lot too much time to that undertaking. (8) So I chose to get a job. (9) Believe it or not, I'm all ready beginning to regret my decision because I don't like having to jump every time someone says "Come hear." (10) Its just not the way I imagined the world of work would be. (11) I guess I had to learn from my own mistakes.

Check the answer key.

APPLICATION IV

Proofread a rough draft of a paper of your own for problems with confusing and misused words. Place the editing symbol *ww* next to each error. Correct all the problems you find. Show your revisions to your instructor or tutor.

22

Spelling

OBJECTIVES:
1. To learn the spelling rules that are presented.
2. To apply these rules correctly.
3. To learn the exceptions to these rules.
4. To proofread paragraphs carefully at least once for mis-spelled words only; the editing symbol is *sp*.

KEY CONCEPT: Poor spelling is not an inherited trait. Usually, poor spelling is the result of mispronunciation, poor word choice, or igno-rance of a few basic rules. Because poor spelling can brand a writer as uneducated or uninterested in effectively communi-cating the message, it is important for you to make a con-certed effort now to improve your spelling habits. Correct spelling is not difficult. A few simple steps are all it takes.

Types of Spelling Errors

Try keeping a list of the words you frequently misspell; then analyze them for the types of mistakes you make. There are three basic kinds of spelling errors:

1. Mistakes caused by mispronunciation:

   - omitting a letter, as in "reconize" (*recognize*)
   - adding an unnecessary syllable, as in "atheletics" (*athletics*)
   - scrambling the sounds, as in "irrevelant" (*irrelevant*)

   Correction: If misspelling is due to mispronunciation, then check the dictionary for the correct pronunciation and use that pronunciation in your speech.

2. Mistakes caused by confused meanings or poor word choice:

   - confused meanings, as with *principal/principle*
   - poor word choice, as with *formerly/formally*

   Correction: Train yourself to distinguish between words that have the same sound but different meanings (**homonyms**) and words that have similar sounds. Again, use the dictionary to clear up your confusion.

3. Mistakes caused by uncertainty about the rules of spelling:

   Correction: Learn the following rules for correct spelling.

Rule #1: Words with ie or ei

If you learn this singsong bit of poetry, you will be able to spell many hard-to-spell words correctly:

RULE: Write *i* before *e*
Except after *c*
Or when sounded like *a*
As in n*ei*ghbor and w*ei*gh.

Does this rule apply all the time? No, there are exceptions, but it does work most of the time for most of the words you use on a daily basis. Now, let's examine the parts of the rule.

"Write i *before* e*"*

Examples: believe   bier   priest

EXERCISE   Fill in the blanks, following the above examples.

ach___ve   p___r   v___w

"Except after c*"*

Examples: rec*ei*ve   dec*ei*ve   rec*ei*pt

EXERCISE   Fill in the blanks, following the above examples.

conc___ve   dec___t   conc___t

"Or when sounded like a/As in neighbor and weigh*"*

Examples: r*ei*gn   f*ei*nt   f*ei*gn

EXERCISE   Fill in the blanks, following the above examples.

v___n   r___ns   w___ght

Have your instructor or tutor check your work.

EXCEPTIONS: Now, let us discuss the exceptions to this rule.

1. The rule applies only when the *ei/ie* cluster is pronounced as one syllable; it does *not* apply when the letters are divided between two syllables, as in *deity, sienna,* and *science.*
2. If the word is borrowed from a foreign language, then the rule may not be applicable; examples are *sheik, weimaraner,* and *reichsmark.*

Here are some words that are exceptions to the rule:

ancient	Fahrenheit	prescience	sleight
caffeine	financier	protein	stein
codeine	height	reveille	surfeit
counterfeit	leisure	seize	their
either	neither	sheik	weird

PRACTICE 1

Complete the following words, using *ie* or *ei,* whichever is correct.

1. s____ve   6. b____ge

2. l____sure   7. sh____ld

3. sl____gh   8. ch____f

4. p____   9. w____rd

5. y____ld   10. v____l

Check the answer key.

PRACTICE 2

Fill in the blanks in each sentence with either *ie* or *ei.*

1. The c____ling needs to be repaired.

2. The attackers bes____ged the fort for a year.

3. Ach____vement-oriented people sometimes get ulcers.

4. Children enjoy rec____ving gifts.

5. I-V tubes are usually inserted into a blood v____n.

Check the answer key.

Rule #2: Adding Prefixes

This rule is simple to remember and simple to apply:

RULE: *When adding a prefix to a root word, merely attach the new syllable to the beginning of the given word.* A **prefix** is a syllable added to the *beginning* of a word to change its form or meaning. A **root** is the base, core, or kernel of a word, the part of the word that contains its essential meaning.

Examples:
prefix + root = *new word*
dis + approve = disapprove
il + legal = illegal
pre + paid = prepaid

EXERCISE Add the given prefix to the given word, following the above examples.

prefix + *root* = *new word*

im + mature = _____

in + continent = _____

post + dated = _____

Have your instructor or tutor check your work.

PRACTICE 3

In the blanks at the right, enter the correct spelling of each word with the given prefix added to it.

1. ir + reversible = _____

2. un + lovable = _____

3. il + licit = _____

4. mis + apprehension = _____

5. re + turn = _____

6. pre + cede = _____

7. com + mission = _____

8. en + able = _____

9. dis + agree = _____

10. poly + theistic = _____

Check the answer key.

Rule #3: Changing y to i

This rule applies when you add a suffix to a word that ends in *y*. A **suffix** is a syllable added to the end of a word to change its form or meaning.

RULE: *If a word ends in the pattern* consonant + y (cy), *change the* y *to an* i *before you add the suffix. If the word ends in the pattern* vowel + y (vy), *simply add the suffix.*

Example: *word   +   suffix   =   new word*

            flabby   +   est   =   flabbiest
            (cy)

            lazy   +   er   =   lazier
            (cy)

            byway   +   s   =   byways
            (vy)

            pray   +   ed   =   prayed
            (vy)

EXERCISE   Following the above examples, add the given suffix to each word.

word   +   suffix   =   new word

lonely   +   ness   =   _____

merry   +   ly   =   _____

prey   +   ed   =   _____

Have your instructor or tutor check your work.

Of course, there are exceptions to this rule.

EXCEPTIONS:

1. The first exception is easy; simply memorize the irregular past-tense pattern of these three verbs:

    Example: *word   +   suffix   =   new word*

              pay   +   ed   =   *paid*
              say   +   ed   =   *said*
              lay   +   ed   =   *laid*

2. If the suffix itself begins with an *i*, then do not change the *y* to *i* before adding the suffix.

    Example: *word   +   suffix   =   new word*

              fry   +   ing   =   frying
              marry   +   ing   =   marrying
              defy   +   ing   =   defying

EXERCISE   Following the above examples, add the given suffix to each word.

word   +   suffix   =   new word

copy   +   ist   =   _____

harry   +   ing   =   _____

supply   +   ing   =   _____

Have your instructor or tutor check your work.

PRACTICE 4

Add the given suffix to each word.

1. hardy + hood = _____

2. defy + ant = _____

3. convey + or = _____

4. happy + ly = _____

5. hasty + ly = _____

6. likely + hood = _____

7. scanty + ly = _____

8. busy + er = _____

9. nasty + ness = _____

10. study + ous = _____

Check the answer key.

Rule #4: Silent e

This rule concerns words that end in a silent *e*, such as *make* and *argue*. In those words, the *e* is not pronounced. This rule has two parts.

1. *Drop the* e *when you add a suffix that begins with a vowel.* (Remember, a suffix is a syllable, such as *ment, ing,* or *tion,* added to the end of the word.)

Example:	*word*	+	*suffix*	=	*new word*
	serve	+	ile	=	servile
	page	+	ing	=	paging
	educate	+	ing	=	educating

EXERCISE Apply the rule to the following words, using the above examples.

word + *suffix* = *new word*

time + ing = _____

dispose + able = _____

create + or = _____

Have your instructor or tutor check your work.

2. *Keep the* e *when you add a suffix that begins with a consonant.*

      Example: *word*   + *suffix* = *new word*

               rampage + d   = rampaged

               time   + ly   = timely

               atone   + ment = atonement

EXERCISE Apply the rule to the following words, using the above examples.

word   + *suffix* = *new word*

attune + d   = _____

excite + ment = _____

bake   + r   = _____

Have your instructor or tutor check your work.

EXCEPTIONS: Once again, there are exceptions to this rule. Memorize the following words:

argument	duly	intervention
bluish	dying	judgment
canoeing	dyeing	shoeing
convention	hoeing	truly

PRACTICE 5

Add the given suffixes to the following words.

1. corrosive   + ness = _____

2. practice   + ing   = _____

3. bride   + al   = _____

4. refuse   + al   = _____

5. degenerate + ly   = _____

6. refute   + ably = _____

7. value   + able = _____

8. write   + ing   = _____

9. due   + ly   = _____

10. intervene + ing   = _____

Check the answer key.

Rule #5: Doubling the Final Consonant

This rule is very useful, but it is a bit more complicated than the previous ones. Yet, it is worth studying, because it explains why there are two *r*'s in *preferred,* but only one in *preference.*
There are two conditions necessary for the correct application of this rule.

1. The word must have only one syllable, or the last syllable must be accented. A syllable is a sound unit that contains at least one vowel. An accented syllable is the one that is emphasized or is the loudest one you hear.

    Examples: mop   sub mit′

2. The word must end in a *vowel-consonant* (**vc**) cluster.

    Examples: m(op)   beg(in)   subm(it)   t(an)
    　　　　　　(**vc**)   (**vc**)   (**vc**)   (**vc**)

    RULE: *If you have both of the above conditions, then you must double the final consonant before adding a suffix that begins with a vowel.*

    Examples: *word*   +   *suffix*   =   *new word*
    　　　　　　mop   +   ing   =   mopping
    　　　　　　begin   +   ing   =   beginning
    　　　　　　submit   +   ed   =   submitted
    　　　　　　tan   +   ing   =   tanning

EXERCISE   Apply the rule to these words:

word   +   *suffix*   =   *new word*

fog   +   ed   =   _____

omit   +   ing   =   _____

wag   +   ish   =   _____

regret   +   ed   =   _____

Have your instructor or tutor check your work.

PRACTICE 6

Add the given suffix to each word below.

1. fob   +   ed   =   _____

2. top   +   ing   =   _____

3. commit   +   ee   =   _____

4. deposit + or = _____

5. refer + ed = _____

6. forget + ing = _____

7. allot + ing = _____

8. kid + ing = _____

9. hot + est = _____

10. limit + able = _____

Check the answer key.

APPLICATION I

Underline and correct the misspelled word(s) in each sentence.

1. To the deelight of all, there was a surfiet of shrimp.

2. Conflictting territoryal claims frequently cause wars.

3. She responded testyly, not with her usual motherlyness.

4. The crew decided to dump the cargo because the ship was heading towards the jettyes.

5. The anceint financier loved to go sleigh-riding.

6. "Ilicit, ilegal, and immoral!" shouted the district attorney.

7. Mediateing grieveance disputes is not a pleasant hobby.

8. The insureance did not cover basement flooding.

9. In order to attain a slimer body, she omited all carbohydrates from her diet.

10. The company sent its regretts.

Check the answer key.

APPLICATION II

Each sentence in this paragraph is numbered. If all the words in the sentence are spelled correctly, write C next to the number of the sentence. If there are any spelling errors in the sentence, write *sp* above its number and correct the misspelled word(s).

(1) In order to acheive perfection, you must constantly be honeing your skills. (2) Acting stodgyly or saucyly won't gain you a clientele. (3) All that it will gain you is a peaceful office, free of all interruptions. (4) This is not to say that you should stand mute and voiceless while others pilfer your clients. (5) No, this is merly a reminder. (6) Instead of standing around, hopping and praying for business, go out and locate it. (7) One place that usualy is usful for druming up clients is a shopping center. (8) There you can astound and mystify people by demonstrateing your skills. (9) With luck, one or two people will approach and ask you for assistance. (10) That will be the begining of your portfolio.

Check the answer key.

APPLICATION III

Each sentence in this paragraph is numbered. If all the words in the sentence are spelled correctly, write *C* above the number of the sentence. If there are any spelling errors in the sentence, write *sp* next to its number and correct the misspelled word(s).

(1) An extremely tragic expereince happenned to me when I bought a mail-order formula that claimed to cure one's acne, to change one's physique, and to improve one's popularity. (2) The product fulfiled its promise, but not in the way I anticipated. (3) The advertisment on the product read, "No one will ever notice your oily skin or your acne." (4) Part of this statement was acurate. (5) True, the oil was removed from my face, but it went straight into my hair. (6) Plus, the formula liftted severel layers of skin from my face. (7) No one noticed my zits because the ointment turned my skin bright red; the pimples now blended with the rest of my skin. (8) When I was questioned about the discolortion, I simply explained that I had a bad sunburn. (9) After a week of useing the product each day, I noticed a complication with my physique. (10) Sure, the product changed my body proprotions; all of my wieght shifted from my legs and arms to my waist. (11) My popularity with the girls was a diasaster. (12) Instead of the Don Juan I wanted to be, I became the funniest-looking male of all time. (13) When I walked through the school coridors, all the girls laughed outragously. (14) The final insult occured when my mother and I went shopping. (15) She told me to walk five feet behind her so that no one would think that we were related. (16) So, I advise all students to beware: don't beleive everything you read. Check the answer key.

APPLICATION IV

Proofread a paper of your own. Check carefully for spelling errors and place the editing symbol *Sp* next to the errors. Correct any misspellings, and show your revisions to your instructor or tutor.

PART VII

The Composing Process

23

The Composing Process

OBJECTIVES: 1. To explore topics through generating ideas, prewriting, narrowing topics, and identifying audience and purpose.

2. To develop topic sentences.

3. To organize details.

4. To revise a paper.

5. To edit a paper.

6. To proofread a paper.

7. To explore the writing process through writing assignments.

KEY CONCEPT: To become an effective, powerful writer, you must employ the entire composing process.

Writing is not an isolated activity. Even though you may compose alone at a desk, your writing will communicate and share your ideas with others who, in turn, will respond to your prose. For this reason, you must be an effective writer, one who can compose reports for academic assignments now and professional correspondence for a career later. As you develop your own writing process, you will also gain the power to discover and explore your ideas and then to share them with an audience. This transmission of ideas allows you to communicate effectively with instructors, professionals, and the larger social world we all share.

Usually, we view only the end product of a writer's work: the published piece or the submitted paper. We rarely observe a writer's mental activity: the writer's thoughts, the knowledge drawn from personal experience and research, the facts selected, the organization chosen, the words employed to convey the writer's meaning best, the sense of audience and purpose the writer has established, the discussions about the piece that the writer has had with others, and the constant revisions made. This mental process makes writing more than the mere recording of black marks on a piece of paper. Through this writing process, you can more thoroughly investigate your own ideas, explore new ones, and share them with others.

Exploring Topics

Generating Ideas

When you consider topics for papers, begin with what you know or would like to investigate. The more interested you, as a writer, are in a subject, the more interesting you can make it for an audience. First, examine your own personal experiences. When you write about personal experience, the final piece is an individual one. For example, you might draw upon your memories of a favorite family vacation to describe a vacation site. Or you could use your experience in a political campaign as background to discuss the roles of campaign workers. By using your memories and knowledge, you will be able to visualize the event and provide specific details for your readers so that they can understand the importance of the event.

Your own experience also provides a starting point for researching a topic. If, for instance, you were asked to describe the conditions of nursing homes in your city for a sociology class, then you could begin by considering those family members who might have been in nursing homes or by interviewing your family members or friends who might have worked in nursing homes. Then, you could research the topic in the library to learn what professionals have discovered. Your inclusion of personal experience will make the piece more interesting to readers than if you relied solely upon statistical evidence. Consider, for example, how reporters approach a topic. Journalists know that most readers are concerned with human experience. Thus, articles on the plight of the homeless often begin with interviews of transients and a description of their days rather than with statistics about the number of homeless people in the nation.

To investigate your knowledge of, and interest in, a topic, use the following questions, based on the ones reporters ask, to guide you.

1. What are your interests in this topic?
   What do you know about it from personal experience?
   What do you want to know about it?
   What can you tell others about it?

2. Why is the topic important?
   Why should others know about it?

3. Who should know about this topic?
   Who has the most current knowledge about it?

4. How is the topic related to everyday life?
   How has it had an impact on others?

5. Where can you find information about the topic?

6. When is knowledge of this topic important?

Answers to these questions will help you approach a topic quickly and effectively. You will be able to determine your knowledge of a topic, your interests in it, and your purpose in communicating your ideas to others.

Sometimes, however, ideas do not come easily. Many writers will admit that the first piece of blank paper, or a blank computer screen, can intimidate them and send them staring into space for a number of minutes; they waste time as they try to force a topic to materialize on paper. Fortunately, when you are faced with such a situation, prewriting techniques will help you get started rapidly.

Prewriting

Prewriting, what a writer does before actually committing sentences and paragraphs to paper, can take many forms. Before writing, you need time to view topics from different perspectives, to discuss these topics with others, and to research topics in the library. Through these activities, you will have a better sense of your ideas, their importance, and your presentation of them. However, this invention—this thinking about writing—does not end when you begin to write. Even after you have started composing, you can still add and delete facts or alter your original ideas or focus. You should remain willing to explore a topic throughout the entire composing process, for this discovery of ideas makes writing worthwhile, both for you and your reader. Through two specific prewriting techniques, brainstorming and freewriting, you can investigate ideas during the entire writing process.

Brainstorming. Brainstorming, quickly generating and listing ideas about a topic, provides a useful starting point in the composing process. During a brainstorming session, which could last only ten minutes, you should record all ideas and facts you have about a general topic. Rely upon your personal experience and knowledge first to generate ideas; then, identify your interests in the topic. By the end of the brainstorming session, you will have generated many ideas to consider for your paper. Consider the following results of a brainstorming session on the topic *concerts*.

Ideas generated for a paper:

- types of concerts—music played
- types of audiences at concerts
- outdoor concerts versus indoor ones
- Fourth of July concert in Central Park with the New York Philharmonic
- variations in performances
- specific performers in concert
- famous concerts—Stravinsky's *Rite of Spring* ballet performed in Paris in 1913 or the Woodstock concert of 1969
- competitions at bluegrass concerts
- rock concerts
- specific rock groups in concert—the Grateful Dead concerts over the years
- changes in concerts over the years
- return of music from 1950s and 1960s in concert
- listening to a radio broadcast versus attending in person
- ambience of concert halls—Carnegie Hall
- weekend-long concerts—Newport Jazz Festival

While this one topic could yield many more ideas, this list gives the writer a starting point. In fact, for most of these ideas, the writer can draw upon personal experience for an original piece about concerts. Since brainstorming allows you to identify a number of ideas quickly, it can be used at any point in the composing process when you need to generate ideas.

PRACTICE 1

Choose three of the subjects below, and complete a brainstorming session on each topic. In each ten-minute session, record your ideas about the topic. Be sure to use your personal experience and knowledge initially; also, identify areas you would like to research. At the end of each session, place a check beside those ideas you believe could be developed into a paragraph. Finally, compare your lists of potential topics with those of other students. What similarities or differences do you notice? Which ideas can be best developed later?

1. Sports
2. Vacations
3. Environmental concerns
4. Your city or neighborhood
5. Education

6. Politics
7. Holidays
8. Restaurants
9. Movies
10. Music

Freewriting. After a brainstorming session, you can be overwhelmed by the number and types of topics generated. You need now to decide upon a topic you can expand successfully in a paragraph. Freewriting can help you effectively identify advantages and disadvantages of topics and explore your knowledge of them. With this method, you can quickly determine one or two potential topics for a paragraph.

In a freewriting exercise, you will write continuously for a specific amount of time, usually ten to twenty minutes, on a particular topic. Without concern for correct sentences, spelling, grammar, or punctuation, you will record specific ideas about a topic as you keep your pen moving for the required time. At times, you may feel that you are straying from your topic; however, this is not the case. As its name suggests, freewriting gives you the freedom to investigate ideas. Even those thoughts that seem to be random and tangential can be useful, for they may evoke sharp memories and details of an event. For example, if you were asked to write about the topic *movies*, then you could initially list those movies that you enjoyed the most. As you continue to write, you may find that one particular movie dominates your prose. Thus, you can use specific details from one movie to write a paper about the impact movies can have upon individuals. If you become "stuck" for ideas in a freewriting exercise, then simply repeat a key phrase or word until new ideas come.

You may be pleasantly surprised when you read your freewriting exercise. You will find that you do, indeed, have something to say about a topic, and you may find that ideas generated in a free-writing exercise are more interesting than your original topic. Freewriting offers several advantages. First, it helps you decide whether a topic can be treated fully by using personal experience and knowledge or whether you need to research the topic before you write. Second, freewriting can generate ideas for use later in a more formally structured paper. Finally, freewriting can be used at any point in the composing process since it quickly provides ideas and supporting details for a topic.

PRACTICE 2

Select three topics from your brainstorming exercise. Within a set limit of fifteen to twenty minutes, complete a freewriting exercise on each one. Using the list of questions below, compare your responses with those of other students.

1. What ideas did you generate?
2. Which of these ideas can be used in a paper?
3. What differences do you note between your freewriting and that of others?
4. What different ideas did others generate?
5. Why might these differences occur?

Narrowing Topics

No matter what their length, paragraphs share a common feature: they usually develop only one main idea. The paragraph's main idea, the topic, indicates the specific idea you will develop and alerts your reader to your purpose in communicating. Without a narrowed topic, you will only generalize for readers who will be unable to determine the purpose of the paragraph.

Depending upon the context into which it is placed, a topic can be either specific (narrow) or general (broad). For example, the topic *zoology* is specific if the writer discusses courses in biology; however, the same topic can be general if the writer discusses only herpetology. A topic is usually too general for development in a paragraph if you can think of several subtopics for it. Consider the topics *education, politics,* and *science*. Each of these broad topics naturally leads to other, more specific topics. For example, *education* encourages readers to question the level of education to be discussed, the standards of education, the country the writer will discuss, and the century or decade the writer will analyze. Certainly, this topic is too general to be developed adequately in a paragraph. However, a topic can be too specific if there is little for you to develop in a paragraph. The topic *the number of students who drive to school* could be too specific. You will need only a sentence or two to support this topic. This topic, however, could be developed into an adequate one if the writer considers other aspects of it. For instance, the topic *student dissatisfaction with campus parking facilities* could provide material for a well-developed paragraph.

To narrow a topic successfully, you should be able to identify stages of subtopics. The following example illustrates how a topic is narrowed through various stages, each more specific than the last, until it is a suitable topic for a paragraph.

> **General topic:**   American politics
>
> > **Specific topic of American politics:**   Presidential primaries
> >
> > **Specific topic of presidential primaries:**   Presidential primaries of 1988
> >
> > **Specific topic of presidential primaries of 1988:**   The impact of media coverage on the presidential primaries of 1988
> >
> > **Specific topic of the impact of media coverage on the presidential primaries of 1988:**   The impact of media coverage in New Hampshire on the presidential primaries of 1988

For each specific topic, the writer chose one aspect of the preceding topic until the final topic, *the impact of media coverage in New Hampshire on the presidential primaries of 1988*, could be developed in a paragraph.

PRACTICE 3

Label each set of topics below from 1 for the most general to 5 for the most specific. Make sure that your stages of development are logical and that each topic really narrows the one preceding it.

Example: _1_   Space exploration by the United States

   _5_   Landing of U.S. astronauts on moon

   _4_   Apollo program

   _3_   NASA's achievements

   _2_   Creation of National Aeronautics and Space Administration

1. ____   Facades of New York skyscrapers

   ____   Architecture

   ____   Urban architecture

   ____   Skyscrapers in New York

   ____   Emergence of classical influences on facades of New York skyscrapers

2. ____   Houses

   ____   Tax advantages of home ownership

   ____   Renting or owning a house

   ____   Deduction of interest on home mortgage from federal taxes

   ____   Advantages of owning a house

3. _____ Renaissance painters

_____ Painting of Sistine Chapel from 1508 to 1512

_____ Current restoration of Sistine Chapel

_____ Michelangelo's paintings

_____ Controversy over restoration of the Sistine Chapel

4. _____ William Faulkner

_____ Characterization in Faulkner's *The Sound and the Fury*

_____ Southern novelists

_____ Faulkner's novels

_____ American novelists

5. _____ Fuel

_____ Environmental effects of Three Mile Island incident

_____ Nuclear power plants

_____ Three Mile Island nuclear-power plant accident

_____ Nuclear power

PRACTICE 4

Return to Practice 1, in which you completed brainstorming sessions on three different subjects. Choose four topics from one brainstorming session, and narrow each topic until you have reached a specific paragraph topic. Be sure to identify the stages of your logical reduction. Compare your responses with those of other students, and discuss the differences you note.

Identifying Audience and Purpose

The discovery of a paragraph topic does not end with selecting a narrowed topic. Your ideas and their presentation depend upon two conditions: audience and purpose. When you speak to others, you naturally address your audience and purpose. Consider, for example, your description of a party to your parents and friends. The details you include and their presentation will differ with each audience. In some cases, you might tell your parents fewer specific details than you tell close friends. In addition, your language may be more formal when you speak with your parents than when you talk with peers. Hence, in each description, you modify your presentation and language to meet the needs of each audience. When you write, use this innate ability to present a single topic in different ways to diverse audiences. Without an understanding of these two crucial components, your final piece will not complete its function: to communicate ideas to others.

Unfortunately, too many writers ignore their audiences and purposes. When they receive an assignment, some writers simply compose a piece. The final product is sometimes flat, contains only generalizations, and lacks direction; in fact, the paper may bore both the writer and the reader. To test this lack of audience, scan some instruction manuals for appliances or some insurance forms. In each case, you may find that the writers simply did not meet their audiences' needs. Instructions for operating microwave ovens or personal computers, for example, are often far more complex than the actual operation. Insurance forms stating the terms of the insurance often require legal assistance to decipher. However, if you identify your audience and purpose, then your message will be focused, and the language, tone, and details will be appropriate for your audience.

Analyze the following topics designed for specific audiences and purposes. Note that one general topic can yield several topics for different audiences.

General Topic	Audience	Purpose
1. Health care	a. Hospital administrators	Discuss how to provide quality health care at a reasonable price
	b. Hospital patient	Discuss changes in the patient's diet and exercise for better health
	c. Paramedics	Explain specific lifesaving techniques to be used in emergencies
2. Economics	a. Stockbrokers	Explain the effect of the overseas value of the dollar and its impact on the stock market
	b. Students in an introductory economics class	Discuss basic economic theory
	c. Consumers	Discuss the effects of inflation on purchasing power
3. American history	a. Tourists	Narrate the events of a certain historical episode
	b. Newspaper readers	Provide background information for a travel article
	c. Students in a literature class	Explain the historical context of a certain novel

To identify your audience and purpose, think first of a specific person to whom you would address the topic; consider also what you want this piece of writing to accomplish. If you have difficulty visualizing a specific audience, then ask the following questions to create a potential audience.

1. Who would be most interested in the topic?
2. What would this person already know about the topic? (What pieces of information must be included or omitted?)
3. What is this person's educational background? What are his or her social and cultural interests?
4. How old is this person? To what generation does the reader belong? How might the person's age determine his or her interests?
5. Is this person sympathetic or hostile to the topic? (How would you respond in each case?)

Finally, determine your purpose in communicating. Do you want to explain, compare and contrast, define, classify, narrate, persuade, or convince? How do you want your audience to respond? Do you want your readers to agree with your argument, comply with your instructions, enjoy the humor of a story, understand a problem and possible solutions, or alter their behavior? Answers to these questions will provide you with a better sense of your audience and purpose for a specific topic.

PRACTICE 5

For each topic below, several audiences are listed. Create and list a possible purpose for each audience.

1. **Topic:**   The homeless in urban areas

   Audience   *Purpose*

   a. City social workers   _____

   b. Hospital administrators   _____

   c. Neighborhood organizations   _____

2. **Topic:**   Part-time jobs for students

   Audience   *Purpose*

   a. Students   _____

   b. Guidance counselors   _____

   c. Employers   _____

3. **Topic:**   Professional football

   Audience   *Purpose*

   a. Players   _____

   b. Owners of franchises   _____

   c. Fans   _____

PRACTICE 6

In Practice 4, you listed specific paragraph topics. For each of your paragraph topics, list two potential audiences and purposes.

Developing Topic Sentences

Each paragraph you write should contain a topic sentence stating your main idea. Usually the first sentence in a paragraph, the topic sentence defines your opinion, predicts your discussion, and controls the development of the paragraph. Paragraphs without topic sentences often leave readers questioning the purpose of the discussion. Such a method may be appropriate if an author wishes to create suspense, but, for most expository paragraphs, this method may cause readers to misinterpret information. Readers can more easily follow your discussion if a paragraph contains a topic sentence. Analyze the example below.

> Demanding, learned, and boundlessly generous with his time, John Sheridan, S.J. (1906–1982) was the most remarkable teacher I ever encountered. He had long been an institution at Loyola High School when I entered

his freshman class in 1964. He seemed glacial, with his withering stare and strident cackling that mocked our every mistake. Hating sloth as much as he loathed ignorance and imprecision, he made no effort to adjust to us during the nine periods of Latin each week and a daily English class. We despised public speaking and recited Shakespeare; one sentence fragment—things were different then—meant an *F* on our weekly composition. Insatiably curious, Sheridan read all the time—novels, poetry, cartloads of biography and history—and remembered everything. He once told me, when I was too young to understand, that the person who reads is never lonely. Where his students were concerned, time meant nothing. He graded for hours each night and met with us before and after school and during the summer. We foolish teenagers were convinced, however, that we had more important things to do than learn a dead language and master the native tongue that we mangled with astonishing ease. Only in retrospect could we fully perceive the magnitude of this thorny figure who spurned familiarity. When I did try to thank him, years later, he grew embarrassed and walked away. Sometimes, when I teach across the hall from Sheridan's old classroom, I try to tell today's students what they are missing. Most don't understand, and I suspect that they humor me. But there are quiet times when I cross that hall and turn the corner to see where time has gone. Some other apprehensive and attentive boy sits along my old wall, but the memory of John Sheridan remains as vibrant as the master who filled this room more than twenty years ago.

This paragraph's topic sentence, located first, explains the author's opinion about a former teacher. The topic sentence also predicts the discussion of the paragraph by listing three of the teacher's qualities: "demanding, learned, and boundlessly generous with his time." The order of these qualities also controls the paragraph's organization. Notice, too, that the topic sentence is more general than the statements that follow it. From this example, you should conclude that, although the topic sentence narrows a limited topic for a paragraph-length discussion, the topic sentence is more general than the specific details that support it. Therefore, a topic sentence has two functions: it unifies the paragraph by supplying a main idea, and it organizes the ideas given in a paragraph.

The topic sentence's *controlling idea,* usually located in the sentence's predicate, accomplishes these two functions. The controlling idea offers an opinion or limitation about the topic; it is the statement the author wishes to make about the topic. Since this controlling idea identifies the purpose for communication, it limits the discussion. Writers know that they must support their opinions or explain the given limits. With this goal in mind, they choose only those details that will help them validate their opinion and, therefore, ensure a unified paragraph. Writers then present those facts logically and, therefore, organize their paragraphs.

Hence, a topic sentence contains two major parts: a subject that identifies the topic and a controlling idea, a word or phrase, that identifies the writer's opinions or limitations. Consider the following topic sentence:

Subject   Controlling Idea

The *technology* developed for space exploration provides *many benefits for consumers.*

In this sentence, *technology* is the subject of the sentence; it also, with the assistance of the adjective phrase "developed for space exploration," is a narrowed topic suitable for a paragraph. The controlling idea of the sentence is *many benefits for consumers.* In the paragraph, the writer will enumerate and explain the advantages of this technology.

Controlling ideas indicate a writer's opinion or limit the topic. Examine the following sentence. Does it offer an opinion or limitation?

Example: All college graduates should be computer literate.

This particular topic sentence states the writer's opinion about computer literacy and college students; the writer will develop the reasons for this opinion in the paragraph.

A controlling idea can also limit the topic in some way. For example, it could list causes, effects, steps in a process, stages of development, or characteristics. Examine the following sentences. Do they offer opinions or limitations?

Examples: Many college students choose to major in business for three reasons.
To change a flat tire correctly and safely, you must complete four tasks.

Both topic sentences limit the writers' discussions to either the three reasons or the four stages. Although the writers have not expressed opinions, they have classified and enumerated essential elements and, thus, have limited the topics further.

Occasionally, a topic sentence can have two controlling ideas that express both opinion and limitation. Analyze the following topic sentence from the example paragraph earlier:

Demanding, learned, and boundlessly generous with his time, John Sheridan, S.J. (1906–1982) was the most remarkable teacher I ever encountered.

In this sentence, two controlling ideas are present. One controlling idea, *the most remarkable teacher I ever encountered,* provides the author's opinion about John Sheridan. The author will provide support for his opinion by developing the second controlling idea: *demanding, learned, and boundlessly generous with his time.* This second controlling idea limits the paragraph's discussion by listing three characteristics of the teacher.

PRACTICE 7

In each of these topic sentences, underline the controlling idea. Label each controlling idea either *O* for opinion or *L* for limitation.

Controlling Idea

Example: _O_ Sociologists believe that the trend toward serial monogamy indicates a serious breakdown in family values.

_____ 1. College registration is often a frustrating, bewildering experience for freshmen.

_____ 2. Buying a new computer requires careful consideration of three items.

_____ 3. The national drinking age should be twenty-one.

_____ 4. Hospitals should be required to care for indigent patients.

_____ 5. Many advertisements should be aimed at members of the "baby boom" generation.

_____ 6. For two primary reasons, colleges must evaluate the academic records of their athletes.

_____ 7. State police should provide checkpoints to detect drivers who have been drinking.

_____ 8. Small towns provide several benefits to families.

_____ 9. All students should be required to take at least four humanities classes.

_____10. Photography is a difficult career.

PRACTICE 8

For each of these general topics, narrow the topic, decide upon a purpose and audience for the narrowed topic, and develop a topic sentence to address a specific audience. Compare your topic sentences with those of other students. In groups, identify the controlling ideas, the audiences, and the purposes of the topic sentences.

1. A campus problem
2. A local or state problem
3. Summer jobs
4. College athletics
5. Television

Before they develop topic sentences, some writers prefer to generate a number of paragraphs to discover what they believe about a topic and what they wish to convey to others. These writers must then analyze their paragraphs to identify specific details. From these details, the writers can generalize about their topic and then develop a topic sentence to unify and organize their paragraphs.

PRACTICE 9

Return to Practice 6, in which you listed potential audiences and purposes for narrowed topics. Complete a freewriting exercise on one of these topics. After you have finished, analyze your prose and list specific details from your freewriting exercise. Develop a topic sentence to unify and organize these details.

The placement of a paragraph's topic sentence depends on your presentation of ideas in a paragraph. The list below indicates the placement and function of topic sentences in paragraphs.

1. If the topic sentence is *first* in a paragraph, then it introduces the details that support or explain the controlling idea. In addition, this topic sentence immediately informs your reader of the purpose of the entire paragraph.
2. If the topic sentence is *last,* then it summarizes the details given in the paragraph.
3. If the topic sentence appears in *both the first and last sentences,* then the topic sentence both introduces and summarizes the details. This dual placement is effective when your audience is unfamiliar with the topic or the material is difficult.
4. If the topic sentence appears in the *middle* of the paragraph, then it serves as a transition between details given at the beginning and at the end of the paragraph. This method is effective when the topic sentence has two controlling ideas.

Organizing Details

When writers finally commit ideas to paper, determine audience and purpose, organize facts, and construct sentences and paragraphs, they use any number of composing techniques. Some writers simply generate thousands of words—many of which will be used in the final paper and others which will be deleted later. Other writers prefer to outline their thoughts and perfect their sentences and paragraphs before they move to the next idea. Because they spend long hours selecting, organizing, and outlining their ideas completely, the act of composing allows them to revise each section as they write. Some writers organize as they compose. Beginning with a general idea of their topic, they write the entire piece first. They then revise and restructure their paragraphs. Ideally, each writer chooses a composing process that best meets the needs of individual papers, for, as all writers have experienced, some papers seem to require little effort while others demand a great deal.

After exploring ideas and discovering a topic in early drafts and freewriting exercises, you should develop an organizational strategy for the generated material to suit your purpose and audience. If you record only your first impressions, then you may create disorganized paragraphs that ignore your audience. Your readers will be forced to organize material because you were unwilling to communicate and share ideas with others. This problem can be avoided, however, if you create unified paragraphs in which all of the supporting sentences develop your topic sentence's controlling idea.

From material you have already generated, select those items that best support your controlling idea, address your audience, and develop your stated purpose. To make material more accessible for your audience, structure details to reflect major ideas (primary support sentences) and minor ideas (secondary support sentences). Primary support sentences directly develop the controlling idea in your topic sentence. Secondary support sentences may contain a specific example or illustration, specific description, or explanation of the primary support sentences. Selected by your audience's needs and by your purpose, these details provide a well-organized paragraph that is accessible to your readers. If, for example, you were asked to describe a new drug-enforcement policy at your school, then you might address students by explaining the legal, psychological, and physiological ramifications of taking drugs. In effect, you will try to convince your peers that they should avoid drugs altogether. To an audience of campus administrators, however, you might explain the legal limits of the college's enforcement policy and the legal rights of students on campus. Each audience needs different details to support these topics. Even though you might have generated details about the legal and physiological effects of drugs, this material would not have a place in your presentation to the administrators since they already know these facts. By keeping your audience and purpose in mind, you will create unified, effective paragraphs.

To organize your ideas, first identify those ideas that directly explain, describe, define, classify, compare or contrast, indicate causes or effects, or provide reasons for arguments. These main ideas will become your primary support sentences. Consider the following topic sentence:

Made in 1942, the movie *Casablanca* remains popular today for three reasons.

The controlling idea in this sentence is *popular today for three reasons*. Thus, the primary support sentences should enumerate the reasons that *Casablanca* remains a popular movie. Examine these primary support sentences:

1. The move describes a poignant love story in which the lovers are separated by a world war.
2. The movie depicts the struggles of many Europeans as they seek to escape the encroaching Nazi occupation of their homelands.
3. With World War II as its background, the movie portrays acts of patriotism as individuals attempt to thwart the Nazi domination and restore democracy.

Although these sentences require further explanation for readers who have not seen the movie, they clearly indicate the reasons for the movie's popularity. In addition, these primary support sentences will provide a structure for the paragraph.

Secondary support sentences explain and illustrate the primary support sentences by giving examples or descriptions. Consider the following paragraph, based on the topic sentence above.

Made in 1942, the movie *Casablanca* remains popular today for three reasons. First, the movie describes a poignant love story in which the lovers are separated by a world war. Second, the movie depicts the struggles of many Europeans as they seek to escape the encroaching Nazi occupation of their homelands. Finally, with World War II as its background, the movie portrays acts of patriotism as individuals attempt to thwart the Nazi domination and restore democracy.

With only four sentences, this paragraph is not adequately developed. Primarily, it lacks the detailed information that secondary support sentences can provide. Without these secondary support sentences, the paragraph will not satisfactorily communicate its ideas to readers.

Analyze the following paragraph. How does it differ from the first one? Does it answer some questions a reader might have?

> Made in 1942, the movie *Casablanca* remains popular today for three reasons. First, the movie describes a poignant love story in which the lovers are separated by a world war. Humphrey Bogart and Ingrid Bergman play the war-torn lovers Rick and Ilsa. Their romance in Paris ends as the Germans occupy the city; they are reunited in Rick's café in Algeria a few years later. However, Ilsa has traveled to Casablanca with her husband, who was once presumed dead but who now strives to unite the underground against the Germans. Second, the movie depicts the struggles of many Europeans as they seek to escape the encroaching Nazi occupation of their homelands. Since Casablanca offers a gateway to the United States from occupied Europe, many refugees must travel there to escape the Nazis. As they gather in Casablanca to await visa clearances and available planes, they tell their stories at Rick's café. Finally, with World War II as its background, the movie portrays acts of patriotism as individuals attempt to thwart the Nazi domination and restore democracy. Even though he professes to be apolitical, Rick eventually helps Ilsa and her husband to escape to America so that they can continue to fight for freedom. The final scene suggests that Rick will join the underground resistance movement to fight against the Nazis. For these three reasons, the movie retains its popularity over the decades.

Added to this revised paragraph, the secondary support sentences explain in greater detail the primary supports. The writer has developed the controlling idea and has answered questions readers might have.

PRACTICE 10

In each paragraph, identify the introductory sentences (*IS*), the topic sentence (*TS*), the primary supports (*PS*), the secondary supports (*SS*), and the concluding sentence (*CS*).

A. _____ 1. Americans have a variety of resources to use for heating their homes. _____ 2. Gas, oil, electricity, and solar power all provide warmth for our homes. _____ 3. However, for all the technological advances in home-heating systems, many Americans are returning to our ancestors' original source of heat: wood. _____ 4. Nearly every new single-family home in America contains a fireplace, and in homes without fireplaces, many people install wood-burning stoves. _____ 5. Consider the advantages of heating with wood. _____ 6. First, wood is economical; while a cord of wood, which could last most of the winter, costs around $100, the equivalent amount of heat produced by gas or oil would cost approximately $400. _____ 7. Second, watching a wood fire provides the intangible qualities of peace and contentment. _____ 8. For both economy and enjoyment, Americans are heating with wood.

B. _____ 1. In 1902, Theodore Roosevelt saved the life of a treed black bear. _____ 2. This humanitarian act, immortalized in a contemporary newspaper cartoon, set the stage for the arrival of a marvelous new companion: the teddy bear. _____ 3. Since 1902, teddy bears have been the first toys of many children; interestingly, this trend continues for adults. _____ 4. Adults value the furry creatures for their investment value and their companionship. _____ 5. Many antique bears are worth far more today than their original purchase price; according to *Newsweek*, three sets of antique bears sold recently for more than $1,500. _____ 6. Even replicas of bears bring high prices. _____ 7. However, bears provide more than a sound economic investment; they are trusted friends. _____ 8. Few human friends are as loyal as a teddy bear. _____ 9. Who else, of all our friends, listens patiently to our complaints and sorrows? _____ 10. Who is a better *confidant* for all of our secrets? _____ 11. Who revels in our joys with an unabashed grin? _____ 12. The answer is simple— the teddy bear. _____ 13. For all of these qualities, bears have captured the hearts of adults as well as children.

C. _____ 1. Purchasing a new car requires the buyer's careful consideration of five items. _____ 2. First, the car buyer must determine a budget. _____ 3. Although many people would appreciate the luxury of a new Mercedes-Benz, few could afford the monthly payments. _____ 4. Second, the buyer must determine the type of car he needs. _____ 5. If the buyer has a large family, then a sports car with only two seats is impractical. _____ 6. Third, the buyer must determine how he will use the car. _____ 7. For example, a rancher who lives in a mountainous area needs a four-wheel-drive vehicle, not a luxury car that requires a tune-up every two months. _____ 8. Fourth, the buyer must choose the options he wants or needs. _____ 9. For instance, if the buyer lives in a subtropical climate, then an air conditioner is a necessity, not a luxury. _____ 10. Finally, the buyer should consider the reputation of the dealer. _____ 11. After all, if there are problems with the machine, then the buyer wants to know that he can rely upon the dealer to have the problems corrected. _____ 12. Following these steps will ensure that a buyer selects the correct car for his needs.

There are no set rules as to the number of primary and secondary support sentences you need to develop a controlling idea adequately. You must rely upon your knowledge of your audience and purpose to determine the amount of support and the degree of its complexity.

As you begin to organize material for the body of the paragraph, be willing to reexamine your topic if you find that you cannot develop it effectively. Analyze your supports carefully; discard those that do not support your main idea and, if necessary, generate new ones by using brainstorming and freewriting techniques.

PRACTICE 11

In Practice 8, you created topic sentences for specific audiences and purposes. Using brainstorming and freewriting, generate supports for one of these topic sentences. Classify your ideas into primary and secondary supports, and then write the paragraph. Compare your paragraph to those of other students. Do your primary and secondary supports actually develop the paragraph sufficiently for others?

Revising

The writing process is not finished once you have produced a first draft of a paragraph. You now must revise the paragraph for problems with organization and content. Revision itself can take many forms. For example, you can produce several drafts of the same paper, each with a specific goal in mind, or you can analyze your first or second draft for specific weaknesses in organization, details, and transitions. In either situation, because there are too many areas to analyze at one time, you should revise in stages. The following checklist will guide you in the revision process.

   I. **Purpose and Audience**
      A. What is your purpose in writing? Can others identify your purpose?
      B. Who is your audience? How do you want this audience to respond? What in the paragraph will lead to this response? Are your level of language and the details you present suited to this audience?

  II. **Topic Sentence**
      A. Does the paragraph have a topic sentence? Where is it located? Is this location effective?
      B. Does the topic sentence have a controlling idea that states your opinion or limitations?

 III. **Organization**
      A. In what order are ideas presented in the paragraph? Is this method of organization effective for your readers? Does it lead your audience to the response you want?
      B. Does the paragraph have primary support sentences? Do they directly develop the controlling idea in your topic sentence? Are these sentences designed to meet the needs of your audience?

C. Does the paragraph have secondary support sentences? Do they explain or illustrate the primary support sentences? Are these secondary support sentences designed to meet the needs of your audience?

D. Are any sentences really tangential? Can you delete these without detracting from the paragraph's development?

E. Are your examples the best ones you could provide? Can you think of better supports now?

PRACTICE 12

Using the checklist above, revise the paragraph you wrote for Practice 11. In groups, compare your first and second versions of the paragraph to those of other students. Be prepared to explain your revisions.

Editing

When you edit a paper, you must examine the individual sentences to ensure that they are concise, effective, and correct. Begin by reading your paragraph aloud. Often this act will alert you to problems with sentences. If some sentences cannot be easily understood when you read them aloud, then you know that you must edit them. The following checklist will guide you as you edit.

I. Clarity

A. Do sentences mean what they say? Or are they ambiguous?

B. Have you used the correct word to describe your meaning? Check unfamiliar words in the dictionary.

II. Diction (See Chapters 19 and 20.)

A. Do you avoid vague words, and use specific ones instead?

B. Do you use adverbs and adjectives correctly?

III. Sentence Construction (See Chapters 6 and 10.)

A. Are sentences varied in structure? Or are they all the same type?

B. Are ideas subordinated effectively?

C. Are equal ideas joined through coordination?

IV. Sentence Correctness

A. Are there any fragments, comma splices, or run-ons? (See Chapters 7, 8, and 9.)

B. Do subjects and verbs agree in number? (See Chapter 11.)

C. Are pronouns correct in case, number, and gender? (See Chapter 12.)

D. Are there any unnecessary shifts in verb tense? (See Chapters 1, 2, and 3.)

E. Are commas, semicolons, colons, and other marks of punctuation used correctly? (See Chapters 14, 15, 16, and 17.)

F. Are words spelled properly? (See Chapters 21 and 22.)

G. Are words capitalized correctly? (See Chapter 13.)

PRACTICE 13

Using the checklist above, edit the paragraph you revised in Practice 12. In groups, check your edited sentences with those of other students.

Proofreading

When you have revised and edited your paper, it is time to produce a clean copy for submission. Because many writers tend to rush through this final stage, they often overlook misspelled words, typing errors, and stray marks of punctuation. Hence, you must proofread the final copy for these errors. You can easily correct the errors in pen and insert words neatly. The following guidelines will aid you in proofreading the final copy.

1. Is each word spelled correctly? (When you read quickly, you may anticipate what you will see and often miss simple spelling or typing errors. To break this pattern of anticipation, read the paper backwards; by doing so, you can isolate each word and easily check its spelling.)
2. Are any words omitted or repeated? (Read each sentence aloud slowly and carefully. Listen to the words. Are there any omissions or repetitions?)
3. Are there any stray marks of punctuation? (Place pieces of paper around each sentence to isolate it; then, read the sentence carefully.)

PRACTICE 14

Using the checklist above, proofread the paragraph you edited in Practice 13. In a group with other students, check your corrections with other students.

Writing Assignments

1. To explore your ideas more, keep a journal in which you write at least a paragraph every other day. Choose any subject of interest, from current events to personal experience, as topics for your journal. This journal is for you; through your paragraphs, you can begin to explore different ideas, diverse styles of writing, and interesting subjects. Some of these entries may provide you with material for formal papers later.

2. To understand the relationships between ideas in a published piece, choose a newspaper or magazine article, and write a summary of the piece in one paragraph. As you read the article, underline the author's main idea and major supports. In your summary, paraphrase this main idea and the supports.

3. For a column in your campus paper, review two restaurants close to school. In your review, focus upon the costs, the types of food served, the service, and the decor of the restaurant. Your purpose is to identify quality restaurants for students.

4. Public transportation is convenient in a highly developed society like the United States, but some people prefer to drive private cars. In a proposal to campus administrators, explain why some students prefer to drive private cars to campus rather than use public transportation. Argue for more parking spaces on campus.

5. Learning without competing for grades or worrying about grades can make learning more enjoyable. However, grades are necessary for a number of reasons. In a letter to campus administrators, explain why grades should be retained at your school.

6. Clothing often reveals what people think about themselves; moreover, people are often judged by the way they dress. In an essay for a popular magazine, such as *Vogue, GQ,* or *Mademoiselle*, explain how clothing is used in these two ways.

7. For a paper in a sociology class, argue that teenagers who commit crimes should be given the same punishment as adults who commit the same crimes.

8. In a letter to television executives, argue that television presents an unrealistic view of life in the United States. Provide some options for the television executives to correct this problem.

9. For an assignment in a sociology class, argue for or against the statement that couples do not take marriage seriously enough these days. Be sure to explain the consequences of such an attitude to society.

10. What kinds of changes does a United States president have the power to make in our society? What kinds of changes would you expect or desire the president to make? Explain your perspective to your local representative by focusing on one or two political issues.

11. To understand our assumptions about words and their definitions, define one pair of words below by distinguishing one word of the pair from the other.

> justice—law
> freedom—order
> truth—belief

12. Years ago, older relatives remained with their families until they died. Today, they often live their last years in a home for the aged. For a newspaper editorial, explain why you approve or disapprove of this change.

13. Choose a figure who, in your opinion, is the best in his or her field, whether politics, the arts (movies, literature, music), sports, or whatever. Justify your choice to a panel that will award a national prize to the figure.

14. Some people believe that the most important things in life are those that make people different from one another; others believe that the most important things are those that make us similar to one another. For a paper in a psychology class, choose the one perspective that represents your own view, and develop an argument to explain your belief.

15. So that a foreign visitor, new to the United States, can understand our celebration of major holidays, describe a typical family gathering during a holiday.

16. For a contribution to a brochure describing your town or city to visitors, discuss some of the major attractions in your town.

17. In preparation for a book describing your family's history, describe a favorite childhood memory.

18. Consider the changes that have occurred in your town or city since your birth. In a letter to the Chamber of Commerce, describe these changes and their impact upon the town and the quality of life there.

19. For a brochure advertising a specific amusement park, describe a local amusement park and its attractions.

20. While many Americans know our country's history, they lack familiarity with the historical importance of their own communities. Choose one historical site in your community, and write an article describing its importance for inclusion in a state historical pamphlet.

Answer Key

Introduction

PRACTICE

1. In—preposition
   tuition—noun
   has risen—verb
2. Boy!—interjection
   gorgeous—adjective
3. and—coordinate conjunction
   must serve—verb
4. seems—verb (linking)
5. society—adjective
   revealing—adjective
   memorable—adjective
6. slowly, gracefully—adverbs
   however—adverbial conjunction
7. although—subordinate conjunction
   she—personal pronoun, nominative case
   and—coordinate conjunction
8. Oh my gosh!—interjection
   kerosene—adjective
   has—helping verb
9. Everyone—indefinite pronoun
   should—helping verb
   to—preposition
10. Warden James—proper noun
    vicious—adjective
    mass—adjective
11. danced, sang—verbs
    before—subordinate conjunction
12. with—preposition
    purple—adjective
    by—preposition
13. Shyness—noun
    characteristics—noun
    of—preposition
14. We—personal pronoun, nominative case
    or—coordinate conjunction
    to—preposition
15. You—personal pronoun, nominative case
    my—personal pronoun, possessive case
    that—demonstrative pronoun
    very—adverb
16. Jerome—proper noun
    failed—verb
    his—personal pronoun, possessive case
    for—coordinate conjunction
17. On—preposition
    summer—noun
    by—preposition
    Andorra—proper noun
    near—preposition
    at—preposition
    of—preposition
18. useful—adjective
    informative—adjective
19. gleefully—adverb
    as—subordinate conjunction
    quickly—adverb
    through—preposition
20. have been rejected—verb
    too—adverb

Chapter 1

PRACTICE 1

1. action
2. linking
3. action
4. action
5. linking
6. linking
7. action
8. action
9. action
10. action

PRACTICE 2

1. he
2. she
3. it
4. it
5. it
6. it
7. they
8. they
9. they
10. we

PRACTICE 3

1. I walk
   you walk
   he, she, it walks
   we walk
   you walk
   they walk
2. I read
   you read
   he, she, it reads
   we read
   you read
   they read
3. I dance
   you dance
   he, she, it dances
   we dance
   you dance
   they dance
4. I hide
   you hide
   he, she, it hides
   we hide
   you hide
   they hide
5. I call
   you call
   he, she, it calls
   we call
   you call
   they call

PRACTICE 4

1. talks
2. runs
3. have, has
4. is
5. are
6. have
7. visit
8. draws, are
9. drives
10. are, is

PRACTICE 5

1. all forms take *danced*
2. all forms take *poured*
3. all forms take *marked*
4. all forms take *painted*
5. all forms take *called*

PRACTICE 6

1. sang
2. wrote
3. went, felt
4. brought, experienced
5. read
6. visited, went
7. was
8. brought
9. enlisted
10. reached, dropped

PRACTICE 7

1. will (shall) complete
2. will ask
3. Will be
4. will run
5. will sell
6. Will meet
7. will travel
8. will benefit
9. will be
10. will succeed

APPLICATION I

1. was
2. flew
3. was
4. offered
5. continued, expressed
6. pleased
7. was
8. knew
9. wanted, sat
10. contained

APPLICATION II

1. will dance
2. will enjoy
3. will explore
4. will participate
5. will (shall) watch
6. will make
7. will steal
8. will visit
9. will be
10. will provide

APPLICATION III

1. shows present time and habitual action
2. add *d* or *ed*
3. something that took place and that was completed before the present
4. present tense of *to be:*

I am	we are
you are	you are
he, she, it is	they are

   past tense of *to be:*

I was	we were
you were	you were
he, she, it was	they were

   present tense of *to have:*

I have	we have
you have	you have
he, she, it has	they have

   past tense of *to have:*

I had	we had
you had	you had
he, she, it had	they had

5. All the forms remain the same as the infinitive except for third-person singular; add *s* or *es* to third-person singular.
6. the basic form of the verb, comprised of the word *to* plus the root form of the verb.
7. 1. change vowels in the basic verb form (knew)
   2. change vowels and add a *t* (taught)
   3. change a *d* to a *t* (built)
8. add the word *will* and the infinitive root; in first-person singular and plural, add *shall* plus the infinitive root

APPLICATION IV

1. saves
2. are
3. make, are
4. portrays
5. is, works
6. relies
7. is, looks
8. proves, is
9. is
10. relies
11. uses
12. give

APPLICATION V

1. offered
2. provided, needed
3. paid
4. supported, increased
5. provided
6. had, arrived, completed, handled
7. planned, studied, worked
8. caused
9. felt
10. gave, required

APPLICATION VI

1. correct
2. decided, fumbled
3. was, began, cooked
4. scraped
5. returned, waited, tossed
6. correct
7. do, run
8. do
9. go
10. put, remain
11. learned

Chapter 2

PRACTICE 1

Infinitive	Past	Past Participle
1. to dive	dived (dove)	dived
2. to sing	sang	sung
3. to write	wrote	written
4. to fly	flew	flown
5. to drink	drank	drunk
6. to steal	stole	stolen
7. to teach	taught	taught
8. to learn	learned	learned
9. to give	gave	given
10. to receive	received	received

PRACTICE 2

1. have had
2. has been
3. has been
4. have visited
5. has become
6. have received
7. has bought
8. has raced
9. have seen
10. have enrolled

PRACTICE 3

1. had been
2. had finished
3. had completed
4. had called
5. had defused
6. had determined
7. had made
8. had completed
9. had chosen
10. had moved

PRACTICE 4

1. will have been
2. will have worked
3. will have finished
4. will have been
5. will have welcomed
6. will have taught
7. will have read
8. will have celebrated
9. will have submitted
10. will have thrown

PRACTICE 5

1. I am asking
2. They had been doing
3. We will be singing
4. He has been hitting
5. You will have been dealing
6. They were swimming

PRACTICE 6

1. will have been dancing
2. is completing
3. was bathing
4. has been working
5. has been going
6. will be leaving
7. was working, is practicing
8. is working, have been burning
9. was running, is operating
10. will be playing

PRACTICE 7

1. should dance
2. has been teaching
3. does plan
4. had crawled
5. was
6. had been doing
7. did live
8. will have been competing
9. had nominated
10. has accepted

PRACTICE 8

1. he *took*
2. players *were*
3. students *fail*
4. it *was working*
5. *The Great Gatsby was published*
6. work processor *will replace*
7. he *turned*
8. he *developed*
9. thousands of athletes *will have arrived*
10. we *missed*

PRACTICE 9

1. would have passed
2. did have
3. correct
4. is
5. have tried
6. attend
7. are
8. manage

APPLICATION I

Verb	Perfect Tense	Progressive Form
1. ride	has/have ridden	am/are/is riding
2. will consider	will have considered	will be considering
3. evolved	had evolved	was/were evolving
4. draws	has/have drawn	am/are/is drawing
5. will answer	will have answered	will be answering
6. will build	will have built	will be building
7. solved	had solved	was/were solving
8. remembers	has/have remembered	am/are/is remembering
9. made	had made	was/were making
10. will discover	will have discovered	will be discovering

APPLICATION II

1. visiting *was*
2. There *were*, I *enjoyed*
3. correct
4. It *was*, we *needed*
5. I *caught*, we *left*
6. Example *was*
7. cousins and I *took*
8. pinto *trotted*
9. meals *pleased*
10. correct
11. It *was*

APPLICATION III

1. correct
2. Two *are*
3. Clemens *paid*
4. correct
5. greenhouse *occupied*
   fireplace *had*

6. residence *had*
7. correct
8. which *was published*
9. house *contains*
10. house *is*
11. Americans *are*, which *sheltered*

Chapter 3

PRACTICE 1

1. transitive
2. intransitive
3. transitive
4. transitive
5. transitive

6. intransitive
7. transitive
8. transitive
9. intransitive
10. intransitive

PRACTICE 3

1. will be given
2. were sent
3. had been driven

4. will have been
   commanded
5. was written

PRACTICE 4

1. were
2. were
3. be

4. be
5. were

PRACTICE 2

1. made
2. saddled
3. received
4. changed
5. cooked

6. lit
7. announced
8. passed
9. made
10. gave

PRACTICE 5

1. To earn—infinitive
2. noted—past participle
3. Driving to the store—present participle
4. to earn extra money this summer—infinitive
5. skiing—gerund; to spend a summer afternoon—infinitive
6. playing in the yard—present participle
7. deserved—past participle
8. "To be, or not to be"—infinitives
9. aged—past participle; photographing birds—gerund
10. ringing the church bells—gerund
11. Dashing to the finish line—present participle
12. After receiving her bachelor's degree—present participle
    to attend law school—infinitive
13. Typing the final word—present participle
14. To dance the limbo—infinitive
15. to see a movie, (to) dine at a restaurant, and (to) dance until midnight—infinitives
16. fading back for a pass—present participle
    rushing—present participle
17. Pivoting quickly—present participle
18. feuding—present participle
    to settle their differences in court—infinitive
19. Building a fire—gerund
20. camping, biking—gerunds

APPLICATION II

1. American people *love* baseball.
2. People *view* it as the true American sport.
3. Abner Doubleday, an American, *invented* baseball in 1839.
4. Since that time, many great players *have dominated* the game.
5. correct
6. Millions of people *fill* the ballparks and stadiums each year.
7. From sandlots and school playgrounds to superdomes, everyone *plays* baseball.
8. correct
9. correct

APPLICATION III

1. which *claimed, marked*
2. Lee *wanted*
3. which he *thought*
4. Maryland, a border state, *would be won*
5. Lee *planned*
6. correct
7. McClellan *failed* and *allowed*
8. correct
9. the Confederacy *would have*
10. Union *remained,* history *took*

Chapter 4

PRACTICE 3

	Verb	Subject
1.	laughs	Terry
2.	swam	I
3.	is	Elvis Presley
4.	play	children
5.	read	defendant
6.	seemed	homework
7.	will be	night
8.	fainted	doctor
9.	hit	bullet
10.	is	Porsche

PRACTICE 4

	Verb	Subject
1.	are	Fords, Chevrolets
2.	hissed, scratched	cat
3.	read, study	Caleb, I
4.	became	Angela
5.	took	He, Martha
6.	seemed	Tina
7.	are	ice cream, cake
8.	are	Puerto Rico, St. Thomas
9.	appears	Nita
10.	leaped, swam	dolphin

PRACTICE 5

	Verb	Subject
1.	are	friends
2.	is	manuscript
3.	are	ball, bat
4.	is	answer
5.	come	boyfriend, girl

PRACTICE 6

	Verb	Subject
1.	will have left	Tom
2.	will have been	senator
3.	had been demolished	car
4.	will be released	animals
5.	was playing	jockey

PRACTICE 7

1. The *cat ran* ~~under the porch~~.
   (s) (v)

2. *Bronco Davis was* a famous football player ~~for twenty years~~.
   (s) (v)

3. The *greyhound* ~~with the matted coat and an evil look in his eyes~~ *frightened* the schoolchildren.
   (s) (v)

4. The *drive* ~~to Orlando~~ *is* a pleasant one.
   (s) (v)

5. *Bing Crosby* and *Bob Hope were* a successful team ~~for more than fifteen years~~.
   (s) (s) (v)

APPLICATION I

	Subject	Verb	Prepositional Phrases
1.	it	becomes	At night
2.	President, Mrs. Reagan	greeted	
3.	Julio	will help	
4.	Bob, Ted	did go	after football practice
5.	members	chose	of the Board, of Trustees
6.	Jerry	is planning	to the Far East
7.	you	Do watch	
8.	Dr. Harper	climbed, reported	to the American Academy, of Scientists
9.	Professors James, Harvey	played, scored	in the student-faculty basketball game
10.	homes	are	in Concord, Massachusetts
11.	Many	encouraged	of the U.S. presidents, from the rest, of the world
12.	Children, adults	like	
13.	(you)	Call, make	for Friday afternoon
14.	Mr. Avery	has saved	by itemizing my deductions
15.	planes	were	In the distance
16.	Department of History	will announce	In the morning, of History, about the new history course
17.	Chad	did go	to Alaska
18.	friend	is going, is going	to school, at the same time
19.	It	is	for students
20.	Firefighters, police officers	have, are injured	
21.	Math, science	are	
22.	Eagles	tried, could do	
23.	All	requested	of the students, of schedule
24.	team, team	practiced	in the gym, during the winter
25.	Delores, Ann	Have decided	on their vacation
26.	Jim	sold, bought	
27.	Many	require	of the new businesses
28.	(you)	Talk, ask	to Sara
29.	All	sold	of the members, of the Women's Club, in order, for their annual dance
30.	People	need	for their good deeds

Chapter 5
PRACTICE 1

Subject	Verb	Format	Subject	Verb	Format
1. child	hopped	1	4. price	has been increased	1
2. lamb	cried	1	5. Jumpin' Jack	sings	1
3. hundreds	fly	1			

PRACTICE 2

Subject	Verb	Object	Format 1 or 2
1. Tom	forgot		1 S-V
2. band	won	contest	2 S-V-DO
3. Helen	completed	novel	2 S-V-DO
4. I	swam		1 S-V
5. dog	crossed	road	2 S-V-DO
6. arrow	struck	tree	2 S-V-DO
7. team	lost		1 S-V
8. toddler	broke	vase	2 S-V-DO
9. drunk	leaves		1 S-V
10. auctioneer	had sold	mansion, contents	2 S-V-DO

PRACTICE 3

Subject	Verb	Object	Format 1 or 2
1. police	caught	thief	2 S-V-DO
2. television	broke		1 S-V
3. horse	won	Triple Crown	2 S-V-DO
4. children	jumped	fence	2 S-V-DO
5. Mary	cried		1 S-V
6. moon	rose		1 S-V
7. fullback	caught	football	2 S-V-DO
8. rooster	crowed		1 S-V
9. airplane	left	runway	2 S-V-DO
10. diver	speared	barracuda	2 S-V-DO
11. shoelaces	broke		1 S-V
12. president	fired	assistant	2 S-V-DO
13. speaker	declined	invitation	2 S-V-DO
14. chair	fell		1 S-V
15. Children	like	ice cream	2 S-V-DO

PRACTICE 4

Subject	Verb	IO	DO
1. Pablo	awarded	Henry	prize
2. boy	bought	girl	flower
3. man	handed	girlfriend	ring
4. teacher	gave	me	mark
5. Hector	fed	dog	dinner
6. bird	built	mate	nest
7. I	gave	friend	umbrella
8. She	brought	Darryl	soda
9. kidnappers	gave	child	bar
10. Sharon	bought	father	sweater

PRACTICE 5

	PA-S	LV	Format
1.	powerful weightlifter	is	S-LV-PA
2.	sad Tom	appears	S-LV-PA
3.	happy Mary	looks	S-LV-PA
4.	good dinner	tasted	S-LV-PA
5.	cooperative Earl Bruce	was	S-LV-PA
6.	angry cat	sounds	S-LV-PA
7.	tired He	seems	S-LV-PA
8.	sour onion	smells	S-LV-PA
9.	rough road	becomes	S-LV-PA
10.	red, delicious apple	was	S-LV-PA

PRACTICE 6

	Verb	PA or DO		Verb	PA or DO
1.	branded	calf-DO	6.	were	pretty-PA
2.	looks	expensive-PA	7.	serves	food-DO
3.	enjoy	books-DO	8.	has	water-DO
4.	struck	rock-DO	9.	looks	interested-PA
5.	are	dirty-PA	10.	seemed	uneasy-PA

PRACTICE 7

	Subject	Linking Verb	Predicate Nominative
1.	senator	is	head
2.	Annapolis	is	capital
3.	desk	is	antique
4.	Shawn	became	astronaut
5.	John	is	player
6.	Jane	is	force
7.	Television	is	one
8.	She	is	actress
9.	girl	is	cousin
10.	alligator	is	symbol

PRACTICE 8

	Subject	LV	PA	PN	Format
1.	She	is		girl	S-LV-PN
2.	ideas	are	ambiguous		S-LV-PA
3.	Students	seem	busy		S-LV-PA
4.	Doctors, lawyers	are		professionals	S-LV-PN
5.	teachers	are	enthusiastic		S-LV-PA
6.	Discos	are		alleys	S-LV-PN
7.	Records, tapes	are	expensive		S-LV-PA
8.	craze	is		mini-skirt	S-LV-PN
9.	Faulkner	was		one	S-LV-PN
10.	Silence, patience	are		virtues	S-LV-PN

PRACTICE 9

	Subject	Verb	IO	DO/PA or PN	Format
1.	She	is		star-PN	S-LV-PN (4)
2.	Coach	gave	Paul	equipment-DO	S-V-IO-DO (3)
3.	bread	tastes		stale-PA	S-LV-PA (4)
4.	dog	caught		stick-DO	S-V-DO (2)
5.	man	gave	child	dollar-DO	S-V-IO-DO (3)
6.	I	walked			S-V (1)
7.	runner	became		hero-PN	S-LV-PN (4)
8.	Women	have joined		clubs-DO	S-V-DO (2)
9.	Kim	sang		aria-DO	S-V-DO (2)
10.	horse	tripped			S-V (1)
11.	Connors	is		player-PN	S-LV-PN (4)
12.	Lawyer	gave	client	advice-DO	S-V-IO-DO (3)
13.	student	was		sick-PA	S-LV-PA (4)
14.	Maria	invited		Brad-DO	S-V-DO (2)
15.	dog	growled			S-V (1)
16.	roses	are		gift-PN	S-LV-PN (4)
17.	Alice	caught		fish-DO	S-V-DO (2)
18.	Doctors	seem		intelligent-PA	S-LV-PA (4)
19.	He	gave	me	present-DO	S-V-IO-DO (3)
20.	picture	appears		faded-PA	S-LV-PA (4)

PRACTICE 10

	Verbal	Function	Code	Format
1.	to give (infinitive)	subject	S-V-PA	4
	to receive (infinitive)	subject	S-V-PA	4
2.	Bailing (gerund)	subject	S-V-DO	2
3.	partying, dancing, swinging (gerunds)	predicate nominatives	S-V-PN	4
4.	to climb (infinitive)	direct object	S-V-DO	2
5.	to see (infinitive)	predicate nominative	S-V-PN	4
6.	Writing (gerund)	subject	S-V-PN	4
7.	reading	direct object	S-V-DO	2
8.	to hide (infinitive)	direct object	S-V-DO	2
9.	snorkeling (gerund)	predicate nominative	S-V-PN	4
10.	mixing (gerund)	direct object	S-V-DO	2

PRACTICE 11

1. Imperative
2. Interrogative
3. Declarative
4. Exclamatory
5. Imperative
6. Declarative
7. Interrogative
8. Imperative
9. Exclamatory
10. Declarative

APPLICATION II

	Subject	Verb	Indirect Object	Direct Object	Predicate Nominative	Predicate Adjective	Format
1.	teacher	taught	John	lesson			S-V-IO-DO
2.	He	had been				rambunctious	S-V-PA
3.	behavior	was disrupting		class			S-V-DO
4.	That	was				unacceptable	S-V-PA
5.	she	sent	mother	note			S-V-IO-DO
6.	note	asked					S-V
7.	mother	agreed		to help			S-V-DO
8.	John	will forget		Tuesday			S-V-DO
9.	view	changed					S-V

APPLICATION III

1. students—noun, subject
   think—verb
   opportunity—noun, object of preposition
2. situations—noun, object of preposition
   it—pronoun, subject
3. holder—noun, indirect object
   interview—noun, direct object
4. is—verb
   guarantee—noun, subject
5. to see—infinitive, noun, direct object
6. are—linking verb
   possibilities—noun, object of preposition
7. Talking—gerund, noun, subject
   time—noun, direct object
8. They—pronoun, subject
   to know—infinitive, noun, direct object
9. should keep—verb
10. hunting—gerund, noun, subject
    business—noun, predicate nominative

Chapter 6
PRACTICE 1

1.
2. C
3. C

4. C
5.

PRACTICE 3

1. D
2. D
3. I
4. D
5. I

6. D
7. D
8. I
9. D
10. I

PRACTICE 4

1. college—subject
   sponsors—verb
   day—direct object
   for students—prepositional phrase
   Format: S-V-DO
2. During the president's vacation—prepositional phrase
   vice-president—subject
   was—verb
   responsible—predicate adjective
   for the administration—prepositional phrase
   of the college—prepositional phrase
   Format: S-V-PA
3. Swimming—subject
   is—verb
   sport—predicate nominative
   Format: S-V-PN
4. sentry—subject
   standing guard duty—participial phrase
   had fallen—verb
   asleep—predicate adjective
   at his post—prepositional phrase
   Format: S-V-PA
5. Harold, Maude—subjects
   made—verb
   couple—direct object
   because of the contrast—prepositional phrase
   in their ages—prepositional phrase
   Format: S-V-DO

6. hiking—participle
   club—subject
   plans—verb
   to visit—direct object
   Format: S-V-DO
7. Distraught—participle
   victim—subject
   refused—verb
   to answer—direct object
   Format: S-V-DO
8. At the sound—prepositional phrase
   of the approaching train—prepositional phrase (approaching—participle)
   deer—subject
   scrambled—verb
   for safety—prepositional phrase
   Format: S-V
9. To enjoy—infinitive
   of one—prepositional phrase
   of Shakespeare's plays—prepositional phrase
   you—subject
   should read—verb
   play—direct object
   to the performance—prepositional phrase
   Format: S-V-DO
10. ambition—subject
    is—verb
    to become—predicate nominative
    Format: S-V-PN

PRACTICE 7

1. compound   Governor Toll was nominated   he decided
                    S   V   S   V

2. simple   Derby, Preakness, Belmont Stakes   form
                      subjects   V

3. compound   firefighters   used   they   use
                   S   V   S   V

4. simple   musicians, composers   were employed
                  subjects   V

5. compound   Mexico   has   some   go
                 S   V   S   V

PRACTICE 8

1. PP (prepositional phrase)
2. DC (dependent clause)
3. DC
4. SW (subordinating word)
5. IC (independent clause)
6. IC
7. PP
8. PP
9. DC
10. PP
11. SW
12. DC
13. IC
14. PP
15. DC
16. PP
17. PP
18. IC
19. DC
20. DC

PRACTICE 11

1. <u>dependent clause</u>   <u>independent clause</u>
   (Whenever the weather is beautiful), <u>they have a picnic</u>.

2. <u>dependent clause</u>   <u>independent clause</u>
   (Although he had household chores), <u>he decided to see a movie</u>.

3. <u>independent clause</u>   <u>dependent clause</u>
   <u>It began to rain</u> (before the boat reached shore).

4. <u>independent clause</u>   <u>dependent clause</u>
   <u>We knew</u> (that he did not go home).

5. <u>dependent clause</u>   <u>independent clause</u>
   (Because she has an exam tomorrow), <u>Kate will study tonight</u>.

6. <u>dependent clause</u>   <u>independent clause</u>
   (After the movie ended), <u>all thirty of us headed to the local pizza parlor</u>.

7. <u>dependent clause</u>   <u>independent clause</u>
   (Before Marvin could shout a warning), <u>the firecracker exploded</u>.

8. <u>dependent clause</u>   <u>independent clause</u>
   (After they buy a house), <u>they will purchase new furniture</u>.

9. <u>independent clause</u>   <u>dependent clause</u>
   <u>Harriet decided to go on the ski trip</u> (even though she had a broken leg.)

10. <u>dependent clause</u>   <u>dependent clause</u>
    [Because many parents believe (that their children should know computers)], <u>they are</u>

    <u>independent clause</u>
    <u>purchasing home computers</u>.

PRACTICE 12

1. complex   <u>independent clause</u>   <u>dependent clause</u>
   <u>Betsy goes to the beach</u> (whenever she can.)

2. compound   <u>independent clause</u>   <u>independent clause</u>
   <u>It is a warm day</u>; <u>the temperature is now 95 degrees</u>.

3. simple   <u>dependent clause</u>   <u>independent clause</u>
   <u>In order to earn enough money to go to college</u>, <u>Terry worked as a waitress</u>

   <u>all summer</u>.

4. compound   <u>independent clause</u>   <u>independent clause</u>
   <u>Jack and Mary entered the haunted house cautiously</u>, for <u>they believed all the</u>

   <u>stories about ghosts</u>.

5. complex   <u>dependent clause</u>   <u>independent clause</u>
   (When the rain was over), <u>the children ran outside</u>.

6. complex   <u>dependent clause</u>   <u>independent clause</u>
   (Because the battery was dead), <u>the car refused to start</u>.

7. compound   <u>independent clause</u>   <u>independent clause</u>
   <u>You must hurry</u>, or <u>you will miss the last bus</u>.

8. simple

    independent clause
Marcello and his brothers gritted their teeth and began the long, slow climb to the top

of the mountain.

    independent clause   *dependent clause*
9. Complex   He told you (that your plan was impossible).

    independent clause
10. Compound   With its varied historical background, New Orleans is a fascinating place to visit;

    independent clause
the Mardi Gras is one example of its French heritage.

PRACTICE 13

    dependent clause   *independent clause*   *independent clause*
1. (When the monster appeared on the screen,) one girl fainted, and the audience clapped.

    independent clause   *dependent clause*
2. The movie's visual effects, (which cost 15 million dollars,) were fantastic; later, the graphic

    independent clause
artists won an Academy Award for their work.

  independent clause   *dependent clause*   *independent clause*
3. I wish (that you had seen the film); we could discuss it.

  independent clause   *dependent clause*   *independent clause*
4. Knitting, (which is a relaxing pastime,) can be profitable, for handmade sweaters have become

a fashion item.

    independent clause   *dependent clause*   *independent clause*
5. Order the pizza (when you get home); I'll be there soon.

    dependent clause   *independent clause*
6. (Because England was America's first mother country), many people believe (that the English

    dependent clause   *independent clause*
do everything better); however, these Americans are not correct.

    dependent clause   *independent clause*   *independent clause*
7. (If you will wait for me), then I'll finish my work, and we can go to the beach.

    dependent clause   *independent clause*   *independent clause*
8. (Before you purchase your textbooks), go to class; the instructor may have changed the reading

list.

    independent clause   *dependent clause*
9. Our surprise birthday party for Jerry failed; (before he entered the room), everyone was

    independent clause
practicing "Happy Birthday."

    independent clause   *dependent clause*   *independent clause*
10. My father always told me to turn the lights off (when I leave a room); he claimed (that such

    dependent clause
a practice would save money).

PRACTICE 15

1. complex

independent clause   dependent clause
<u>She is a person</u> (whom we admire.)

2. complex

independent clause   dependent clause   independent clause
<u>The dog</u> (that wins the contest) <u>will be used in the commercial.</u>

3. complex

dependent clause   independent clause
(Because he has left), <u>we must stay here.</u>

4. compound-
   complex

dependent clause
(Because the panda's natural habitat in China is threatened), <u>many Chinese</u>

independent clause
<u>zookeepers wish to export them to other countries</u>, and <u>the Chinese</u>

independent clause
<u>government has agreed.</u>

5. complex

independent clause   dependent clause
<u>Close the door</u> (when you enter).

6. complex

dependent clause   independent clause
(Before we leave for a vacation), <u>we always have the car checked for problems.</u>

7. complex

independent clause   dependent clause
<u>Have Dave and Hank decided</u> (when they will paint the house)?

8. simple

independent clause
<u>We decided to see *The Rocky Horror Picture Show* at midnight.</u>

9. compound

independent clause
<u>Curt and Stacy played the romantic leads in *Romeo and Juliet*</u>; however, <u>the</u>

independent clause
<u>performance reminded one of *The Taming of the Shrew*.</u>

10. simple

independent clause
<u>Each section of the country, from New England to the West Coast, boasts of its</u>

<u>native foods.</u>

APPLICATION I

1. simple
2. complex
3. complex
4. compound
5. complex
6. compound-complex
7. complex
8. complex
9. complex
10. compound
11. compound
12. compound
13. complex
14. complex
15. complex
16. simple
17. compound
18. simple
19. complex
20. compound-complex

Chapter 7
PRACTICE 1

1. Frag
2. Frag
3. C
4. Frag
5. C
6. C
7. Frag
8. Frag
9. C
10. Frag

Have your instructor or tutor check your corrections.

APPLICATION I

1. Frag	6. Frag	11. Frag	16. Frag
2. Frag	7. Frag	12. C	17. C
3. Frag	8. Frag	13. Frag	18. Frag
4. Frag	9. Frag	14. Frag	19. C
5. C	10. Frag	15. Frag	20. Frag

Have your instructor or tutor check your corrections.

APPLICATION II

1. C	6. C	11. C	16. C
2. Frag	7. Frag	12. Frag	17. C
3. Frag	8. Frag	13. C	18. C
4. Frag	9. Frag	14. Frag	19. Frag
5. C	10. C	15. C	20. C

Have your instructor or tutor check your revisions.

APPLICATION III

1. Frag	6. C	11. C	16. Frag
2. C	7. Frag	12. C	17. C
3. C	8. C	13. Frag	
4. Frag	9. Frag	14. Frag	
5. Frag	10. C	15. C	

Have your instructor or tutor check your revisions.

Chapter 8
PRACTICE 1

1. CS
2. CS
3. CS
4. CS
5. CS

PRACTICE 2

1. C
2. CS   job; she *or* and, she
3. CS   high; I
4. CS   beach; however,
5. CS   Park, for
6. C
7. C
8. CS   inadequate; each
9. C
10. CS   poet; he

APPLICATION I

1. C		11. CS drought; this
2. CS here; on		12. C
3. CS best; fiberfill		13. CS college; this
4. CS ways; students		14. CS fun; it
5. CS understanding; teenagers		15. CS improving; the
6. CS nutritious; however,		16. CS cooks; everyone
7. CS commodities; in		17. CS accident; therefore,
8. CS time; the		18. CS nineteen, but
9. C		19. C
10. CS events, for		20. CS hobby; then

APPLICATION II

1. CS days; I		11. C
2. C		12. C
3. C		13. CS cares; it
4. C		14. CS existence; it
5. CS birthdays; the		15. CS hypocrites; they
6. C		16. C
7. C		17. C
8. CS do; the second		18. CS birthdays; then
9. CS favored; we		19. C
10. C		

APPLICATION III

1. C		18. C	
2. CS	advice. We	19. C	
3. C		20. CS	rolling. I'll
4. C		21. CS	essay; next
5. CS	October. We	22. C	
6. CS	begin; everything	23. CS	write; however,
7. C		24. C	
8. C		25. C	
9. CS	requirements; however, they	26. C	
10. C		27. CS	gratifying; however, a recommendation
11. C		28. C	
12. CS	choice; however, the best	29. CS	January; the
13. C		30. C	
14. C		31. C	
15. CS	times, but enough	32. C	
16. C		33. CS	arrives, and
17. C			

Note: Because there are a number of ways to correct comma splices, have your instructor or tutor check your corrections.

Chapter 9

PRACTICE 1

1. RO	friend/he	4. RO	dancer/she
2. C		5. C	
3. RO	move/many		

PRACTICE 2

1. C		6. C
2. RO		7. RO
3. RO		8. RO
4. RO		9. C
5. C		10. RO

Have your instructor or tutor check your corrections

APPLICATION I

1. RO	11. RO
2. C	12. C
3. RO	13. RO
4. C	14. C
5. RO	15. RO
6. RO	16. RO
7. C	17. RO
8. RO	18. C
9. RO	19. RO
10. C	20. RO

Have your instructor or tutor check your corrections.

APPLICATION II

1. C	9. C
2. RO	10. RO
3. RO	11. C
4. C	12. RO
5. C	13. C
6. C	14. RO
7. RO	15. C
8. C	

Have your instructor or tutor check your corrections.

APPLICATION III

1. C	8. RO
2. C	9. C
3. RO	10. RO
4. RO	11. C
5. RO	12. RO
6. C	13. C
7. C	14. RO

Have your instructor or tutor check your corrections.

(*Chapter 10: Many answers are acceptable; have your instructor or tutor check your work.*)

Chapter 11
PRACTICE 1

1.	S	6.	P
2.	P	7.	P
3.	P	8.	P
4.	S	9.	S
5.	P	10.	S

PRACTICE 2

1. The boys laugh at the clown.
2. The mice hide in the pantry.
3. The examinations seem difficult.
4. The puppies nip at my heels.
5. The girls dive into the water.

PRACTICE 3

S or P		Subject	Verb
1.	S	cat	carried
2.	S	child	screamed
3.	P	dolphins	are
4.	S	Hank Thompson	answers
5.	P	gardens	grow
6.	P	grades	depend
7.	S	Tim	works
8.	S	Chrysler	was
9.	P	dogs	bark
10.	P	They	sat
11.	P	millionaires	own
12.	P	headaches	are caused
13.	S	desk	was
14.	S	actor	is
15.	P	books	make
16.	S	adolescent	faces
17.	S	bowl	is
18.	S	chair	is
19.	S	song	was
20.	S	player	smashes

PRACTICE 4

1. The student always feels. . . .
2. A dog is usually considered. . . .
3. A child loves. . . .
4. The nation has amassed. . . .
5. The plant needs. . . .

PRACTICE 5

S or P		Subject	Verb
1.	S	each	enjoys
2.	S	All	was
3.	P	Some	have
4.	S	Each	plays
5.	S	Neither	wants
6.	P	All	enjoy
7.	S	teenager	wants
8.	P	horses	gallop
9.	P	adults	enjoy
10.	S	Half	was

PRACTICE 6

S or P		Subject	Verb
1.	S	gaggle	has
2.	S	*The Crusaders*	is
3.	S	measles	is
4.	P	trousers	have
5.	S	pounds	is

PRACTICE 7

S or P		Subject	Verb
1.	P	Jack and Eileen	want
2.	P	union representatives	want
3.	S	George	swims
4.	S	husband	has
5.	P	quiche, hash	don't

PRACTICE 8

S or P		Subject	Verb
1.	S	who (refers to Fitzgerald)	was
2.	P	who (refers to lawyers)	select
3.	S	that (refers to one)	is
4.	S	which (refers to monument)	is
5.	S	who (refers to only one)	enjoys

PRACTICE 9

S or P		Subject	Verb
1.	P	people	are
2.	P	courthouse, church	stand
3.	P	letters	are
4.	P	forms	were
5.	S	fortune	lies

APPLICATION I

	Subject	Verb			Subject	Verb
1.	students	go		14.	Most	was
2.	Spring, fall	are		15.	reasons	are
3.	All	were		16.	stereo, television, radio	were
4.	Dogs, cats	make		17.	Washington, Oregon, California, and Alaska	border
5.	who (refers to men)	were		18.	He, I	are
6.	books	are		19.	group	is
7.	She, I	are		20.	Half	is
8.	salesmen	are		21.	Many	play
9.	dollar	was		22.	governor	is
10.	teachers	have		23.	blacksmith, horse	were
11.	media	have		24.	army	is
12.	Harry	is		25.	problems	are
13.	Half	is				

APPLICATION II

1. The record is being catalogued now.
2. The car speeds down Mt. Royal Avenue each day.
3. Her song is selling quite well.
4. Their child insists on staying awake until midnight.
5. Our new puppy cries all night.
6. A hurricane is a natural phenomenon.
7. The scientist declares that one day a person may live to be one hundred.
8. A statistician has been known to manipulate data.
9. A steel door offers more protection than a wooden door.
10. A swimmer exercises all the muscles in his body.

APPLICATION III

1. s-v agr.   leader who teaches, conducts
2. s-v agr.   have
3. correct
4. correct
5. s-v agr.   type stresses
6. correct
7. s-v agr.   player who fails
8. correct
9. correct
10. s-v agr.   is the coach
11. s-v agr.   team is required
12. s-v agr.   team that is quite well prepared
13. correct
14. correct
15. s-v agr.   coach does expect
16. correct
17. s-v agr.   each type exists
18. s-v agr.   they all want

APPLICATION IV

1. agr   there is a big difference
2. C
3. agr   which include
4. agr   you always have
5. agr   you have
6. agr   Families provide
7. agr   person changes, he or she grows
8. agr   family helps, each life affects
9. C

Chapter 12
PRACTICE 1

	Nominative	Objective	Possessive
1. dock	it	it	its
2. dog	it	it	its
3. Harry and Ellen	they	them	their, theirs
4. James and I	we	us	our, ours
5. Sara	she	her	her, hers

PRACTICE 2

1. she
2. they
3. their
4. my
5. its/her/his

PRACTICE 3

Pronoun	Antecedent
1. her	Maria
2. you	Mr. Roberts
3. her	teacher
4. his	radiologist
5. her	lawyer
6. we	Steve and I
7. its	horse
8. them	books
9. her	grandmother
10. it	industry
11. it	pen
12. you	Bonnie and Jack
13. them	plants
14. her	mother
15. it	novel

PRACTICE 4

1. it
2. She
3. We
4. he
5. he or she
6. her
7. his
8. it
9. their
10. He
11. It
12. they
13. They
14. It
15. they

PRACTICE 5

Pronoun	Antecedent
1. their	societies
2. its	herd
3. his/her	Everybody
4. their	players
5. their	some
6. its	company
7. its	class
8. her	neither
9. its	board
10. their	women
11. its	flock
12. their	students
13. their	dean, associates
14. their	doctor
15. its	*New England Journal of Medicine*

APPLICATION I

1. his
2. their
3. its
4. its
5. their
6. his
7. its
8. our, them
9. their
10. their
11. his
12. its
13. his
14. his
15. her
16. her
17. their
18. their
19. their
20. her, her
21. his
22. his
23. my
24. their
25. its

APPLICATION II

1. The dogs barked at their owner.
2. The judges announced their decision on Monday.
3. They told their versions of the accident to the officer.
4. Both boys plan not to continue their education.
5. The cars' engines smoked and coughed before they finally quit.
6. They told their parents that they had received a scholarship.
7. The pandas ate their bamboo at the Washington Zoo.
8. The crews of the space shuttle perform their duties.
9. The airplanes lost two of their engines.
10. The referees recognized that they had made a poor call.

APPLICATION III

The following sentences have pronoun reference errors:

1. *it* holds
4. *his* novel
5. *our* galaxy
6. *their* vision
8. *their* amazing
9. as if *he, his* universe

Have your instructor or tutor check your work.

APPLICATION IV

1. C
2. C
3. C
4. ref they can offer, for their choice
5. C
6. ref enables them
7. ref it is actually
8. ref assure their offspring, spends its money
9. ref these purchases
10. ref demand their time, to their careers
11. C
12. C
13. ref left for themselves

Chapter 13

PRACTICE 1

1. There
2. I, In, I
3. Ye, I
4. According
5. He, Close, Ringed

PRACTICE 2

1. President, Ford's Theater
2. *Mountain Eagle*
3. American Workers Association, Tall Oaks Community Hospital
4. none
5. Wheaties, Rice Krispies

PRACTICE 3

1. none
2. Freud's, Jungian
3. Middle Ages, Renaissance
4. Napoleonic France, Regency England
5. Declaration of Independence, Revolution
6. Even, I, God
7. Missouri
8. Although, Judge
9. none
10. Christmas

PRACTICE 4

1. .
2. ?
3. ?
4. ! *or* .
5. ?
6. .
7. .
8. .
9. !
10. value. so?

APPLICATION I

1. C
2. The, he, place. Rather, works there, it's incredible.
3. He treats
4. to give me an order. I let
5. job. Can you beat that! *or* ?
6. inventory. Because, we did not
7. C
8. However, shoppers. Before, customers
9. That
10. We'll, inventory.
11. problem, me. Today
12. there. I, surf. (Such, establishment.)
13. I, the solution, give in. At three o'clock

APPLICATION II

1. the Preakness, the second race
2. C
3. Maryland
4. warm spring weather
5. pre-Hunt Cup, social
6. days. It covers
7. preppie, "Eat, drink, and be merry."
8. hand.
9. hot dogs
10. tailgate, lawn, golden retriever, MacDuff
11. *The Preppie Handbook*
12. strangers.
13. it, grounds
14. C
15. knows. Even the, "How are you?"
16. Harvard crew team, Hopkins lacrosse team
17. Cup
18. afternoon
19. spring
20. wagon. My

Chapter 14

PRACTICE 1

1. C
2. C
2. P   schoolyard, for
4. P   hour, but
5. P   hour, and

PRACTICE 2

1. P   Datsuns, Toyotas, and
2. P   Ways, M&Ms, and
3. C
4. P   Christmas, Thanksgiving, and
5. P   cleaner's, . . . milk, and

PRACTICE 3

1. P   harsh,
2. C
3. P   dirty,
4. P   short,
5. C

PRACTICE 4

1. P   before,
2. C
3. P   road,
4. P   him,
5. P   graded,

PRACTICE 5

1. P   December 7, 1941
2. P   Avenue, Washington, D. C.
3. C
4. C
5. P   July, 1988

PRACTICE 6

1. P   jumping,
2. P   nine,
3. P   old,
4. P   thirty,
5. C

APPLICATION I

1. P   September, 1971, January 23, 1981
2. C
3. P   cold,
4. P   hitting,
5. P   womb,
6. P   safe,
7. P   items,
8. C
9. C
10. P   bureau, . . . bed, or
11. P   large housekeeping
12. C
13. C
14. P   architect, but
15. P   tall, lean
16. P   raining, the
17. C
18. P   toy, a book, and
19. P   old, dilapidated
20. P   Tacoman, Mississippi, Finleyburg, Missouri

APPLICATION II

The following sentences have comma errors:

1. year,
2. campus,
4. schedules, tastes
5. second,
6. do, plans, classes,
8. example, eyes,
11. However,
12. rewarding, exciting,

Have your instructor or tutor check your corrections.

APPLICATION III

The following sentences have comma errors.

3. ocean, feasts,
10. test,
13. early, briefcase,

15. later,
16. desk, it, head,
20. it, it,

22. testing,
24. enough,
27. school, world,

33. adulthoods,
34. benefits,
36. medium,

Chapter 15

PRACTICE 1

1. MacBride,
2. thinks, Charles,
3. Honor,
4. parade,
5. tonight,

PRACTICE 2

1. understand,"
2. "Bugs," . . . primly, "are
3. emphatically,
4. interested,"
5. declared,

PRACTICE 3

1. C
2. P   Smith, Sally's neighbor,
3. P   George, a famous panhandler,
4. P   Carter, . . . executive,
5. P   brother, Harry,

PRACTICE 4

1. P   child, bright and witty,
2. P   man, . . . undaunted,
3. P   spring, . . . uplifting,
4. P   boy, . . . time,
5. C

PRACTICE 5

1. P   Parrots, . . . speech,
2. P   Puppies, . . . tricks,
3. P   dress, . . . often,
4. C
5. C

PRACTICE 6

1. P   fact,
2. C
3. P   Surprisingly,
4. P   conclude,
5. P   Darlingston, . . . not,

APPLICATION I

1. P   student, . . . hand,
2. P   dog, . . . Pomeranian,
3. P   jockey, . . . alert,
4. P   said,
5. P   honestly,
6. P   Oh,
7. C
8. P   students, generally speaking,
9. P   action," she stated,
10. P   Andy,
11. P   player, muscular and tanned,
12. C
13. C
14. P   D'Arcy, the Dean of the College,
15. C
16. C
17. P   brother, who loves to golf,
18. P   Plants, not dogs,
19. P   decided, young man,
20. C

APPLICATION II

1. P   students, writers,
2. C
3. C
4. P   "Hello, dear,"
5. C
6. P   Terrible, Nancy,
7. P   "boss, idiot, Harry, imbecile,"
8. P   that,
9. P   wife, upset,
10. C
11. P   job, interesting and well-paying,
12. P   "something,"
13. P   readers, critics,
14. C
15. P   writing, task,

APPLICATION III

1. P   game, memorable, School,
2. C
3. C
4. P   team, Vikings,
5. P   Fleming, quarterback, suddenly,
6. C
7. C
8. C

9. P   myself,
10. C
11. C
12. P   however,
13. P   gone,
14. C
15. P   defender,
16. C

Chapter 16

PRACTICE 1

1. school's rules
2. someone's idea
3. some people's responses
4. agency's regulations
5. Thelma and Gene's child
6. Mr. Grant's and Mr. Stone's families
7. my mother-in-law's quilt
8. the thief's motives
9. the congregation's responses
10. the crowd's insults

PRACTICE 2

1. the team's ball
2. the rabbi's work
3. the bus's passengers
4. the buses' passengers
5. someone's record
6. Ms. Jones's credit cards
7. the tennis pro's racquet
8. today's weather conditions
9. the Marines' motto
10. America's national anthem
11. the commander-in-chief's responsibilities
12. his grandparents' refrigerator
13. Jack and Tony's restaurants
14. Jack's and Tony's restaurants
15. the movie's special effects
16. the people's concern
17. I won't
18. he can't
19. they've
20. *several*'s
21. *yet*'s
22. Brazil's jungles
23. the salespeople's wares
24. the soldier's uniform
25. *z*'s

APPLICATION I

1. family's, it's
2. It's, one's
3. isn't
4. Everyone's, father's
5. men's
6. you're, team's
7. 10's, 20's, 100's
8. *ah*'s, *okay*'s
9. They're, rabbits' feet
10. '20s
11. Hank's, *r*'s
12. It's, woman's
13. children's
14. Rick's
15. Son's, isn't
16. heaven's
17. they'll
18. New Hampshire's
19. children's
20. officers'

APPLICATION II

1. students'
2. *F*'s
3. correct
4. correct
5. couldn't
6. *but*'s, *sure*'s, *okay*'s
7. mother-in-law's
8. *gonna go*'s, *should of*'s
9. correct
10. correct
11. *A*'s, *B*'s, *C*'s, *D*'s, *F*'s
12. marks
13. correct

Have your instructor or tutor check your work.

APPLICATION III

1. C	6. C	11. apos	standards, yours
2. apos *don't*	7. apos breaks	12. apos	I've, I've, rules
3. apos don't	8. C	13. apos	I've, 60's, 65's
4. C	9. apos standards	14. C	
5. apos *do*'s	10. C	15. apos	I'll, fits

Chapter 17

PRACTICE 1

1. disdain, "I . . . operas."
2. "Sailing to Byzantium"
3. blood: "He . . . unpunished."
4. "I . . . pay. . . ."
5. "Nerd," "turkey," and "buster"

PRACTICE 2

1. thing:
2. *Bankruptcy:*
3. never-ending:

APPLICATION I

1. P "The . . . Taken" best-known
2. C
3. P "Had . . . time. . . ."
4. P "Do . . . 'manatee' means?"
5. P changes:
6. P Supply-side
7. P well-paid
8. C
9. C
10. P Harding (most . . . name)
11. P [1660]
12. P —I . . . believe—
13. P qualifications:
14. P ex-spouse—we're . . . terms— *or* (we're . . . terms) is
15. P "Time will tell"
16. P [1928]
17. P "Tyger! . . . night . . ."
18. P tomorrow—or is it the next day?—
19. C
20. C

PRACTICE 3

1. brother—, doctor—, soft-hearted
2. you—
3. well-known, star—, two-thirds, time—
4. thirty-two, dollars!—
5. heir-apparent, old-fashioned

PRACTICE 4

1. (which . . . fought),
2. [1989]
3. (which . . . understood)
4. [ten pounds]
5. (he . . . wives)

APPLICATION II

1. P proverb-ridden
2. P (usually . . . add)
3. C
4. P examples:
   "When in Rome . . . ,"
   "A stitch in time . . . ,"
   "Don't count your chickens. . . ."
5. C
6. C
7. P award-winning
   ["Choose Your Mate!"]

APPLICATION III

The following sentences have punctuation errors:

1. P "[I]f
4. P counterfeiter (in . . . money) safecracker (which is—as is the previously mentioned occupation—illegal)
7. P earn—
8. P advertise ("We . . . way: we earn it.") old-fashioned
12. P "work"
21. P matters:
22. P forty-hour
27. P characteristics:

Chapter 18

PRACTICE 1

1. dm   To run in the Boston Marathon, Beth needed many hours of practice.
2. dm   Dancing all night, we saw the dawn.
3. dm   To earn an A, you need many hours of study.
4. mm   The teacher received her report, written by Jan.
5. dm   At the age of six, I moved to Colorado with my family.

APPLICATION I

1. mm   There are only two weeks left. . . .
2. C
3. mm   The athletes were frequently told. . . .
4. dm   While hanging by a thread, the spider attacked the fly. . . .
5 C
6. C
7. mm   Al wants to pass his economics examination, if at all possible.
8. mm   I told him to meet me on Friday at the train station.
9. mm   My car, which had a flat tire, was towed. . . .
10. C
11. mm   The bright light hanging from the ceiling was reflected.
12. mm   Mr. Smythe sat in a chair with a cane bottom.
13. mm   Students who study diligently succeed. . . .
14. C
15. mm   The robber with a masked face mugged. . . .
16. mm   To fulfill the requirements completely, . . .
17. dm   After studying all day, the girls attended a party.
18. C
19. mm   The vagrant was approached by the officer with his police dog.
20. mm   The horse with the star on his forehead was ridden. . . .

APPLICATION II

1. dm   Shaking with a tremendous jolt and finally stopping, the car was pushed to the curb by the middle-aged man.
2. mm   He recognized that it was obviously time. . . .
3. C
4. mm   The man, unfortunately, had nearly a hundred. . . .
5. C
6. mm   A dealer with shifty eyes approached him.
7. C
8. C
9. C
10. mm   The car looked to the dealer like a mammoth pile of glass and twisted metal with a rusty fender.
11. dm   The man gazed at the car, hanging by a bolt.
12. C
13. C
14. C
15. mm   There is nothing we can do for you unless you want to see only a new car with all the accessories.

APPLICATION III

1. C
2. C
3. mm   I usually went with a friend.
4. C
5. mm   It then took us only a while . . .
6. dm   This walking . . . stream; we avoided the water at all costs.
7. C
8. C
9. mm   We eventually . . . stream where the banks narrowed from fifteen to five feet.
10. mm   Here, the banks were made of clay that could be moistened and molded.
11. C
12. mm   Here, we often tried to dam the creek.
13. C
14. C
15. C
16. mm   Cold and wet, I would arrive home from the stream with a pail of crayfish in tow.
17. C
18. dm   I felt like a famous explorer who had just returned from fabulous lands.
19. C
20. C
21. mm   However, I now have new challenges, new places to explore.

Chapter 19

PRACTICE 1

Column A	Column B
really adv.	is
great adj.	holiday
nationalistic adj.	fervor
historic adj.	patriotism
perfectly adv.	combine
warm adj.	weather
summer adj.	weather
fully adv.	enjoys
hardly adv.	is
any adj.	dissension
this adj.	holiday
most adj.	people
willingly adv.	participate
joyfully adv.	participate
national adj.	heritage

PRACTICE 2

1. gaunter	gauntest
2. tinier	tiniest
3. more high-minded	most high-minded
4. more flexible	most flexible
5. shrewder	shrewdest
6. sleepier	sleepiest
7. more obvious	most obvious
8. crazier	craziest
9. gaudier	gaudiest
10. more vivid	most vivid

APPLICATION I

1. Ad foolishly		11. Ad happy
2. Ad properly		12. Ad normally
3. C		13. C
4. Ad bored		14. C
5. Ad cuter		15. Ad bold
6. Ad wisest		16. Ad suspiciously
7. Ad Most		17. C
8. C		18. Ad biggest
9. C		19. Ad lowest
10. Ad seriously		20. C

APPLICATION III

1. Ad writing well
2. C
3. Ad vast majority, stoutly and adamantly maintains
4. Ad is evident
5. Ad persistently and consistently, most shameful
6. Ad task publicly
7. C
8. Ad obvious fact, spelling correctly
9. C
10. Ad very carefully

APPLICATION IV

1. Ad good idea
2. Ad long brown hair, bright blue eyes, perfectly applied make-up
3. Ad long legs
4. Ad *Pleasant* is rather general. See if you can supply a more concrete and specific word.
5. Ad perfectly formed body
6. Ad highly polished looks, the most effervescent personality, the most generous soul
7. C
8. Ad converse seriously
9. Ad the happiest man
10. Ad Truly

Chapter 20

PRACTICE 1

These are suggested revisions of the given sentences. Other versions are possible, though. Check with your instructor or tutor if you are not sure of your answer.

1. Every night at ten o'clock we are hungry, so we go to the refrigerator.
2. Despite the bad weather conditions, the team decided to climb the mountain.
3. Being a member of the hassled and tense crowds in the central city every day is very depressing.
4. A stitch in time saves nine.
5. Basic math rules are easy to learn.

PRACTICE 2

These are suggested revisions of the given sentences. Other versions are possible, though. Check with your instructor or tutor if you are not sure of your answer.

1. Substitute "smell" for "sniff."
2. Substitute "walking" for "strolling."
3. Substitute "think" for "cogitate."
4. Substitute "rites" for "obsequies."
5. Substitute "lying" for "prevaricating."

PRACTICE 3

The following are suggested revisions. Check your revision with your instructor or tutor.

1. Substitute "fired" for "excessed."
2. The principal decided not to allow the student to be promoted, for the student's own benefit.
3. . . . and act like an executive.
4. My son's grades were satisfactory this year. *or* My son's grades were excellent this year.
5. This child's intellectual development was hampered by her very premature birth.

APPLICATION I

The following are possible revisions. Check your revision with your instructor or tutor.

1. Substitute "hit" for "bopped."
2. Substitute "bad" or "poor" for "bum."
3. Substitute "increased" or "greater" for "enhancing."
4. Substitute "a perspective on" for "an overview of."
5. Substitute "to confer" for "to conference."
6. Substitute "there" for "yond."
7. Substitute "computer disk" for "floppy disk."
8. Substitute "dead" for "pushing up daisies."
9. C
10. The gang decided to murder the informer.
11. . . . my income has been depleted, and my budget is unbalanced.
12. C
13. . . . become more and more negative.
14. Substitute "productive" for "pleasant."
15. That dress fits you well.
16. C
17. Substitute "hard" or "efficiently" for "prodigiously."
18. Substitute "worthwhile" or "excellent" for "the cat's pajamas."
19. Substitute "chubby" or "fat" for "portly."
20. C

APPLICATION II

Only sentences 13 and 15 are correct.
Show your revised sentences to your instructor or tutor.

APPLICATION III

Only sentences 7 and 9 are correct.
Show your revised sentences to your instructor or tutor.

Chapter 21
APPLICATION I

1. it's, a, accept, your
2. Two, too
3. and, affected, their
4. used
5. Here, there
6. you're, lose, your, breath
7. choose, among, your
8. supposed
9. passed
10. advice, bought, capital
11. Who's, weather
12. quite, compliment, dessert
13. advised, quite
14. Whether, used
15. past, quite
16. leave
17. fewer, than
18. a lot
19. Capitol
20. an, teach, learn
21. brake
22. burst, rights
23. site
24. led
25. preceding
26. raised
27. thorough
28. sights
29. cite
30. rites

APPLICATION II

1. ww   to the store, and Mary, along too
2. ww   compliment
3. ww   by asking, would accept
4. ww   to do
5. ww   was used, principle
6. ww   advice
7. C
8. ww   capital
9. ww   quite well
10. ww   bought her two
11. ww   whether

APPLICATION III

1. ww   principal's advice, accept
2. ww   among, a job
3. ww   choose whether, an authority
4. C
5. C
6. ww   borrow, capital to start
7. ww   to allot
8. C
9. ww   already, here
10. ww   It's
11. C

Chapter 22

PRACTICE 1

1. sieve
2. leisure
3. sleigh
4. pie
5. yield
6. beige
7. shield
8. chief
9. weird
10. veil

PRACTICE 2

1. ceiling
2. besieged
3. achievement
4. receiving
5. vein

PRACTICE 3

1. irreversible
2. unlovable
3. illicit
4. misapprehension
5. return
6. precede
7. commission
8. enable
9. disagree
10. polytheistic

PRACTICE 4

1. hardihood
2. defiant
3. conveyor
4. happily
5. hastily
6. likelihood
7. scantily
8. busier
9. nastiness
10. studious

PRACTICE 5

1. corrosiveness
2. practicing
3. bridal
4. refusal
5. degenerately
6. refutably
7. valuable
8. writing
9. duly
10. intervening

PRACTICE 6

1. fobbed
2. topping
3. committee
4. depositor
5. referred
6. forgetting
7. allotting
8. kidding
9. hottest
10. limitable

APPLICATION I

1. delight, surfeit
2. conflicting, territorial
3. testily, motherliness
4. jetties
5. ancient
6. illicit, illegal
7. mediating, grievance
8. insurance
9. slimmer, omitted
10. regrets

APPLICATION II

1. sp   achieve, honing
2. sp   stodgily, saucily
3. C
4. C
5. sp   merely
6. sp   hoping
7. sp   usually, useful, drumming
8. sp   demonstrating
9. C
10. sp   beginning

APPLICATION III

1. sp   experience, happened
2. sp   fulfilled
3. sp   advertisement
4. sp   accurate
5. C
6. sp   lifted, several
7. C
8. sp   discoloration, simply
9. sp   using
10. sp   proportions, weight
11. sp   disaster
12. C
13. sp   corridors, outrageously
14. sp   occurred
15. C
16. sp   believe

Chapter 23

Answers to the practices will vary; have your instructor or tutor check your work.